Research Methods in Social Studies Education

Contemporary Issues and Perspectives

A volume in
Research in Social Education
Series Editor: Merry M. Merryfield

Research in Social Education

Merry M. Merryfield
Series Editor

Critical Issues in Social Studies Research for the 21st Century (2001)
edited by William B. Stanley

Education for Democracy: Contexts, Curricula, Assessments (2002)
edited by Walter C. Parker

Critical Race Theory Perspectives in Social Studies: The Profession, Policies, and Curriculum (2003)
edited by Gloria Ladson-Billings

Critical Issues in Social Studies Teacher Education (2004)
edited by Susan Adler

Research Methods in Social Studies Education: Contemporary Issues and Perspectives (2006)
edited by Keith C. Barton

Research Methods in Social Studies Education

Contemporary Issues and Perspectives

Edited by

Keith C. Barton
University of Cincinnati

INFORMATION AGE
PUBLISHING

Greenwich, Connecticut 06830 • www.infoagepub.com

Library of Congress Cataloging-in-Publication Data

Barton, Keith C.
  Research methods in social studies education : contemporary issues and
perspectives / by Keith C. Barton.
      p. cm. – (Research in social education)
  Includes bibliographical references and index.
  ISBN 1-59311-453-2 (pbk.) – ISBN 1-59311-454-0
  1. Social sciences–Research–Methodology. 2. Social sciences–Study and
teaching. I. Title. II. Series.
  H62.B345 2006
  300.71–dc22

                                                                2005029950

Printed in the United States of America

LIST OF CONTRIBUTORS

Keith C. Barton	University of Cincinnati
Christine Woyshner	Temple University
Cynthia A. Tyson	The Ohio State University
Marilyn Johnston	The Ohio State University
Fionnuala Waldron	St. Patrick's College, Dublin
Simone A. Schweber	University of Wisconsin–Madison
Carole L. Hahn	Emory University
Deborah L. Cunningham	Primary Source, Watertown, MA
Wendy K. Richardson	University of Maryland–College Park
Bruce VanSledright	University of Maryland–College Park
Timothy Kelly	University of Maryland–College Park
Kevin Meuwissen	University of Maryland–College Park

CONTENTS

CHAPTER 1

INTRODUCTION

Keith C. Barton

As social studies educators, we fulfill many roles. Depending on whether we work primarily in schools, at universities, or for state agencies and non-profit organizations, we may teach courses for children or adults, create curriculum and testing programs, supervise beginning teachers in field placements, give workshops for practicing teachers, develop policy guidelines, teach graduate courses, oversee theses and dissertations, give presentations and write articles for practitioners, and serve on all the committees that keep our organizations running. In fulfilling these diverse and sometimes conflicting responsibilities, we would do well to pay particular attention to how empirical research contributes to our work. Whether we conduct such research ourselves or apply that of others, the importance of research looms large in our professional careers.

THE ROLE OF RESEARCH IN SOCIAL STUDIES

The most familiar purpose for social studies research is its contribution to the knowledge base for teaching and learning. Research provides insight, for example, into how students think and learn, into their cares and concerns, and into the contexts in which their ideas and attitudes have developed. To take just three examples from among the contributors to this volume: VanSledright (2002) has found that fifth graders can use primary sources to construct historical accounts and that their facility in doing so

Research Methods in Social Studies Education, pages 1–10
Copyright © 2006 by Information Age Publishing
All rights of reproduction in any form reserved.

improves with instruction; Schweber (together with Irwin) has shown how students of fundamentalist religious backgrounds attribute persecution of Jews during the Holocaust to religious beliefs rather than biological racism or Christian anti-Semitism (Schweber & Irwin, 2003); and Richardson (with Torney-Purta) has demonstrated that students' reports of open classroom climate are positively related to both their civic knowledge and their intention to vote as adults (Torney-Purta & Richardson, 2002). Nor are these isolated or idiosyncratic studies, unconnected to other scholarship; each is part of a growing body of empirical research, and each builds on previous work while also inspiring further investigation (on elementary students' use of primary sources, see, e.g., Barton, 1997; on students' religious interpretations of the Holocaust, see Spector, 2005; on classroom factors associated with civic knowledge and participation, see Hahn, 1998).

Other bodies of social studies research have contributed to our knowledge of how teachers make instructional decisions and how social and cultural forces influence the school curriculum. Again drawing only from among contributors to this volume, Cunnigham (2003) has documented the variety of goals that history teachers in England take into account as they teach for empathetic historical understanding; Hahn (1998) has traced the relationships among classroom civic education practices and cultural and political forces in five countries; and Woyshner (2004) has examined the PTA's role in promoting civic education in the first half of the 20th century. These too are part of larger research traditions that involve a number of investigators working on similar problems, and the result is an accumulating body of knowledge that informs our understanding of education in the social studies. Studies of both students and teachers not only provide evidence for the impact of educational experiences but move us beyond "common sense" by challenging our beliefs and assumptions and helping us better understand the possibilities for teaching and learning.

Collectively, research on social studies contributes to academic knowledge, just as any research in the social and behavioral sciences does—it adds to our understanding of human thought and action. Most of us who work in education, on the other hand, are more interested in the application of research, and this is where we find particular value in social studies research. By knowing how teachers make decisions, we can design better coursework and field experiences. By knowing how students interpret history, civics, or other subjects, we can build better curricula, develop more meaningful assessments, and design more effective forms of instruction. And by knowing how larger forces influence social studies in schools, we can be more thoughtful about our efforts to reform the subject. The fact that we don't yet know as much about any of these topics as we'd wish, like the fact that some educators don't utilize such knowledge as much as we think they should, is beside the point; as anyone familiar with the field can attest, social studies researchers are producing a growing body of empirical evidence that can be used to make decisions about teaching and learning.

This is not to suggest that social studies research is objective, neutral, or value-free, or that it can be applied in a purely technical way to solve educational problems. The implications of research rarely are simple or straightforward, and in order to become meaningful, research findings must always be filtered through the practical reality of our own contexts. Moreover, in light of conflicting ideas about the purpose of social studies (and of schooling generally), the implications of research depend in large part on our own educational values and assumptions. Even more basic, all knowledge is socially and historically situated—the result of our contemporary interests and perspectives—and thus educational studies inevitably reflect the concerns of individual researchers, of their community of inquiry, and of the larger society. But neither the situated nature of inquiry, nor the practical and value-laden character of educational decisions, detracts from the usefulness of research. After all, it's helpful to know that students draw on their religious backgrounds in making sense of the Holocaust, whether one wants to encourage such interpretations or provide alternatives to them.

But social studies research has another important application. Not only can it provide a knowledge base for our educational efforts, it can also serve as the very means by which we undertake such endeavors. That is, we can use the *process* of research—and not just its scholarly products—to improve the educational experiences of those with whom we work. Tyson (Chapter 3) argues that we cannot simply use the communities in which we do our research as "data plantations"; we must commit ourselves to addressing concerns of those communities and must design studies that benefit participants. Johnston's discussion of action research (Chapter 4) illustrates one way of doing that. By helping teachers carry out their own, practice-based research projects, scholars might be able to influence schools more directly than they could through studies that derived solely from the concerns of researchers. Waldron, meanwhile, applies a similar perspective to involving students in research (Chapter 5). She argues that rather than being content with a generalized benefit to the educational community, researchers should make sure that students benefit directly from their participation in research; one way of accomplishing that is by involving children, to the extent possible, in the design of studies and the interpretation of results. Furthermore, the benefits of research need not be limited to those with whom we work; international and comparative research helps us reflect on our own educational assumptions (Hahn, Chapter 7), and self-studies provide information on the nature and effects of our own instructional practices (Johnston, Chapter 4). Thus, while much research aims at a general benefit to the entire educational community, other approaches attempt, in whole or in part, to influence participants more directly.

RESEARCH DISCUSSIONS IN SOCIAL STUDIES

Improving teacher preparation, changing instruction, influencing policy, helping communities—these are lofty aims, and not all social studies research is equally successful in contributing to such efforts. Some questions and theoretical constructs are more productive than others, some designs achieve their objectives better than others, and some instruments yield more useful data than others. As researchers, knowing about the range of available methods should allow us more effectively to select those that suit our needs, and such knowledge should make us more thoughtful in applying those methods. And it seems self-evident that we would be better educated about research methods if discussion of the topic were a part of the public discourse of our field. Given our mutual interest in improving our own research, and of better understanding the research of others, one might expect that such discussions would appear frequently at academic conferences and in journal articles. Yet that is not often the case. The last book-length treatment of research methods in social studies was Cornbleth's (1986) edited volume, *An Invitation to Research in Social Education*, and in 1991 the *Handbook of Research on Social Studies Teaching and Learning* (Shaver, 1991) carried just three chapters on methodology (one each on critical, quantitative, and qualitative methods). Since that time, research methods have only rarely been the focus of presentations at annual conferences such as the College and University Faculty Assembly of the National Council for the Social Studies (NCSS) or the Research in Social Studies Education Special Interest Group of the American Educational Research Association (AERA). Articles on the topic are rarely found in *Theory and Research in Social Education*, and international journals and conferences are just as unlikely to feature discussion of research methods in social studies or its constituent subjects. When we talk about research, we understandably focus on our findings, but why is discuss of our methods so rare?

Reasons for the paucity of methodological discussion in social studies are open to interpretation, but two factors may have dampened enthusiasm for the topic. The first may be a lurking self-doubt, a fear that we are doing something wrong. When I first entered the field in the early 1990s, one of the few times I heard research methods discussed publicly was at business meetings of the College and University Faculty Assembly of NCSS. Each year Jack Fraenkel, then editor of *Theory and Research in Social Education*, would end his annual report by admonishing the audience not to submit papers in which they used inferential statistics inappropriately. Over the years, I have come to appreciate the importance of Fraenkel's advice (and the depth of his frustration) as I have read countless manuscripts that made the mistakes he warned against—usually by conducting tests of statistical significance to evaluate the magnitude of differences found in convenience samples (see also Fraenkel & Wallen,1991).

Advice about the proper use of statistical tests are perfectly fitting for the research community, and there may be other areas in which such warnings are justified—such as the need to adhere to ethical standards in the protection of participants. Unfortunately, however, the idea that research methods can be sorted into correct and incorrect applications has extended beyond topics such as inferential statistics. There really are correct and incorrect uses of such tests, but few research methods can be so neatly dichotomized. There are no correct and incorrect ways of interviewing participants, observing classrooms, or designing surveys; there are only more and less productive ways of doing these with given populations for particular purposes. Although the social studies research community would surely benefit from discussing the range of such possibilities, many researchers may not perceive the field as being open to such discussions.

In the first volume of this series on *Research in Social Education*, for example, Shaver (2001) decried the fact that social studies was not "imbued with a common research culture" (p. 240) and argued that deficiencies of research in the field were due to its "intellectual uncertainty" (241), the "disruptive effects of conflicting epistemologies" (p. 241), and a "lack of consensual thought" (p. 244). The effect of this kind of argument can be chilling: If social studies researchers think the field is closed to diverse perspectives and innovative approaches, they are unlikely to initiate discussion of methods, either in print or in person. Although it is tempting to think that this exclusivity is limited to proponents of positivistic research designs, such warnings can also be found among advocates of ethnographic, phenomenological, critical, or other interpretive traditions. Such advocates are sometimes perceived as asserting authority over their territory by establishing what counts as a legitimate application of their favored method. If social studies researchers find that their attempts to apply such perspectives are dismissed as "misuses," they will have little incentive to expand their repertoire. In both these cases—calls for methodological conformity and assertions of ownership of given methods—open discussion of alternatives becomes too risky, particularly for newcomers to the field. Who wants to discuss research methods if they might be told they're either disruptive or mistaken? Each of the chapters in this book, on the other hand, aims to open up consideration of alternatives rather than to foreclose such discussion.

A second factor that may have diminished enthusiasm for methodological discussion in social studies is the legacy of the "quantitative versus qualitative" debate. This was a hotly contested issue in education in the 1980s and 1990s, and on those rare occasions when research methods have been discussed in the social studies community, this has often been the focus. Yet this debate has not always been a productive one. To portray quantitative and qualitative data as though they were mutually exclusive—indeed, as though they inevitably reflected different epistemological and even moral positions—is short-sighted, and several of the chapters in this volume show how irrelevant such dichotomies are. Richardson (Chapter 8), for example, explains how cognitive interviews can be used to explore respondents' understanding of (and response to) survey items, and thus how qualitative research can improve quantitative measures. Hahn (Chapter 7) also notes that the validity of international quantitative surveys relies on an appreciation of context, which necessarily derives from qualitative inquiry. VanSledright, Meuwissan, and Kelly (Chapter 10), meanwhile, describe their attempt to construct a scale that would measure qualitative changes in teachers' ideas about history. Indeed, construction of any quantitative measure always depends on qualitative research (whether formal or informal), because the content of those measures always derives from concepts that have been expressed in verbal terms—people don't speak in numbers, and thus no research can be purely quantitative. Similarly, anytime a qualitative study uses terms such as "one," "some," "most," or "nearly all," it has reported quantitative data, however inexact.

Evaluating this debate as though true scholarship or morality lay on one side or the other is similarly unproductive. Proponents of quantitative research often dismiss qualitative studies for their lack of precision, but the fact that so many quantitative studies misuse inferential statistics indicates that numbers are no guarantee of academic quality. Advocates of qualitative research, on the other hand, sometimes portray quantitative studies as inherently conservative and repressive, as though they existed only to reinforce the status quo; qualitative studies, conversely, may be described as fundamentally reflexive, participatory, and even emancipatory. But as Tyson (Chapter 2) suggests, the emancipatory potential of research derives, in part, from its responsiveness to community concerns and its benefit to participants. Plenty of qualitative researchers collect data without giving thought to such issues, and sometimes their work may even harm the communities that have given them access. Just as important, in many cases teachers, parents, and even students may want researchers to collect not qualitative but quantitative data (e.g., what portion of minorities take advanced courses?). The distinction between qualitative and quantitative data simply does not map neatly onto political or ethical positions. The chapters in this volume raise a number of sophisticated questions about research, yet nowhere in them will you find a discussion of "quantitative versus qualitative" research. The bluntness of such a conceptual tool may have slowed the course of methodological discussions in our field, but these chapters suggest that we are ready to move forward in new directions.

OPENING UP DISCUSSION OF RESEARCH METHODS

The lack of discussion of research methods in the public forums of social studies—its journals and conferences—sometimes leaves researchers ill-prepared to make informed choices about their questions, designs, instruments, and analytic procedures. Doctoral students in particular may find themselves relying on research courses taken from faculty in educational foundations, and these are not always appropriate to the kinds of studies they hope to undertake. Quantitative courses, for example, typically focus on precisely the statistical procedures that are of little use in school- and classroom-based studies. Qualitative courses, meanwhile, often emphasize ethnographies, yet many studies of teaching and learning in social studies do not revolve around the concept of culture (as ethnographies traditionally have done), nor do they involve the kind of comprehensive investigation that is characteristic of ethnographies. As a result, beginning researchers may spend their time focusing on procedures that have little use for them, and that may even be counterproductive. To take one example: Students in qualitative methods courses may learn how to explain their presence in schools through the use of "cover stories," but classroom researchers often need no such subterfuge. Usually we can tell participants exactly why we are there—because we want to know what students think about the Holocaust (Schweber, Chapter 6), or national identity (Waldron, Chapter 5), or how teachers include empathy (Cunningham, Chapter 9) or primary sources (VanSledright et al., Chapter 10) in their lessons. At the same time, qualitative research courses may not address the range of instruments that can be used in interviews, because ethnographic studies typically rely on informal or semi-structured conversations. In social studies, on the other hand, we often use sorting tasks, stimulated recall, think alouds, ranking exercises, visual images, hypothetical scenarios, and a range of other devices designed to help participants articulate ideas about topics they may have little practice discussing.

When doctoral students need to go beyond the methods covered in research courses, they understandably rely on the expertise of their doctoral advisors, and that's usually a good way of being apprenticed into the use of productive research methods. But none of us are experts on everything, and when students' interests diverge from those of their mentors, they would benefit from the kinds of public discussions that are lacking in our field. Such discussions could lead to expanded ideas about research questions, designs, sampling procedures, instruments, and methods of analysis. Although most members of our profession are probably happy to discuss such matters informally with their peers and junior colleagues, beginners may not always feel comfortable initiating such contacts, or they may not move in the same professional circles as those who would be most helpful to them. All of us would benefit if discussions of research methods were more public and accessible.

This volume represents an initial attempt to contribute to such discussions. The authors of the following chapters address a number of important issues in social studies research, and they illustrate those with examples from their own experience. Three chapters emphasize the conceptualization of research questions. In reviewing the historiography of social studies, Woyshner (Chapter 2) identifies three approaches that have dominated the field, suggests how these could be expanded, and offers new questions that might be pursued. VanSledright and colleagues (Chapter 10) point to the need for greater conceptual clarity in designing research, and although their examples focus on history education, their call for theoretical precision is applicable to any topic. And Tyson (Chapter 3), as already noted, explores how researchers could attend more closely to the needs and concerns of the communities in which they work.

The next two chapters focus on the design and implementation of research, and both build on Tyson's suggestions for more directly attending to participants' perspectives. Johnston (Chapter 4) provides a rationale for action research and self-study, and she details their defining characteristics and common elements. Waldron (Chapter 5) describes how children can be more fully incorporated into the research process, and she discusses the ethical justification for doing so. Tyson, Johnston, and Waldron all focus on how researchers can connect more closely with participants; however, not all research allows for such connections, and the next two chapters illustrate some of the challenges of studies in which distance is inescapable. Schweber (Chapter 6) describes the issues she faced in conducting research at two sites where she was clearly perceived as an outsider—one a fundamentalist Christian school, the other a fundamentalist Jewish school—and the ways in which her personal identity intersected with the demands of her research. Hahn (Chapter 7) addresses international and comparative studies, in which researchers and participants are typically separated by cultural, educational, and linguistic differences. She examines the benefits of this kind of distance—for researchers, at least—and identifies factors that facilitate such research.

The final three chapters focus more directly on data collection, and particularly on ways in which we can better ensure that we are accurately representing participants' perspectives. Richardson (Chapter 8), as noted earlier, explains how cognitive interviews can be used to improve the design and interpretation of surveys. Cunningham (Chapter 9) emphasizes teachers' ability to reflect on their own practice; in contrast to much received wisdom in the field, she found that teachers could represent their thoughts and practices clearly and thoughtfully. The range of methods she used to encourage this effort should serve as a model for other studies. Finally, VanSledright and colleagues (Chapter 10)—in addition to advocating greater conceptual clarity, as already noted—explore the challenges of getting at the thinking of students and teachers, and particularly the ways in which our instruments require constant interrogation and rethinking, lest we place more confidence in them than they merit.

This volume is by no means comprehensive. There are far more topics, more perspectives, more suggestions and advice than could be covered in a scant nine chapters. I have tried, however, to include contributions from researchers who work with varied methods, in diverse settings, and from multiple theoretical frameworks, and I hope that these chapters will prove as useful to other researchers as they have been to me. With any luck, they may inspire further discussion of methods, and such conversations may become a regular and ongoing part of the public discourse of our field.

ACKNOWLEDGEMENTS

I deeply appreciate the efforts of each of the volume's authors. They have produced chapters that are stimulating and insightful, and I particularly appreciate their willingness to open up their own research challenges for public scrutiny—no easy matter. I am also indebted to reviewers of individual chapters for their careful and thoughtful suggestions; these include Kathy Bickmore, Margaret Smith Crocco, Todd Dinkelman, Cynthia Hartzler-Miller, Alan Sears, and Elizabeth Yeager. Thanks are also due to series editor Merry Merryfield, who suggested the project, and to Diana Hess and Stephen Thornton for their thoughtful suggestions.

REFERENCES

Barton, K. C. (1997). "I just kinda know": Elementary students' ideas about historical evidence. *Theory and Research in Social Education, 25*, 407–430.

Cornbleth, C. (1986). *An invitation to research in social education* (Bulletin No. 77, National Council for the Social Studies). Washington, DC: National Council for the Social Studies.

Cunningham, D. L. (2003). *Professional practice and perspectives in the teaching of historical empathy.* Unpublished doctoral dissertation, Oxford University.

Fraenkel, J. R., & Wallen, N. E. (1991). Quantitative research in social studies education. In J. P. Shaver (Ed.), *Handbook of research on social studies teaching and learning* (pp. 67–82). New York: Macmillan.

Hahn, C. L. (1998). *Becoming political: Comparative perspectives on citizenship education.* Albany: State University of New York Press.

Scheweber, S., & Irwin, R. (2003). "Especially special": Learning about Jews in a fundamentalist Christian school. *Teachers College Record, 105,* 1693–1719.

Shaver, J. P. (Ed.). (1991). *Handbook of research on social studies teaching and learning.* New York: Macmillan.

Shaver, J. P. (2001). The future of research on social studies—For what purpose? In W. Stanley (Ed.), *Critical issues in social studies research for the 21st century* (pp. 231–252). Greenwich, CT: Information Age.

Spector, K. (2005). *Framing the Holocaust in English class: Secondary teachers and students reading Holocaust literature.* Unpublished doctoral dissertation, University of Cincinnati.

Torney-Purta, J., & Richardson, W. K. (2002). An assessment of what 14-year-olds know and believe about democracy in 28 countries. In W. C. Parker (Ed.), *Education for democracy: Contexts, curricula, assessments* (pp. 185–210). Greenwich, CT: Information Age.

VanSledright, B. A. (2002). *In search of America's past: Learning to read history in elementary school.* New York: Teachers College Press.

Woyshner, C. (2004). From assimilation to cultural pluralism: The PTA and civic education, 1900–1950. In C. Woyshner, J. Watras, & M. S. Crocco (Eds.), *Social education in the twentieth century: Curriculum and context for citizenship* (pp. 93–109). New York: Peter Lang.

CHAPTER 2

NOTES TOWARD A HISTORIOGRAPHY OF THE SOCIAL STUDIES

Recent Scholarship and Future Directions

Christine Woyshner

The history of the social studies is a critical yet underrealized branch of educational research, and it is a relatively recent line of inquiry among social studies scholars. Examining the history of a curriculum field is central to understanding that area, however, as it informs policy, practice, and curriculum development. Most historians of the social studies suggest ahistoricism can and should be avoided, as historical antecedents "illuminate critically important subtleties of context and relationship that are crucial to policy and practices" (Davis, 1981, p. 26). Furthermore, researchers can benefit from having some sense of the historical context within which the field developed, as well as from knowing the various interpretive frameworks that historians of the social studies bring to the narrative, so that they can develop a more critical eye.

This chapter assesses the body of scholarship that has been developed over the last several decades and discusses common interpretations used by social studies historians since the time when leaders such as O.L. Davis, Jr. (1980, 1981) called for an understanding of the subject's history. However,

Research Methods in Social Studies Education, pages 11–38
Copyright © 2006 by Information Age Publishing

unlike Davis, who issued important caveats but refrained from offering a research agenda, I suggest additional lenses through which researchers may write the history of the field. In reviewing the scholarship on the history of social studies, I also began to wonder whether its multiple and conflicting definitions have made for multiple and conflicting histories. That is, might the fact that social studies has been defined in different ways, and has not always been a popular school subject, have played a role in shaping an equally discordant historiography? For instance, some scholars laud the progressive origins of the field as an important birthright that gives social studies credence in the school curriculum, while others use its progressive roots to argue for the field's lack of rigor. It is the purpose of this chapter to bring these and other interpretations to the fore in order to prompt further inquiry.

HISTORIOGRAPHICAL REVIEWS

A growing area of scholarship in the last three decades, historical analyses of the social studies have offered various and conflicting views of this content area's origins, meaning, and applications.[1] Paul Robinson (1980) noted a "modest surge of interest" (p. 65) in social studies history nearly a decade after Hazel Hertzberg (1971) pointed out that the field had been neglected as a subject of historical inquiry. Ten years after Robinson, Michael Bruce Lybarger (1991) declared that there was a "revival of interest in the history of social studies" (p. 8), and he cited as evidence the beginnings, in 1975, of National Council for the Social Studies (NCSS) conference presentations and publications that were dedicated to the history of social studies. In 1977, O.L. Davis, Jr., Oliver Keels, and Paul Robinson were among those who founded an NCSS special interest group on the Foundations of Social Studies.[2]

Several scholars have offered observations on this recent spate of studies into the past of the social studies. Davis (1980, 1981, 1995) has called for more nuanced investigations into the field's past that include "more sharply focused case studies within specific school contexts" (1995, p. 52) and histories that treat broader movements as well as the lives of individuals and institutions. Davis has been at the vanguard of promoting the importance of the history of social studies, and he has denounced studies that lack attention to historical research standards and do not involve systematic, thorough investigations of evidence within its historical context. Arguably, these and other appeals for more exacting scholarship have resulted in more sophisticated interpretations in the area. Davis's invitation to conduct further inquiry into the history of social studies marks a turning point in the field's historiography, from "impatient probing and haphazard sifting of evidence" (1995, p. 52) to more careful analyses in the late 20th and early 21st centuries.

Other scholars have followed Davis's suggestions and added their own commentaries on the historiography of social studies. Lybarger (1991), for example, claims that historians of social studies have not "as yet developed a sufficiently diverse range of writings" (p. 4); he offers direction to those undertaking such studies and implores scholars to attend to broader intellectual and social contextual factors. In his analysis of methods textbooks, David Warren Saxe (1992a) cautions would-be social studies historians against subscribing to the misguided notion that the subject either originated spontaneously in the early 20th century or was invented by the National Education Association's Committee on Social Studies in 1916. He argues for a more thorough investigation of the roots of the subject.

More recently, a special issue of *International Journal of Social Education* explored the history of social studies by looking at critical episodes, crucial issues, and controversies and dilemmas. Each of these themes or directions represented further thinking about the focused case studies that Davis called for. Special issue editor Ronald W. Evans (2004) noted that earlier histories of the field situated "changes in thought and practice in internal developments within social studies" (p. 3), whereas more recent histories looked at broader trends in education and society that influenced social studies. For this special issue, Evans invited scholars to follow the second line of inquiry and submit articles that included biographies of social studies leaders "writ large," suggesting greater attention to historical context than in previous analyses. Evans, like Davis, declared a need for "full, rich, and multi-sided portrayals of social studies' past replete with multiple schools of interpretation" (Evans, 2003, p. viii).

Finally, an edited collection by Christine Woyshner, Joseph Watras, and Margaret Smith Crocco (2004) takes up the mantle of broader social, political, and economic contexts to examine the development of social studies in the twentieth century. Echoing Davis's call, the authors issue a caveat against drawing "oversimplistic conclusions about the field's past," but they claim that such conclusions are due to the "thin and uneven nature of the historiographic evidence found in social studies" (p. xix). In contrast to Davis's optimistic outlook regarding the increasing availability of primary sources, Woyshner and colleagues argue that the field has been hindered by issues in documentation, such as the lack of primary sources that shed light on actual classroom practices. This has always been the challenge facing the curriculum historian, because far more official reports and prescriptive pronouncements have been saved for posterity than evidence of application and interpretation (Cuban, 1991). As Davis suggests, the "impressive inventory of activity in the social studies" (1981, p. 33) during the early years of the 20th century is the reason that a fair amount of the historiography is dedicated to interpreting the intentions and bent of social studies committees in that period, rather than looking at other curricular endeavors over time. Scholars have tried creative means to tap into the history of social studies practices, but this line of inquiry has yet to be developed.[3] Nonetheless, it is worth remembering that even prescriptions can offer insight into what a group of people held to be important or valuable, and it is this perspective that has sustained much of the historical research in the field (Davis, 1981; Kliebard, 1992).

In what follows I outline three recurrent and overlapping interpretive frameworks in the historiography of the social studies. For the purposes of this chapter I stay close to the subject area usually labeled social studies and do not include works that investigate histories of more specific content areas (e.g., economics, history education) unless the researcher considers that domain synonymous with social studies. As one might expect, it was difficult at times to parse histories of social studies from those that dealt with narrower disciplines. Therefore, while this analysis does not represent a comprehensive review of the field's historiography, I believe it offers scaffolding that will allow others to deconstruct existing histories and forge new paths of inquiry.

The first narrative orbits around the Progressive-era origins of the field and highlights changes in the history profession and the rise of social efficiency and child-centered pedagogy.[4] While I could locate no dispute as to the progressive origins of the social studies, I did observe that oftentimes these origins were used either to support or undercut the importance of the subject. Closely linked to this controversy, the second of the three frameworks relies on a metaphor of struggle and usually casts that conflict in terms of history versus social studies. This perspective holds that social studies and history are at odds with each other, as if the school curriculum were a zero-sum entity in which one must lose for the other to gain. Indeed, much of the scholarship that applies the struggle metaphor revolves around the Progressive-era origins of the social studies, though the narrative of conflict continues in scholarship that extends well beyond that era and arguably to the present day. Finally, a significant portion of the historiography addresses biography—of individuals, institutions, and groups (such as committee members and professional associations). This may be considered a method—biographical investigation—but it also is an interpretive framework, because most of these studies seek to explain or recover the importance of an institution, leader, or group of leaders to the history of the social studies.

I discuss these frameworks separately in order to consider the central or driving interpretation of each, even though the three typically overlap. (For example, some histories rely on biographical data to argue for the progressive origins of the field.) Also, as I discussed above, many works that position history against social studies draw on the progressive roots of the subject to support one or the other stance. In my categorizing efforts, therefore, I attempted to determine the most salient interpretation and oftentimes considered the historical study biographical if a person's name or references to social studies leaders appeared in the title.[5] Certain works are discussed in more than one section because their analyses warrant it, or because I wished to use aspects of these works to highlight particular points. As I reviewed the historiography, I found most striking the extent to which scholars have debated so fervently the worth (or lack thereof) of a school subject. I can think of no other subject area in which this is the case. Can we envision a history of the chemistry curriculum that makes the argument that the subject area is not important? Are there histories of mathematics that argue for its rigor? Would any scholar dare put forward the notion that teaching English has outlived its usefulness? Missives for and against the relevance of social studies are lobbed in the historiography of the social studies and form a cacophonous subtext in this body of research.

THE PROGRESSIVE-ERA ORIGINS OF SOCIAL STUDIES

Investigations of the Progressive-era origins of the social studies form a major line of inquiry in the field's historiography. This interpretation holds that the history of social studies is shaped by its roots in progressivism, and I could find virtually no history to take the contrary position—that social studies did not emerge in the Progressive era or as a result of progressive endeavors—though some scholars have looked at precursors to the formal social studies curriculum (e.g., Keels, 1980, 1993, 1994). Some scholarship uses progressivism as the context within which social studies and its ideals emerged (e.g., Hertzberg, 1989; Lybarger, 1980; Reuben, 1997), while another segment of the literature applies progressivism as an argument to support or refute social studies' relevance (e.g., Bohan, 2004; Ravitch, 2003). The literature that supports social studies argues that it was a much-needed development amid an irrelevant and stodgy curriculum. These scholars, for whom the progressive bent of the social studies is an advantage, set the origins of the field against a tedious, traditionalist sphere in order to claim its relevance and appropriateness for a new student body and a new century. In particular, this interpretive framework appears to be utilized when a scholar wishes to counter the position, often found in the debates of the mid-to-late 20th century, that social studies is nondescript, has no substance, or is not as rigorous as disciplines such as history, geography, and political science. The other perspective, which holds that the presumed lack of rigor in social studies is due to its progressive origins, is based on an understanding of "progressive education" as more concerned with young people's feelings and attitudes than with rigor and content. This group of historians charges social studies with being too child-centered, nebulous, and ineffective.

The emphasis on progressivism and progressive education requires consideration of how social studies historians have defined these terms.[6] Unfortunately, the literature lacks definitional consistency regarding the notion of progressivism. A rare treatment is found in Hertzberg's chapter, "History and Progressivism: A Century of Reform Proposals" (1989); her outline of different types of progressive education is instructive in discussing social studies historiography. The first of Hertzberg's types is humanistic progressivism, which focused on the teaching and learning of academic subjects. It held that the student was an inquirer, not a receiver of information, and that the school curriculum included humanities and social sciences (the center of which was history) to help students exercise skills of judgment and interpretation. Hertzberg considers two other types of progressivism—scientific management and social efficiency—to be similar; within the social studies literature, both suggest an emphasis on social control through curriculum and pedagogy.[7] Finally, child-centered progressivism is the type most often associated with the notion of progressive education. It maintains that education should be focused on the developmental stages of childhood and that curriculum should focus on children's needs and interests. This understanding appears infrequently in the historiography of the social studies, perhaps because much of the field is centered on secondary education reports. According to Hertzberg, the three types appeared sequentially—humanistic progressivism appeared in the 1890s, social efficiency came to the fore in the 1910s, and child-centered progressivism enjoyed popularity in the 1920s.

A key debate that draws on the notion of humanistic progressivism focuses on whether the Committees of Ten (1983) and Seven (1899) reflected progressive ideals or whether those ideals were only embodied later, in the 1910s, in the social studies committee reports of the National Education Association (NEA).[8] Hertzberg (1989) argues the former: In the 1880s, a common core of beliefs that characterized "progressive education in history and other social subjects was emerging in the literature of reform" (p. 71; see also Hertzberg, 1988). She maintains that the work of the history committees of the Committee of Ten "set the agenda for what the members considered to be progressive education in the social subjects in purpose, content, and method" (1989, p. 74). These methods included question and discussion, non-textbook resources, and investigation by students. Building on Hertzberg's ideas, Chara Bohan (2004) uses humanistic progressivism to argue that the Committee of Ten and the American Historical Association's Committee of Seven did not argue for a pure subject of history for history's sake, but proposed a "broadened conception of history" and called for "a more complete program in history." Given this, and her reading of documents alongside biographical backgrounds of the committee members, Bohan argues that calls for this type of history were "quite progressive" (pp. 4–5). She asserts, "The authors of the Committee of Ten report should be viewed as the vanguards of early progressive thought, not traditionalists committed to upholding the status quo," because they "sought to create a prominent place for history in the school curriculum" (p. 6).

This interpretation contrasts with that of historian of education R. Freeman Butts (1977), who considers social studies to have emerged as part of what he labels "The Civics of Progressive Modernization, 1876–1926." His major sources include texts used to teach history and social studies in this era, and his discussion of civic education focuses on the development of social studies in the early 20th century. Butts characterizes the Committees of Ten and Seven as favoring history in the schools and promoting the goal of teaching "high school students a historian's grasp of the nature of evidence" (p. 56). This he contrasts with the progressive leanings of the NEA committees on social studies of the 1910s, which, "reflecting Progressive views of reform, explicitly brought citizenship to the forefront of the social responsibility of the secondary school" (pp. 57–58). Butts uses a humanistic progressive interpretation to explain social studies' emphasis on government and history and the change in pedagogy from rote memorization to investigation. However, he argues that despite appeals for a change in pedagogy, lecturing and other traditional methods held on in classrooms (p. 59).

Following Butts's line of thinking, Saxe (1991, 1992a) argues that the Committees of Ten and Seven valued history, and he contrasts this position with the progressivism of the social studies committees of the 1910s. He therefore sets up a dichotomy between those who preferred history and the "insurgents" who favored a social science emphasis in the curriculum. Saxe (1991) writes that by 1916 "the insurgents' movement was gaining attention" (p. 137) as they sought to reorganize secondary education. At this point in his narrative, Saxe introduces the influence of the second type of progressivism, the doctrine of social efficiency, and explains that it came about "during the political transition from conservative programs to the progressive agenda" (p. 140).

Scholars reveal virtual unanimity in their assertion that the second type of progressivism, that of social efficiency and/or scientific management, characterized the work of the NEA committees on social studies of the 1910s.[9] Accompanied by a shift from university professors to school leaders, curriculum-making arose as a distinct specialty in this period and was led by individuals such as W. W. Charters, Franklin Bobbitt, and David Snedden (Hertzberg, 1988; Kliebard, 1986; Robinson, 1980). Hertzberg

(1988) argues that "social efficiency" was integral to the NEA social studies committees, which promoted community civics and the "Problems of Democracy" course as two aspects of a new, functional social studies curriculum. As N. Ray Hiner (1972) explains, social efficiency meant cultivating both individual development and cooperation in a differentiated curriculum, a notion that contrasted with the Committee of Ten's promotion of "aristocratic education for all" (p. 44).

Social efficiency is central to Saxe's (1991) study of the origins of social studies. His social studies insurgents were an integral part of the group of social efficiency experts who led the charge to reform the school curricula in the early 20th century, and he argues that the traditional history curriculum faded quickly once the "social studies movement embraced social efficiency as its battle cry" (p. 25). Social efficiency, according to sociologists such as Snedden, meant that the school curriculum would be differentiated and the social sciences would provide educators with important data about curriculum and pedagogy. Saxe argues that ultimately, however, history was viewed as an "inefficient discipline" by such social efficiency experts. Therefore, the Committee on Social Studies "established that public education and in particular social education (social studies) needed to be centered on working toward the goal of social efficiency. [This] appealed to urban educators overburdened by the massive influx of immigrants from Europe as well as from the southern states" (Saxe, 1991, p. 169).

Child-centered progressivism is less apparent in the scholarship on the past of the social studies. One notable exception is Julie A. Reuben's (1997) research on how community civics was influenced by changing notions of citizenship at the turn of the 20th century. Reuben argues that the changes in the school curriculum during this time, most notably the creation of the social studies, cannot be accounted for solely by rising immigration. (Ironically, the widely accepted notion among historians of education, that increased immigration accounted for sweeping changes in schools and the school curriculum, appears infrequently in the social studies historiography, which tends to focus its analysis on internal development and is typically only incidentally related to broader historical frameworks [Robinson, 1980].) Reuben embeds the development of community civics in the radical shift from the "rigorous and elitist 'republican citizenship'" of the mid-19th century to the more democratic concept that broadened the definition of citizenship beyond voting and political rights. Likewise, she argues, community civics was "aimed at younger children and incorporated progressive pedagogical theories" (p. 400), and in so doing, the new curriculum involved younger children in the study of civics and aimed to teach them about community participation.

Why do scholars dedicate so much energy to these early reports and the progressive origins of the social studies? Although this era was one of ferment in civic and social education ideas, my impression is that these efforts seek either to establish or to deemphasize the importance of social studies by beginning at the beginning, which for many historians is the series of reports produced by the NEA social studies committees of the 1910s. If one can show that the subject of social studies was supported by early historians and educationists, one might be able to convince readers of the importance of the subject. Or, depending on how the reader views progressive education, a case may be made that undercuts rather than supports social studies in the school curriculum. In fact, Davis (1981) has lamented this overemphasis on the early years—an overemphasis that since then, thankfully, has been remedied with analyses that cover much more ground. Nonetheless, it is well worth asking what other eras and movements shaped the social studies. Looking across the 20th century, one notices that the field has been influenced by such movements as civil rights, feminism, and postmodernism (Crocco, 2004; Howard, 2004; Segall, 2004). Society's political and intellectual revolutions must certainly have had an impact on the ways that citizenship education has been conceptualized and taught in schools. I address recent scholarship that explores these and other episodes at the conclusion of this essay.

THE STRUGGLE METAPHOR,
OR HISTORY VERSUS SOCIAL STUDIES

The interpretive framework of struggle seeks to emphasize differences between two or more competing groups, each with a stake in the social education curriculum. In 1991, Lybarger called for further research that applied Kliebard's (1986) notion of struggle, at around the same time that this interpretation was already inundating scholarship in the field. Some scholars frame the struggle as one between historians and social studies leaders (Hiner, 1972; Keels, 1980; Saxe, 1991), while others seek to reveal how other interest groups played a role in the development of the field (Evans, 2004). This interpretation extends well beyond the Progressive era to the present day, though a substantial portion of the historiography focuses on the years 1893 to 1916. Histories that identify interest groups tend to follow the schema outlined by Kliebard (1986), who identifies social meliorists, social reconstructionists, and social efficiency experts. Social studies historians have been slower to incorporate Davis's (1981) and Lybarger's (1991) suggestion that they include other community groups, such as settlement houses, fraternal associations, and charity organizations (e.g., Zimmerman, 2002). For example, Evans (2003) argues that

20th-century social studies scholarship has looked at "history versus social science versus social efficiency versus social meliorism versus social reconstructionism" (2003, p. viii), a characterization that hinges on a framework of struggle among factions. This depiction of conflict among competing groups is the most accepted narrative of social studies' development in the 20th century.

The narrative has the general contours of the following plot, which may include two or more groups: Historians argue for a disciplinary bent to social education in the schools, with history at the core. They may or may not support the notion that history makes for good citizenship; if not, they emphasize the importance of learning history for its own sake. Meanwhile, the more progressive camp of social studies leaders—whether individuals or interest groups or both—are portrayed as idealistic educationists who forge a curriculum of relevance and democracy for the 20th century. In works that favor history, social studies educationists are sometimes cast as softhearted progressives who promote a toothless curriculum.[10] This line of inquiry creates an oppression narrative, to borrow a trope from women's history (Lerner, 1981), in that social studies, the subject area that is new or has been marginalized, seeks to attain legitimacy in the traditional canon.

Histories of the social studies written in the 1970s and 1980s took up this debate to varying degrees. Hiner (1972, 1973) was among the first to look at these two groups in terms of what he construed as "changing relations" between educators and historians of the early twentieth century. This changing relationship—and the degree to which historical study was accepted in the high school curriculum—depended on what kind of history was in favor (e.g., modern or ancient, history focused on social relevance, etc.). He writes that the "firm alliance" between historians and educators was due in part to historians' willingness to "embrace citizenship as the primary objective of history in the schools and the educators' acceptance of the thesis that historical mindedness was an essential characteristic of the good citizen" (1972, p. 41). Hiner thus suggests a potential disagreement between those favoring history as a distinct subject and those favoring a social-science approach to the curriculum.

However, the distinctions between history and social studies were not always so stark. Hertzberg (1988) downplays these differences as she discusses method and content in teaching history. Her interpretation utilizes the phrase favored by those in the early 20th century, *history and the allied subjects*. Consequently, Hertzberg uses the terms history, social studies, and social sciences virtually interchangeably. Her argument, one that is challenged by Saxe, holds that the history that was put forth in the Committee of Ten's 1893 report focused on practical matters and preparation for life through its emphasis on history and civil government. She writes, "The Committee of Ten sought to bring the incipient social sciences into the curriculum" (p. 16). Nonetheless, Hertzberg upholds the history-versus-social studies dichotomy by accepting as fact that there were two camps, though she posits that for over 50 years, historians were the "chief friend and defender" of social studies (p. 13).

While Hertzberg's writings on social studies history are lauded (Lybarger, 1991), they are also problematic because she cites virtually no secondary sources, a glaring oversight in historical method (Saxe, 1992a). Her histories refer to important secondary works, such as those by David B. Tyack and Raymond Callahan, but they are not cited in the references, nor are their interpretations used as context in any way. One scholar went so far as to point out that she is among those to use a thesis to support a political position (Cuban, 1991).

Shortcomings in method also characterize other publications that employ the struggle metaphor, the major offense being selective blindness when it comes to the secondary literature. One example is Stephen Correia's (1999) article, "The De-evolution of Social Studies." In his discussion of whether social studies or history has dominated, he draws simplistic conclusions about the type of history proposed by the Committee of Ten, connecting it to a "cultural transmission" brand of citizenship education (p. 34). This interpretation does not take into account the many writings on the history of social studies and the tensions around history education of this time, and it does not interject any thorough discussion of the history and meaning of citizenship education through a review of the secondary scholarship in this area. Such approaches fail to heed Davis's (1981) caveat regarding ahistoricism in writing the history of social studies; Davis writes that scholars' "search for evidentiary support of reform proposals routinely yields a catalogue of precedents, ordinarily snatched from context and threaded together with slogans in lieu of meaning" (pp. 19–20). This myopia is a significant aspect of calls for greater attention to broader contexts in the historiography, and historians of the social studies should be well cautioned against linking current trends to past precedents, and particularly against doing so in a manner that does not follow historical methodology.

Another sin of omission in social studies historiography is the converse of failing to attend to existing secondary literature: not securing adequate primary source documentation. In reviewing Saxe's *Social Studies in the Schools*, Keels (1993) chides Saxe for his choice of sources—"solely public utterances"—and claims, "Saxe makes no reference to archival sources, and he fails even to employ any of the available published collections of correspondence" (p. 185). Keels also refers to Saxe's most egregious error in method, that of making claims beyond the evidence. This particular misstep is all too common in a historiography that expends significant energy interpreting official pronouncements of what the social studies curriculum should be rather than focusing on what actually transpired in school districts and classrooms.

Nonetheless, the most thorough application of the struggle metaphor is found in Saxe's writings (1991, 1992a, 1994, 2003). Saxe details the emergence of social studies with the early 20th century National Education Association committees and argues that the central issue in the origins of the social studies is the conflict between traditional historians and the social studies "insurgents" who wrestled for control of the social and civic education curriculum. In terms of evidence, Saxe relies heavily on the committee reports of this era and employs a common historiographic strategy by examining the membership of the NEA and AHA committees to establish his position (see also Bohan, 2004; Hertzberg, 1988; Hiner, 1972). He attributes the origins of the social studies to the NEA committees of 1913, 1915, and 1916 and argues that social studies has its origins not in history but in the social science fields (1991, 1992a). Saxe calls the argument that social studies originated in history the "historical foundation research" and includes Keels, Hertzberg, and Hiner in this group (1992a, p. 264).

Saxe's 1991 book is extremely detailed in its description of the work of the early history and social studies committees, and his writings might prompt other scholars to pursue questions he raises, including whether such inquiries are "picky and arcane as counting angels on heads of pins" (Saxe, 1992a, pp. 266–267). Saxe and others have been unable to answer that question thoroughly, yet much must be at stake inasmuch as the metaphor of struggle has been applied in recent years to call for the end of social studies. In his article "On the Alleged Demise of the Social Studies," Saxe (2003) uses the progressive roots of social studies and the metaphor of struggle to argue for the field's obsolescence in a high-stakes testing environment, and he asks whether social studies should survive in the 21st century. So, while his support of social studies has changed, the interpretive framework remains the same: history and the social studies are presented as adversaries.[11] Saxe's proclivity for the history-versus-social studies narrative—in which history is or should be the victor—is evident as he argues that "the eclectic wing of the social studies continued to drift from one curricular fad to another, [as] the field's history-centered, disciplinary-focused wing remained entrenched in certain quarters, poised to return" (p. 96). He denigrates social studies for its eclecticism—its ability to encompass a wide range of ideas in the social sciences, along with curricular programs such as values clarification, inquiry teaching, and life adjustment approaches. Saxe characterizes the social studies as having "one curricular foot in a scattering of subject areas and the other in a multitude of processes," and argues that "social studies were everything and nothing" (p. 97), leading him to call for a return to traditional, rigorous history instruction. This particular publication is an example of how scholars use the metaphor of struggle to position history against social studies, thereby attempting to directly impact current policy and practice.

One of the most blatant examples of using the struggle metaphor to support an overt political agenda is Diane Ravitch's application of the history-versus-social studies narrative (e.g., 1985a, 1985b, 2003). Ravitch calls for a return to history in the schools by pitting the rigor of the pure subject area of history against the "mishmash of courses" that is social studies (2003, p. 1). Unlike Saxe (2003), who argues that social studies and history coexisted over the course of the 20th century, Ravitch claims, "Over the past century, the teaching of chronological history was steadily displaced by social studies" (p. 1).[12] She traces the origins of the social studies to the commission reports of the 1910s and claims that by the end of the 20th century, many social studies educators regarded history with "open disdain, suggesting that the study of the past was a useless exercise in obsolescence that attracted antiquarians and hopeless conservatives" (p. 2). Though more polemical than other scholars writing the history of social studies, Ravitch's work merits mention because of the widespread acknowledgment of—and potential adherence to—her recommendations by policymakers. It should be noted, however, that social studies historians have taken both Ravitch and Saxe to task for their "suspect views of the past" (Whelan, 1997a, p. 257; see also Keels, 1993). Whelan (1997a) comments on both scholars' work in pointing to the problem of social studies historians that are decontextualized and that tailor research to support a political position.

Lest we start to believe that the metaphor of struggle is used only by those who have an agenda, we can turn to other recent works that employ the narrative in more even-handed ways. These studies either incorporate multiple constituencies into the historiography or seek to add nuance to a caricature of social studies educators pitted against historians. A recent book by Evans (2004) will serve as an illustration of the former, in its examination of various competing groups within the history-versus-social studies framework. Evans applies Kliebard's interest-group theory, rightly arguing that this particular direction tenders a "richly textured history" (p. 3). He outlines the activities of no fewer than five competing camps, all with a stake in the school curriculum, including Kliebard's descriptors of social meliorists, social reconstructionists, and social efficiency experts.[13] An additional camp works toward consensus in the history-versus-social studies narrative. Although Evans admits that the history of social studies is more accurately one of negotiation among interest groups (and thus suggesting dialogue), his use of the combat metaphor is striking as he explains that he wrote the study as a story of "civil war, with competing armies of American educators clashing on the battlefield of curriculum development and their recommendations breaking over the anvil of classroom constancy" (p. 4). To his credit, Evans incorporates the multiple contexts called for by Davis (1981) in his attempt to write a full history of the clashes among competing groups within social education. Many recent works adhere to the caveat of minding the rich contexts approach that I discuss in the concluding section of this chapter (e.g., Blount, 2004; Lybarger, 1980, 1987; Reuben, 1997).

In an effort to produce scholarship that goes beyond a simplistic narrative of historians against social studies educators, and building on the scholarship of Hertzberg (1971, 1988, 1989) and Whelan (1994, 1997b), Watras (2004) has written about the development of the field by looking at both similarities and differences between the two camps. He cautions us to avoid the simplistic understanding of an image of historians and educators falling into "distinct, uniform groups whose members held fast to specific aims and sought to have all schools affirm them" (2004, p. 193). Watras's research thereby troubles the notion of separate and distinct groups. Although this research rests on the central theme of history versus social studies, it presents a much more subtle interpretation than those found in previous studies, while also seeking to challenge the centrality of the metaphor of struggle.

One wonders why this metaphor has been so widely applied in the history of the social studies. It could be because the available documentary evidence supports the notion, which is how it came to be in the first place. Or, it could be that this trope is so widely accepted that historians do not question its salience or seek to offer other ways of construing the past.[14] This is not to fault current historians working in this area; it merely points to the legitimacy and importance of the interpretation. Yet it is still important to build on it and even counter it with other ways of looking at the past. It is critical to follow the path of expanding Kliebard's list of constituents with a stake in the social studies curriculum, and to do so without employing the metaphor of struggle. For example, a recent investigation into the role of women's voluntary associations looks at their supportive role in informing and promoting the community civics curriculum of the NEA's Committee on Social Studies (Woyshner, 2003). This interpretation does not hinge on clash and conflict but seeks to uncover a synergy between male professional leaders and women volunteers. Historians of social studies must continue to consider who is left out of the research, and this involves attending to those voices that are harder to hear in the historical record.

BIOGRAPHY: OLD MASTERS, GREAT MEN, AND WOMEN SOCIAL EDUCATORS

An emphasis on biography of intellectual leaders of the social studies is, in large part, the result of the availability of primary source documentation. A substantial line of inquiry in social studies historiography focuses on individuals—the accomplishments of men and women leaders—and relies heavily on biographical data, along with the major reports and formal curriculum recommendations of learned societies and professional groups. These leaders include the officers of the National Council for the Social Studies, the National Education Association, and other professional associations, as well as important scholars in the field. Often these studies point to the necessity of remembering a scholar's contribution and demonstrate how he or she shaped the curriculum or influenced thinking about the social studies.

Thus, the "Old Masters" approach is one that investigates, for example, the lives of the Progressive-era committee members and other important figures by "trying to reconstruct what they read, learned, and taught" (Lybarger, 1991, p. 11). While Lybarger argues this is "one of the most promising approaches to the history of social studies today" (p. 11), this promise has been more than kept by now; the "Old Masters" approach is one of the most widely used in the historiography of the field (e.g., Butts, 1986; Chilcoat & Ligon, 2003; Keels, 1988, 1994; McAninch, 1990; Nelson, 1987, 1988, 1999; Robinson, 1980; Saxe, 1991, 1992b; Stallones, 2002, 2003; Whelan, 1991, 1994, 1997a, 1997b). Often a central element of this approach is the argument that certain leading figures have been virtually unknown until the scholar's research brought them to the fore. For example, Whelan writes, "Despite the many contributions [Albert Bushnell] Hart made to the development of social studies education, his achievements in this regard have been the subject of very little scholarly research" (1994, p. 423). Keith C. Barton (2005) goes so far as to refer to Mary G. Kelty as "the most important social educator no one has heard of." In yet another example, Murray Nelson (1988) explains that "despite [Merl R. Eppse's] unique contribution to education, [he] has been forgotten and ignored academically" (p. 84).

Unlike other research on Old Masters, however, Nelson's study of Eppse is important due to the dearth of information on African American leaders in social studies, and thus I believe he is justified in his indignation over Eppse's absence in the historiographical record. Other instances of social studies historians' attention to African Americans can be found in Crocco (1999b), Dilworth (2003), and Watkins (1995). This is a dimension of the historiography that is in need of further exploration.

Related to the notion of uncovering heretofore unheard-of social studies leaders is the recent surge in scholarship on women in the history of the social studies (e.g., Crocco, 2004; Crocco & Davis, 1999, 2002). The lens of gender has challenged the Old Masters approach in two ways. First, it has had to rely on an expansive understanding of the definition of social studies, and it sometimes uses the more inclusive term "social education"

(Crocco, 1999a). Second, it has had to consider women's practical work and not just their intellectual leadership. As Margaret Smith Crocco (1999a) argues, one of the central challenges for women working in social education was that their contributions were often positioned "as low-status 'practice' rather than high-status 'theory'" (p. 3). By highlighting the contributions of women social educators, historians seek to render them visible in a field that has marginalized them (Crocco, 1999a). However, scholars such as Crocco are clear that rather than interpreting these women's lives in essentialist terms, their "experiences should be seen as responses to a set of concrete, historical situations shaped by a cultural ideology around gender" (1999a, p. 5). In some of the historiography on women social educators, subjects who are highly regarded in one arena are investigated in order to uncover their role in social studies curriculum development; one example is Petra Munro's look at Jane Addams's critique of classical liberal democracy (1999). Other works reveal the important contributions of the woman-behind-the-man, as in Crocco's study of Mary Ritter Beard's writing of history for schools (Crocco, 1997).

Researchers working along these narrative lines have faced the additional challenge of the paucity of sources on women social educators. Along with being relegated to practical activities over more theoretical ones, women in social studies typically wrote shorter, less theoretical tracts, textbooks, speeches, and curriculum projects (Crocco, 1999a). However, the nature of the researchers' questions can reveal much about their approach to historiography at the same time that it provides important insights about the past. For example, Crocco (2002) writes that the traditional historiographer asks, "Have there been any important women in social studies?" while her work asks, "Over our nation's history, how have women's lives and work reflected a concern with citizenship education?" (p. 12). Such questions inform the historiography by beginning with the assumption that women *were* working in social studies, or social education, and seeking to uncover their work. The same approach would hold for African American social studies leaders: One should not inquire whether there were any but begin with an exploration of what role their work played in shaping social studies. This area of research has raised important questions for other scholars to address. How has gender shaped the field? What have women leaders accomplished? Do their ideas, ideals, and activities look different than those of male leaders? It also is important to look at differences among women, something few studies have done.

Closely related to research on individuals is that on institutions and associations, or institutional biography. Such works explore the history of professional associations and their journals, usually through a focus on leaders. For example, a special issue of *Social Education* addressed the history of the National Council for the Social Studies by taking an era-by-era view (Smith & Palmer, 1995).[15] Similarly, scholars took a retrospective look at the journal *Theory and Research in Social Education* for its 25th anniversary (Shaver, 1997). These works add another perspective to the historiography, though they can be limited if one interprets their subjects as sole or primary influences in the field.

Biographical studies vary in the degree to which they explore the role of broader social, political, economic, and intellectual contexts, or of multiple contexts (Davis, 1981). It is widely believed among scholars that the more compelling histories use biography to illustrate an episode or development in the field. This is the case, for example, with Stuart A. McAninch's (1990) exploration of the educational theory of Mary Sheldon Barnes. McAninch uses Barnes's writings to illustrate early efforts to justify history as an important secondary school subject. He refers both to the intellectual context of Barnes's work—the influence of Pestalozzi—and to changes in the secondary school curriculum of the early 20th century. Likewise, McAninch does not present an entirely sympathetic biography of Barnes but notes that her "educational work also entailed a considerable degree of indoctrination" (p. 46). He thereby meets one of Davis's (1981) criteria for historical scholarship—being critical instead of overly sanguine toward a person's contribution. More narrowly focused biographies spend too much time discussing the individual, are too removed from context, and are apt to be overly positive about the individual's contributions. For example, Jane Bernard-Powers refers to Jared Stallones's (2002) book on Paul Robert Hanna as "an unselfconsciously subjective tribute" (p. 452) that reports more of what Hanna thought was important about his life than what the biographer believed was significant. In biography, sympathy can be anathema if overdone.

On the flip side, being overly critical also can have its drawbacks and may reflect a contemporary political agenda. One example is Donald Johnson's (2000) hypercritical interpretation of the role and legacy of Thomas Jesse Jones. Before Jones became chair of the NEA's Committee on Social Studies, he taught at Hampton Institute, where he crafted a social studies curriculum that focused on educating African American and American Indian students for vocational work and sought to keep them in the lower strata of society. Indeed, Jones is a controversial figure in the history of social studies, but most scholars have handled his legacy with thoroughness and complexity, potraying Jones as a product of the early 20th century (e.g., Dilworth, 2003; Saxe, 1992b; Watkins, 1995). As William H. Watkins (1995) explains, "Jones's social studies met the hegemonic political and social mandates of the time" (p. 132).

However, Johnson's detailed study of Jones's racist educational activities forms the basis of an argument that social studies is no longer appropriate for the school curriculum. In a surprising turn, Johnson (2000) concludes that Jones's ideas are still applied today and asks, "Has the legacy of racism and its key role in the shaping of the field of social studies inadvertently resulted in new teachers being trained to assume that certain groups of students won't, or worse, do not have the innate ability to do homework, read primary documents, or deal with abstractions?" (pp. 91–92). Davis (1981) warns that historians must be careful to avoid the trappings of assuming continuity in ideas over time, yet Johnson ahistorically fails to consider the changing meanings of social studies over the course of more than 80 years.

What does a focus on individuals have to offer? Biography is an accessible means of studying the past because it is more interesting to read about a person or group than a series of events. Also, primary source documentation on individuals often is readily available, whereas it is less abundant on such ephemeral activities as classroom practices. Yet biography can limit our view of the past by making individuals the central players and suggesting they have more control and oversight over curricular changes and reform than they actually do.[16] Biographical studies of famous firsts in social studies constitute a well-worn path that sheds light on the contributions of individuals, organizations, and institutions, but it should be considered one of several lenses through which historians of social studies might view the evolution of the field. However, biographical studies of those whose voices have been absent from the historical record, such as women and African Americans, have been important additions to this body of the literature, and this effort still needs to be expanded to other marginalized groups.

CONCLUSION: OTHER WAYS OF LOOKING

Commenting on the contributions of early social studies historians Henry Johnson, Rolla Tryon, and Edgar Wesley, Paul Robinson (1980) explains that these three structured a conventional view of social studies' past that has tended to dominate our perception of the field's historical development. Characteristics of this view include examining the chronological development of the social sciences in schools; relying on reports of national organizations and scholarly surveys; analyzing internal development of the field at the expense of broader historical frameworks; and focusing on persistent tensions between citizenship goals and intellectual aims in the social studies. In the discussion above I demonstrated that these pitfalls remain in the second generation of scholarship, which began in the 1970s, despite the advent of revisionist and radical history (Lybarger, 1991). However, these pitfalls do not reflect the entirety of the historiography, as some works do take context into account, look beyond the early years, and consider the role and influence of marginalized groups.

Nonetheless, the impression one gets when reviewing the historiography of social studies is one of contested curricular territory—territory that leaders define, constituents must vie for, and some people denounce. Whether noting the field's progressive origins, employing a metaphor of struggle, or focusing on influential leaders, many scholars appear compelled to take a position for or against social studies. These analyses form a central thread in the history of the field, as narratives are organized around accounts of struggle and triumph. Competing interest groups struggle amongst themselves, progressives are triumphant in carving out a new subject area, and important leaders are brought to the fore. Yet, as a group, these interpretations have the potential to create a canon in the historiography that obscures other important and insightful analyses that can shed new light on how social studies as a field was defined in theory and practice. Moreover, different ways of looking at the past can help scholars reconceptualize the questions and directions that inform contemporary policy and research.

How else might scholars frame the development of social studies? I conclude with a glimpse at different ways one might approach the history of the field that builds on work accomplished to date. This is merely a beginning list, in no particular order, and my hope is that other scholars add their perspectives to the directions in which the historiography needs to proceed.

My first suggestion is to continue to expand the timeline beyond the early 20th century. There are many additional episodes and critical periods in the development of social studies that are worthy of study beyond the Progressive-era origins of the field, particularly those of more recent years (e.g., Fraenkel, 1994; Oswald, 1993). For example, there is much to be learned about major developments in the social studies such as the history of issues-centered approaches (Evans, 1989) or the intercultural education movement (Montalto, 1982). Some historians have begun to explore the application of intercultural education in the classroom (Pak, 2004), while others have investigated the symbolic implications of such a curriculum and have critiqued facile assumptions that it continued under the rubric of multicultural education (Olneck, 1990). Also, recent inquiries exploring the New Social Studies of the 1960s have shed light on important developments of that time (Beyer, 1994; Dow, 1991). Researchers need only examine the historiography to find mention of important developments that are in need of further investigation. For instance, in several works, the Harvard Social Studies project under the direction of Donald Oliver is hailed as one of the best of the "new social studies" curricula of the 1960s (Hunt & Metcalf, 1968), yet there is little in the historiography that fully examines its role and impact in schools. A look at these eras would remedy the continuity problem of many studies that look at the early years of the field and then connect an idea or curriculum to the present day. It would take into account the many changes and permutations in the social studies that have occurred over time and, hopefully, lead to enhanced conclusions about what has transpired.

Next, I would like to reiterate a call to explore the multiple constituencies that have had a stake in the social education curriculum. It is well worth asking what other groups and associations were part of the discussion of the meaning and application of social studies, and to extend such consideration beyond the boundaries of the professional interest groups delineated by Kliebard. While AHA and NEA committees are well represented in scholarship, other major professional associations have virtually escaped detection by historians. For example, several scholars mention the American Political Science Association (APSA) in their discussions, yet these comments are akin to sidebars alongside the major narrative of the NEA and AHA.[17] Recent scholarship that is beginning to pursue this line of inquiry is Iftikhar Ahmad's (2004) examination of the role of the APSA in shaping the early social studies curriculum. Broadening the historical view in this manner reveals a more complex history, one of multiple constituencies with a say in the education of citizens through the school curriculum. Many individuals and groups were involved in these discussions in the past, and their ideas should be added to the historical record.

Additional histories could reconceptualize these interest groups by taking into account other purposes and paradigms, such as race. What if the early history of social studies were examined as a narrative of accommodationism versus a liberal arts or talented tenth view? Such a lens would be based, of course, on the writings and speeches of Booker T. Washington, W.E.B. DuBois, and other educational leaders of this era. Applying this lens to the data could highlight previously unnoticed themes in the development of social studies, and work has already begun in this area (e.g., Dilworth, 2003; Watkins, 1995). Also, it would be well worth investigating the role and impact of women's professional associations, such as the American Association of University Women, League of Women Voters, or the National American Woman Suffrage Association. How did women leaders view the development of social studies and what role did they play in the direction the field took (Crocco, 2004)? Voluntary and civic organizations also had much to say about social and civic education over the course of the 20th century, and some recent works have begun to explore these themes (Gross, 2004; Woyshner, 2003, 2004; Zimmerman, 2002). Overall, these works demonstrate the influence of voluntary and civic associations in producing textbooks and popularizing social studies programs.

Finally, the importance of pursuing the role of broader social, political, and economic contexts cannot be overstated. As discussed above, Reuben's

(1997) study of community civics is grounded in changing notions of childhood at the turn of the 20th century and evolving definitions of citizenship. Other works take a wide view as well, such as Jackie Blount's (2004) research on gender and sexuality in social studies over the course of the 20th century. She argues that "schools have played powerful roles in assuring the normative sexuality and gender of their charges" (p. 176) and investigates the curricular endeavors that have supported these ends. Along similar lines, Crocco (2003) considers how notions of cultural and ideological difference have been addressed in social studies and identifies three phases in this history: cultural amelioration (1910–1940), psychological compensation (1941–1980), and knowledge transformation (1981–the present). The work of Reuben, Blount, and Crocco can inform future historiography by providing scaffolding for others to follow, particularly by introducing ways of looking beyond the struggle metaphor or the emphasis on biography. Additional works by Tyrone C. Howard (2004) and Avner Segall (2004) explore civil rights and postmodernism, respectively, offering reminders about two important political and intellectual contexts for other researchers to consider.

For the past several decades, calls for greater attention to the history of social studies have emerged, as have the actual studies themselves. With each new publication the foundation of knowledge in social studies' past becomes fuller and more detailed. To date, however, these studies comprise an important if incomplete view of the field's history, as scholars seek still to write a fuller historiography. In 1981, Davis suggested that historians of the social studies should pay greater attention to discourse in their research. In a prescient move, he wrote that discourse "must be recognized as an essential key to uncovering meaning and to constructing understanding" in the history of the social studies (p. 29). Therefore, I will conclude with a word about discourse. In preparing this chapter, I drafted the title early on, using the term "toward" as a way to suggest the ongoing work that is necessary in the history of social studies. Only after I began the research for this chapter did I notice I was not alone in choosing this particular term. I found it striking how frequently the term "toward" was used in syntheses of the historiography. The title of one of Davis's reflections includes the phrase "Toward a Usable Past of the Social Studies" (1995, p. 52). Evans titled his guest editor's foreword, "Toward a New History of Social Studies" (2003, p. vii). Were I to take a cue from Davis's (1981) call to interweave discourse analysis into this research, I would note that this discursive construction of the historiography reveals much about how social studies historians view their charge. My hope is that we actually get to a point where we cease thinking about moving toward and know that we are already there.

NOTES

1. For the purposes of this chapter, I chose to focus on published works in the history of the social studies. Therefore, I have not included doctoral dissertations, but I encourage readers to consider the myriad dissertations written on the history of the social studies. As Murry R. Nelson (1999) argues, dissertations offer the best in-depth studies of the field, though they are typically read only by other graduate students.

2. Interestingly, this group was "declared dead" at the 2004 annual meeting in Baltimore, after fewer than five members participated (NCSS, 2005, p. 5).

3. One rare example is Sherry L. Field's (1994) article, "Scrap Drives, Stamp Sales, and School Spirit: Examples of Elementary Social Studies during World War II," which uses teachers' magazines for insight into classroom practices. This is a research model that is worth emulating.

4. For the purposes of this chapter, I consider the Progressive era to have lasted from approximately 1890 to 1920.

5. This was not a foolproof approach. For example, Donald Johnson's (2000) study of Thomas Jesse Jones's and W. E. B. DuBois's social education theories is so broadly contextualized in intellectual and educational history that even though the names of the two men appear in the title, I do not consider it a biographical study. Conversely, Michael Whelan's (1997a) article, "A Particularly Lucid Lens," uses the biography of Albert Bushnell Hart to examine history committee reports of the 1890s, even though Hart's name does not appear in the title.

6. For a thorough discussion of progressivism in education, see Lawrence A. Cremin's (1962) *The Transformation of the School: Progressivism in American Education, 1876–1957.*

7. As Hertzberg (1989) notes, social efficiency was also embraced by John Dewey, but it was of a much different variety. To Dewey, social efficiency meant teaching students to be self-directed so that all in society might live in harmony. Both views of social efficiency are found in the historiography.

8. The central committee reports that social studies historians refer to fall into two groups. The first includes those of the 1890s, which are generally considered the history reports because they were prepared by leading historians of the era. These include the Committee of Ten's report (1893) and the American Historical Association's Committee of Seven report of 1899. The second group are the social studies reports of 1913, 1915, and 1916 of the NEA's Committee on the Reorganization of Secondary Education.

9. While use of the term "social efficiency" is virtually unanimous, there is some disagreement around whether it was the kind of social control of David Snedden or the more liberal view of John Dewey. Space does not permit an exploration of these two threads, but readers might want to begin with William G. Wraga's "A Progressive Legacy Squandered" (2001) as an overview of the historiography on the Commission for the Reorganization of Secondary Education.

10. I am aware of the use of "educationists" as a pejorative (e.g., Arthur Bestor, 1953), but I use it in this chapter as a more neutral, inclusive term of those working as education professionals, including teachers, administrators, and education professors.

11. I thank Keith Barton for bringing this insight to my attention.

12. These kinds of contentions appear in the literature with much contradiction. For example, other scholars, such as Hertzberg, argue just the opposite, that social studies over time was steadily displaced by history.

13. Several other scholars use this approach, along with one or more of Kliebard's interest-group terms. See Gross, 2004; Johnson, 2000.

14. Robinson (1980) suggests as much of the work of the first generation of historians of the social studies—Henry Johnson, Rolla Tryon, and Edgar Wesley.

15. Readers should peruse the issue of *Social Education* that marked the 75th anniversary of the National Council for the Social Studies (November/December 1995).

16. I thank Margaret Smith Crocco for suggesting the drawback of the "great man theory of change."

17. One notable exception to this is David Jenness (1990), *Making Sense of Social Studies.*

ACKNOWLEDGMENTS

I would like to thank Keith Barton and Margaret Smith Crocco for their helpful comments and suggestions, though any errors in interpretation are my own. I am especially grateful for their suggestions of additional sources that I had overlooked.

REFERENCES

Ahmad, I. (2004, November). *Teaching government and social studies: The theory and history of citizenship education.* Paper presented at the College and University Faculty Assembly of the National Council for the Social Studies, Baltimore.

Barton, K. C. (2005). Mary G. Kelty: The most important social educator no one has heard of? In L. M. Burlbaw & S. L. Field (Eds.), *Explorations in curriculum history* (pp. 161–184). Greenwich, CT: Information Age.

Bernard-Powers, J. (2004). Review of the book *Paul Robert Hanna: A life of expanding communities. History of Education Quarterly, 41,* 452–454.

Bestor, A. E. (1953). *Educational wastelands: The retreat from learning in our public schools.* Urbana: University of Illinois Press.

Beyer, B. K. (1994). Gone but not forgotten—reflections on the New Social Studies movement. *The Social Studies, 85,* 251–255.

Blount, J. M. (2004). Same-sex desire, gender, and social education in the twentieth century. In C. Woyshner, J. Watras, & M. S. Crocco (Eds.), *Social education in the twentieth century: Curriculum and context for citizenship* (pp. 176–191). New York: Peter Lang.

Bohan, C. (2004). Early vanguards of progressive education: The Committee of Ten, the Committee of Seven, and social education. In C. Woyshner, J. Watras,

& M. S. Crocco (Eds.), *Social education in the twentieth century: Curriculum and context for citizenship* (pp. 1–19). New York: Peter Lang.

Butts, R. F. (1977). Historical perspective on civic education in the United States. In National Task Force on Citizenship Education (Ed.), *Education for responsible citizenship: The report of the National Task Force on Citizenship Education* (pp. 47–68). New York: McGraw-Hill.

Butts, R. F. (1986). A personal appreciation of Hazel Whitman Hertzberg. *Social Education, 53,* 304–305.

Chilcoat, G. W., & Ligon, J. A. (2003). "It is democratic students we are after:" The possibilities and the expectations for the social studies from the writings of Shirley H. Engel. *International Journal of Social Education 18*(2), 76–92.

Correia, S. (1999). The de-evolution of social studies. *Southern Social Studies Journal, 24*(2), 33–46.

Cremin, L. A. (1962). *The transformation of the school: Progressivism in American education, 1876–1957.* New York: Knopf.

Crocco, M. S. (1997). Forceful yet forgotten: Mary Ritter Beard and the writing of history. *The History Teacher 31,* 9–31.

Crocco, M. S. (1999a). Introduction. In M. S. Crocco & O. L. Davis, Jr. (Eds.), *"Bending the future to their will": Civic women, social education, and democracy* (pp. 1–16). Lanham, MD: Rowman & Littlefield.

Crocco, M. S. (1999b). Shaping inclusive education: Mary Ritter Beard and Marion Thompson Wright. In M. S. Crocco & O. L. Davis, Jr. (Eds.), *"Bending the future to their will": Civic women, social education, and democracy* (pp. 93–124). Lanham, MD: Rowman & Littlefield.

Crocco, M. S. (2003). Dealing with difference in the social studies: A historical perspective. *International Journal of Social Education 18*(2), 106–126.

Crocco, M. S. (2004). Women and the social studies: The long rise and rapid fall of feminist activity in the National Council for the Social Studies. In C. Woyshner, J. Watras, & M. S. Crocco (Eds.), *Social education in the twentieth century: Curriculum and context for citizenship* (pp. 142–159). New York: Peter Lang.

Crocco, M. S., & Davis, O. L., Jr. (Eds.) (1999). *"Bending the future to their will": Civic women, social education, and democracy.* Lanham, MD: Rowman & Littlefield.

Crocco, M. S., & Davis, O. L., Jr. (Eds.) (2002). *Building a legacy: Women in social education, 1784–1984.* Silver Spring, MD: National Council for the Social Studies.

Cuban, L. (1991). History of teaching in social studies. In J. P. Shaver (Ed.), *Handbook of research on social studies teaching and learning* (pp. 197–209). New York: Macmillan.

Davis, O. L., Jr. (1980). On exploring three trails. *Journal of Social Studies Research, 4*(2), 44–46.

Davis, O. L., Jr. (1981). Understanding the history of the social studies. In H. D. Mehlinger & O. L. Davis, Jr., (Eds.) *Eightieth Yearbook of the National Society for the Study of Education: Part II. The social studies* (pp. 19–35). Chicago: University of Chicago Press.

Davis, O. L., Jr. (1995). And miles to go until we sleep: Toward a usable past of the social studies. *Theory and Research in Social Education 23,* 52–59.

Dilworth, P. P. (2003). Competing conceptions of citizenship education: Thomas Jesse Jones and Carter G. Woodson. *International Journal of Social Education 18*(2), 1–15.

Dow, P. B. (1991). *Schoolhouse politics: Lessons from the Sputnik era*. Cambridge, MA: Harvard University Press.

Evans, R. W. (1989). A dream unrealized: A brief look at the history of issue-centered approaches. *The Social Studies, 80*, 178–184.

Evans, R. W. (2003). Toward a new history of the social studies. *International Journal of Social Education 18*(2), vii–viii.

Evans, R. W. (2004). *The social studies wars: What should we teach the children?* New York: Teachers College Press.

Field, S. L. (1994). Scrap drives, stamp sales, and school spirit: Examples of elementary social studies during World War II. *Theory and Research in Social Education, 22*, 441–460.

Fraenkel, J. R. (1994). The evolution of the Taba curriculum development project. *The Social Studies, 85*, 149–159.

Gross, S. J. (2004). Civic hands upon the land: Diverse patterns of social education in the Civilian Conservation Corps and its analogues, 1933–1942. In C. Woyshner, J. Watras, & M. S. Crocco (Eds.), *Social education in the twentieth century: Curriculum and context for citizenship* (pp. 42–56). New York: Peter Lang.

Hertzberg, H.W. (1971). *Historical parallels for the sixties and seventies: Primary sources and core curriculum revisited*. Boulder, CO: Social Science Education Consortium. (ERIC Document Reproduction Service No. ED051066)

Hertzberg, H. W. (1988). Are method and content enemies? In B. R. Gifford (Ed.), *History in the schools: What shall we teach?* (pp. 13–40). New York: Macmillan.

Hertzberg, H.W. (1989). History and progressivism: A century of reform proposals. In P. Gagnon & The Bradley Commission on History in Schools (Eds.), *Historical literacy: The case for history in American education* (pp. 69–99). New York: Macmillan.

Hiner, N. R. (1972). Professions in process: Changing relations between historians and educators, 1896–1911. *History of Education Quarterly, 12*, 34–56.

Hiner, N. R. (1973). Professions in process: Changing relations among social scientists, historians, and educators, 1880-1920. *The History Teacher, 6*, 201–218.

Howard, T. C. (2004). Social studies during the civil rights movement, 1955–1975. In C. Woyshner, J. Watras, & M. S. Crocco (Eds.), *Social education in the twentieth century: Curriculum and context for citizenship* (pp. 127–141). New York: Peter Lang.

Hunt, M. P., & Metcalf, L. E. (1968). *Teaching high school social studies: Problems in reflective thinking and social understanding* (2nd ed.). New York: Harper & Row.

Jenness, D. (1990). *Making sense of social studies*. New York: Macmillan.

Johnson, D. (2000). W. E. B. DuBois, Thomas Jesse Jones and the struggle for social education, 1900–1930. *Journal of Negro History 85*(3), 71–95.

Keels, O. M. (1980). The collegiate influence on the early social studies curriculum: A reassessment of the role of historians. *Theory and Research in Social Education, 8*, 105–120.

Keels, O. M. (1988). Herbert Baxter Adams and the influence of the American Historical Association on the early social studies. *International Journal of Social Education, 3*, 37–49.

Keels, O. M. (1993). Still a seemless web. *Theory and Research in Social Education, 21,* 183–191.

Keels, O. M. (1994). In the beginning—Albert McKinley and the founding of *The Social Studies. The Social Studies, 85,* 198–205.

Kliebard, H. M. (1986). *Struggle for the American curriculum, 1895–1958.* New York: Routledge.

Kliebard, H. M. (1992). *Forging the American curriculum: Essays on curriculum history and theory.* New York: Routledge.

Lerner, G. (1981). *The majority finds its past: Placing women in history.* New York: Oxford University Press.

Lybarger, M. (1980). The political context of the social studies: Creating a constituency for municipal reform. *Theory and Research in Social Education, 8,* 1–28.

Lybarger, M. B. (1987). Need as ideology: A look at the early social studies. In T. S. Popkewitz (Ed.), *The formation of school subjects: The struggle for creating an American institution* (pp. 176–189). New York: Falmer.

Lybarger, M. B. (1991). The historiography of social studies: Retrospect, circumspect, and prospect. In J. P. Shaver (Ed.), *Handbook of Research on Social Studies Teaching and Learning* (pp. 3–15). New York: Macmillan

McAninch, S. (1990). The educational theory of Mary Sheldon Barnes: Inquiry learning as indoctrination in history education. *Educational Theory, 40,* 45–52.

Montalto, N. V. (1982). *A history of the intercultural education movement, 1924–1941.* New York: Garland.

Munro, P. (1999). "Widening the circle": Jane Addams, gender, and the re/definition of democracy. In M. S. Crocco & O. L. Davis, Jr. (Eds.), *Bending the future to their will: Women, social education, and democracy* (pp. 73–82). Lanham, MD: Rowman & Littlefield.

National Council for the Social Studies. (2005). Foundations of Social Studies SIG (1977–2004) expires. *The Social Studies Professional, 186,* 5.

Nelson, M. R. (1987). Emma Willard: Pioneer in social studies education. *Theory and Research in Social Education, 15,* 245–256.

Nelson, M. R. (1988). Merle R. Eppse and studies of blacks in American history textbooks. *International Journal of Social Education, 3*(3), 84–90.

Nelson, M. R. (1999). *Foundational dissertations in the foundations of the social studies.* (ERIC Document Reproduction Service No. ED437330)

Olneck, M.R. (1990). The recurring dream: Symbolism and ideology in intercultural and multicultural education. *American Journal of Education 98,* 147–174.

Oswald, J. M. (1993). The social studies curriculum revolution, 1960–1975. *The Social Studies, 84,* 14–19.

Pak, Y. (2004). Teaching for intercultural understanding in the social studies: A teacher's perspective in the 1940s. In C. Woyshner, J. Watras, & M. S. Crocco (Eds.), *Social education in the twentieth century: Curriculum and context for citizenship* (pp. 57–75). New York: Peter Lang.

Ravitch, D. (1985a). From history to the social studies. In C. E. Finn, Jr., D. Ravitch, & P. H. Roberts (Eds.), *Challenges to the humanities* (pp. 80–95). New York: Holmes & Meier.

Ravitch, D. (1985b). *The schools we deserve: Reflections on the educational crisis of our times.* New York: Basic Books.

Ravitch. D. (2003). A brief history of the social studies. In J. Leming, L. Ellington, & K. Porter (Eds.), *Where did social studies go wrong?* (pp. 1–5). Washington, DC: Thomas B. Fordham Foundation.

Reuben, J. A. (1997). Beyond politics: Community civics and the redefinition of citizenship in the Progressive era. *History of Education Quarterly, 37,* 399–420.

Robinson, P. (1980). The conventional historians of the social studies. *Theory and Research in Social Education, 8,* 65–87.

Saxe, D. W. (1991). *Social studies in schools: A history of the early years.* Albany, NY: State University of New York Press.

Saxe, D. W. (1992a). Framing a theory for social studies foundations. *Review of Educational Research, 62,* 259–277.

Saxe, D. W. (1992b). An introduction to the seminal social welfare and efficiency prototype: The founders of 1916 social studies. *Theory and Research in Social Education, 20,* 156–178.

Saxe, D. W. (1994). Establishing a voice for history in schools: The first methods textbooks for history instruction, 1896–1902. *Theory and Research in Social Education, 22,* 482–514.

Saxe, D. W. (2003). On the alleged demise of social studies: The eclectic curriculum in times of standardization—A historical sketch. *International Journal of Social Education, 18*(2), 93–105.

Segall, A. (2004). Social studies and the discourses of postmodernity. In C. Woyshner, J. Watras, & M. S. Crocco (Eds.), *Social education in the twentieth century: Curriculum and context for citizenship* (pp. 160–175). New York: Peter Lang.

Shaver, J. P. (1997). The past and future of social studies as citizenship education and of research on social studies. *Theory and Research in Social Education, 25,* 210–215.

Smith, B. A., & Palmer, J. J. (1995). A history of NCSS. *Social Education, 59,* 391–398.

Stallones, J. (2002). *Paul Robert Hanna: A life of expanding communities.* Stanford, CA: Hoover Press.

Stallones, J. (2003). Paul Hanna and "expanding communities." *International Journal of Social Education, 18*(2), 33–46.

Watkins, W. H. (1995). Thomas Jesse Jones, social studies, and race. *International Journal of Social Education, 10*(2), 124–134.

Watras, J. (2004). Historians and social studies educators. In C. Woyshner, J. Watras, & M. S. Crocco (Eds.), *Social education in the twentieth century: Curriculum and context for citizenship* (pp. 192–209). New York: Peter Lang.

Whelan, M. (1991). James Harvey Robinson, the new history, and the 1916 Social Studies Report. *The History Teacher, 24,* 191–202.

Whelan, M. (1994). Albert Bushnell Hart and the origins of social studies education. *Theory and Research in Social Education 22,* 423–440.

Whelan, M. (1997a). A particularly lucid lens: The Committee of Ten and the Social Studies Committee in historical context. *Journal of Curriculum and Supervision, 12,* 256–268.

Whelan, M. (1997b). Social studies for social reform: Charles Beard's vision of history and social studies education. *Theory and Research in Social Education, 25,* 288–315.

Woyshner, C. (2003). Women's associations and the origins of the social studies: Volunteers, professionals, and the community civics curriculum, 1890–1920. *International Journal of Social Education, 18*(2), 15–32.

Woyshner, C. (2004). From assimilation to cultural pluralism: The PTA and civic education, 1900–1950. In C. Woyshner, J. Watras, & M. S. Crocco (Eds.), *Social education in the twentieth century: Curriculum and context for citizenship* (pp. 93–109). New York: Peter Lang.

Woyshner, C., Watras, J., & Crocco, M. S. (Eds.) (2004). *Social education in the twentieth century: Curriculum and context for citizenship.* New York: Peter Lang.

Wraga, W. G. (2001). A progressive legacy squandered: The *Cardinal Principles* report reconsidered. *History of Education Quarterly, 41,* 494–519.

Zimmerman, J. (2002). *Whose America? Culture wars in the public schools.* Cambridge, MA: Harvard University Press.

CHAPTER 3

RESEARCH, RACE, AND SOCIAL EDUCATION

Cynthia A. Tyson

It is not cruel to inflict on a few criminals sufferings which may benefit multitudes of innocent people through all centuries.

—First-century encyclopedist Celsus

At the end of World War II, Nazi doctors and scientists were put on trial for the murder of concentration camp inmates who were used as research subjects. In the Willowbrook Hepatitis Study, beginning in the mid-1950s, children with developmental disabilities at an institution on Staten Island were deliberately infected with a mild form of hepatitis in order to study the progression of the disease and to test the effectiveness of gamma globulin as an agent for inoculation. In 1971, a number of Mexican American women in San Antonio, Texas, took part in a study to determine side effects of an oral contraceptive. These women had come to a clinic seeking contraceptives, but without their knowledge or consent, they received a placebo during half of the trial. Ten of the seventy-six participants became pregnant. And in the "Tea Room Trade" study, which focused on homosexual practices in public restrooms, the researcher went undercover and gained the confidence of subjects by acting as a lookout. He then identified participants by tracing their license plates and later distributed a "social health survey" in their communities (Bankert & Cooper, n.d.)

Research Methods in Social Studies Education, pages 39–56
Copyright © 2006 by Information Age Publishing

The study that affected my community—the Public Health Service Syphilis Study—was a 39-year investigation (1932–1971) aimed at investigating the development of syphilis in African American men. At the time the study began, there was no known treatment for syphilis (Bankert & Cooper, n.d.). Thomas (1999, ¶ 3) describes the ordeal of participants:

> The 600 black men in the study (399 with syphilis and a control group of 201 who did not have the disease) were the sons and grandsons of slaves. Most had never been seen by a doctor. When announcements were made in churches and cotton fields about a way to receive free medical care, the men showed up in droves. Little did they know the high price they would pay over the next four decades as they were poked and prodded by an endless array of government medical personnel. Even as some men went blind and insane from advanced (tertiary) syphilis, the government doctors withheld treatment, remaining committed to observing their subjects through to the predetermined "end point"—autopsy. To ensure the families would agree to this final procedure, the government offered burial insurance—at most fifty dollars—to cover the cost of a casket and grave.

Bankert and Cooper (n.d., ¶ 4) note:

> Even after penicillin was found to be a safe and effective treatment for syphilis in the 1940's, the men were denied antibiotics. The study continued to track these men until 1972 when the first public accounts of the study appeared in the national press. The study resulted in 28 deaths, 100 cases of disability, and 19 cases of congenital syphilis.

In 1997, Hollywood even found these events fodder for a television movie, *Miss Evers' Boys* (Sargent, 1997). A quarter century after the end of the study, on May 16, 1997, President Bill Clinton issued a long overdue formal apology for the Tuskegee Study of Untreated Syphilis in the Negro Male.

These research events are a few among many that raised the question of ethics in human subjects medical research and gave rise to *The Belmont Report*, which laid out principles designed to protect human research subjects. For those of us engaging in social science research, however, we may feel we would never cause the harm that resulted from the lack of ethical behavior in the medical studies mentioned above. After all, we are now governed by the "principles" of rigorous human subjects review boards. Nevertheless, the common thread of the studies above is unmistakable: Those who were disenfranchised by the many forms of social oppression (racism, anti-Semitism, sexism, heterosexism, classism) were disproportionately represented among the research subjects. This raises other concerns with regard to issues of research, race, privilege, and power in educational research.

The musings for this chapter began with a dialogue that began in 1997. As an African American, female researcher of social education, I addressed the topic of race-based epistemologies (Tyson, 1998) with a continuation of an earlier question raised in response to Scheurich and Young's (1997) *Educational Researcher* article titled "Coloring Epistemologies: Are Our Research Epistemologies Racially Biased?" The question was: If a race-based epistemology can be African American (or feminist, or gay/lesbian, or First Nation), what is it that makes this epistemology different when developing a formalized research methodology?

My answer was then, and still is rooted now, in the "specificity of oppression—the response to which is not based solely on victimization but on struggle and survival" (Tyson, 1998, p. 22). The specificity of oppression made it necessary for the creation of a specific theory of knowledge in response to distinctive kinds of nationally sanctioned inhumanity. To be black in America, for example, specified historically, and continues to specify, the ways in which systemic forms of racism—from enslavement through Jim Crow laws and onto racial profiling—manifest themselves in our experience. Across these historical periods, what counts as knowledge about racism has changed as attempts to redress problems have yielded continued oppression.

This chapter continues that conversation and reflects an effort to address how critical questions related to race and research in social education continue to challenge the direction of traditional epistemologies and research methodologies in the social sciences. This discussion is a more in-depth consideration of a theoretical framework that evokes emancipatory epistemologies and methodologies and examines how they can influence research in the social studies.

The first example that I present is the use of critical race theory (CRT) to examine the teaching of the historical era of Jim Crow—legalized racial segregation in the south. The legal and social addressing of Jim Crow laws and practices was deeply entrenched in the varieties of racism that characterized earlier times. Even challenges to the Constitution and later amendments only yielded returns that reflected the legal system from which they grew. Critical race theory, a countertheory based in critical legal studies, began to deconstruct mainstream legal ideology, which ignores racial oppression, and placed at its center the endemic racism in law and society that is often devoid of contextual and historical examination (Crenshaw, Gotanda, Peller, & Thomas, 1995; Delgado, 1995; Matsuda, Lawrence, Delgado, & Crenshaw, 1993; Parker, Deyhle, Villenas, & Nebeker, 1998).

In other words, critical race theory involved the examination of external practices—such as laws and policies—that restricted African Americans from full participation and citizenship in society. It accomplished this through a series of counterstories that kept race as the central unit of analysis. In this regard, counterstories and storytelling functioned as a type of counterdiscourse, as a means of analysis to examine the epistemologies of racially oppressed peoples. Under this framework, the metanarrative shifts to identify and account for the continuing anguish of racism in the face of legal and social "fixes." It is the very ignoring of the role of race and racism that CRT aims to challenge by analyzing the traditions, "presuppositions and received wisdoms that make up the common culture about race that invariably render African Americans" and other disenfranchised groups powerless (Delgado, 1995, p. xiv).

It is this specificity of oppression that has a collective and empirical impact on the epistemological backdrop of research. As I stated in my earlier work (Tyson, 1998, p. 22):

> I reflect on the experience of being Black in America. I weave together the African tribal and American familial, community, and religious traditions—folktales, foods, medicine men, priests and priestesses, Black churches—but I must also weave in the thread of realism in the politics, economics, and so-called intellectual thought that allowed for the atrocities perpetuated by the Nazis in the holocaust, for the Middle Passage and the enslavement of millions of Black Africans, for Japanese interment camps, and for the annihilation of indigenous peoples.

It is the understanding of lived oppression—the struggle to "make a way out of no way"—that propels us to problematize the dominant ideologies in which knowledge is constructed. Postcolonialism and the so-called "standpoint" positions highlight the role of racism in societal ideology as endemic to the theoretical frameworks that underpin research epistemologies. These research frameworks represent blindness to the ways of knowing that come from the specific experience of oppression.

An example of this can be illustrated in a study I conducted with middle-grade students who used literature to explore the development of civic participation and social/political action (Tyson, 2002). When selecting the site and participants, several factors supported using the theoretical framework of critical race theory. Using socially constructed ideas of race as the unit of analysis evoked a historical critique of how sites in this predominately black community had been involved in research initiatives. Often they were used in ways that allowed the school and broader community to serve as a "data plantation" (Irvine, 1997)—that is, researchers came in to collect data and left without any real involvement of participants, even in the form of member checks. I needed to develop relationships with the participants, their families, and the community with a specificity that recognized how some outsiders had failed to position these economically fragile students and families as experts in the arena of civic participation. The use of CRT led me to pay particular attention to what it means to be a citizen in this community—historically, intergenerationally, and legally (e.g., the Voting Rights Act of 1964 and 1968). Therefore, the objective of the research was to explore the ways in which students could read particular pieces of literature written for children and young adults and develop a sense of social/ political civic action, but placing race at the theoretical center of this research dictated methodological moves that broke from the traditional and that used historical knowledge in its broader context to influence data collection. Again, let me illustrate. At the onset of the study, I approached students' parents before I talked with the teacher with whom I wanted to work. I wanted parents and the community to discuss the project with me and to give me feedback related to how this construction of knowledge, this data-gathering event, would serve larger questions related to their civic concerns. I could not only focus on my research questions. I felt compelled to engage in a critique of the existing civic participatory climate of the community and discuss ways that children's parents could see how involvement in this study might simultaneously present opportunities for individual emancipatory work.

It is my contention that such experiences set the stage for inquiry from a different plane. As a result, the experience of racism and oppression moves the oppressed "Other" into a paradigm of survival, and this creates a view of the world that is not shared by those gatekeepers who legitimize academic discourse and research. This paradigm of survival can be compared to the difference between rowing a life boat from the middle of a vast lake to shore and swimming there. While there is an expenditure of energy and a concern for personal safety in both instances, "a paradigm of survival" for the swimmer creates an alternative frame of reference from which decisions are made.

A new question then arises: How do we begin to analyze the pervasiveness of race and the need for it to move from the margin to the center of our social education research paradigms? In answering this question, the initial challenge is to understand the complexity of such epistemological moves—moves that will require a multifaceted lens, much like a kaleidoscope, in an attempt to understand the implications for inquiry. For example, a small ball, when viewed with the naked eye, has discernable elements—for example, color, shape, and texture. The same ball, when viewed through a kaleidoscope, is multidimensional, with a semblance of new textures. Moreover, the once smooth, round edges may now be flat in places and appear to have different textural properties.

In like fashion, racism, when viewed through a racialized social science lens, may also have different properties from those deeply established in the consciousness of U.S. society. These different perspectives engender many possibilities, particularly opportunities to transform an ideology of oppression into one of economic, political, and social equality. An example of this can be found in work done with Asian American social studies teachers. In his study, Subedi (2002) argued that teachers' perceptions of citizenship and culture contradicted mainstream ideas of citizenship/culture. By speaking of their own experiences in everyday lives, teachers pointed out the need to consider racial, linguistic, and gender differences in discussions of citizenship and culture. They also shared information about the cross-racial aspect of relationships that are formed in schools and that help them cope with societal marginalization. Examining the teachers' classroom practices, Subedi used a racialized lens, putting race in the center and using it as the unit of analysis to gather data. Because of this theoretical approach, Subedi's findings filled a gap in the literature related to the ways that pedagogy, which is infused with the lived experiences of students, helped them cope with multidimensional and complex societal marginalization.

Another example of research from an emancipatory or liberatory epistemology is Condron's (1997) study of women computer scientists working in engineering environments. To be female historically has specified systemic forms of oppression of girls and women. This specifies what women are capable of, what they have access to within their societies, and what they are expected to think about and value. It even specifies what counts as feminine. Thus the specificity of women's place in their social settings restricts their perceived expertise and their access to technical knowledge, education, and careers. Women with computer science expertise who work in engineering environments work in traditionally highly masculinized, exclusive realms, and certainly the percentage of women in technical careers is lower than that of men. The percentages, however, cannot disguise the fact that women do have successful careers in and make valuable contributions to the technical realm. There are many stories that can be told about women with respect to the technical realm throughout history. Some of these stories contradict each other and some complement each other, yet they represent women as fully credentialed and competent in their technical careers. Through their stories these women computer scientists are nudged from the margins toward the center of technical endeavor. The complexities of gender and the technical are brought to the fore, women and girls are brought out of the shadows, and others can see them in their roles as engaged and productive citizens of their own self-perceptions.

With regard to race, however, such a transformation requires work on two fronts. First, we must systematically and consciously resist the injustices of racism. Second, we must work constructively to improve the ways in which racism surfaces in the vocalized assumptions of those in power. In essence, we simultaneously attack the causes and heal the effects. We must work, at both the macro level and the micro level—with systems and with individuals—in order to have an impact on ideology.

Working at two levels, however, raises yet another question: What effect does this rhythmic alteration have on researchers of color? The unending "dual consciousness" that DuBois (1903) spoke of places enhanced demands on marginalized researchers—most often, African American, Chicana(os), Latinas(os), Asian American/Pacific Islander, American Indian/First Nation, gay/lesbian/transgender.[1] It also places demands on the development of our research agendas, particularly with and in relation to our community responsibilities (see also Abu-Lughod, 1990; Behar, 1993; Behar & Gordon, 1995; Delgado Bernal, 1998; Nayaran, 1993; Trinh, 1990; Villenas, 1996).

To awaken this stance and enact racial realism, to move race from the margin to the center of our research paradigms, entails a deconstruction of white racial ideology as the normative stance. As discussed by Mazzei (2004) in her work with white teachers, it is the "notion of what we see and don't see as Whites and how we define others in relation to ourselves as *Other* (i.e., different, exotic, inferior)" (p. 27) that is important in a decentering of whiteness. In other words, the status of being "white" is not necessarily superior; rather, all "others" are measured against it in terms of their "differences." While whiteness, on the surface, has politically shifted from a claim of supremacy to the role of victim (as in reverse affirmative action suits), it retains, and potentially gains, power through being the standard against which everything else is compared. Whiteness remains the center and retains its control through "othering," a process that demeans the efforts of "others."

In her ongoing work with white teachers, Mazzei (2004) engages the "effect of the racial positioning of White teachers in a non-White environment on their perception of themselves in relation to their students" (p. 26). She engages in this work in order to shift the gaze from the *other* (nonwhite student) to the *self* (white teacher). In other words, her project in this decentering work with white teachers is to catch a glimpse of both her own and her participants' whiteness, "not the nonWhiteness (blackness, browness, redness) of others" (Mazzei, 2003, p. 357). Her intent is to explore with these teachers how this shifting of gaze changes their relationship to their students: "We discovered that simply because we were in the minority in our schools, our Whiteness was not always visible to us; in other words, we still saw ourselves as normative and everyone else as other" (p. 358).

In discussions among educational researchers (e.g., López, 1997), the question has been asked, "Shall the master's tools dismantle the master's house?" (Lorde, 1984). To accept the colonial codification of the master and his tools in relation to our work suggests that we are, in essence, workers on "data plantations" (Irvine, 1997): enslaved, and in need of emancipation. This metaphor, though, is not to suggest that the research machine traps scholars of color (and some women), that we can never transcend our subordinate position because we rely on the master's toolbox for our livelihood. Rather, as Ladson-Billings (1998) has pointed out, all we can do is "add different voices to the received wisdom or canon" (p.23). By offering counterstories, and different ways of viewing the world, emancipatory research is generated.

EMANCIPATORY RESEARCH

The ways of white folks, I mean some white folks, is too much for me. I reckon they must be a few good ones, but most of 'em ain't good—leastwise they don't treat me good. And Lawd knows, I ain't never done nothin' to 'em, nothin' a-tall. (Hughes, 1934/1990, p. 181)

In his 1934 book (republished 1990) from which the above quote was taken, Langston Hughes reveals the protagonist's knowledge of race while defining the dominant white ideology from a nonwhite perspective. This definition "from the outside" renders visible the thinking and actions that stem from assumptions made invisible by their pervasiveness within the ideology. In other words, these assumptions cannot be made visible from within the ideology itself. The invisibility of these principles arises from a blindness that fails to legitimate perspectives that are not beneficial to white society (Bell, 1995).

Such an act requires us to create emancipatory epistemologies from which liberatory research methodologies are born. If privileges achieved by individuals at the expense of others constitute an act of oppression, then educational research achieved by individuals at the expense of others is also an act of oppression. It is incumbent upon researchers, therefore, to stop trying "to 'hide' in what we regard as the neutrality of scientific pursuits, indifferent to how our findings are used, even uninterested in considering for whom or for what interests we are working" (Freire, 1985, p. 103). In other words, if we are to engage in emancipatory research, we must stop trying to benefit ourselves and engage in the process of researching for the greater good of our communities.

Consider the work of Erchick (2001, in review), who challenges the dominant epistemology in research on women and girls' experience with mathematics. While much of mathematics education continues to focus on a deficit model where the norm continues to be a masculine epistemology and where females' performance and choices are measured in comparison to those of males, Erchick works to define an epistemology grounded in the mathematics experience of the women and girls in her research. She defines "mathematical voice" (2001) as that which develops in the presence of mathematics, and she works from a definition generated by the women and girls in her work. In turn, that epistemology, and the women and girls' sense of agency that clearly emerges out of their relationships with mathematics, fuels Erchick's work and further serves both women who encounter mathematics as teachers and girls who are establishing agency and voice in the adolescent years. In a developing spiral of growth, the women and girls contribute to the research, benefit from it, and develop further. They are the participants in, contributors to, and beneficiaries of their own epistemology of mathematics.

If our goal is to do emancipatory research, we must ask ourselves, "Who really benefits?" The reward(s) of the academy can deceive us into believing that our work is emancipatory when it is not. Emancipatory research cannot be built on the "participants' backs" but must have a simultaneous commitment to radical social change as well as to those individuals most oppressed by social and cultural subordination.

Often when I conduct literature reviews I come across research that is done on the "participants' backs." An examination of the theoretical frames in such research suggests that hierarchical relationships go unchallenged. These modes of inquiry could rest on epistemologies that create methodologies responsive to issues of race, privilege, and power. Instead, I find research methodologies that marginalize, depoliticize, and reify institutional racism. One such example is that of a researcher who used black graduate students to collect data in urban high schools that were predominately black. While some may think that was a wise methodological move by a white female researcher who wanted to get to students' understandings and beliefs related to social science learning, the published research omitted this methodological move. As a result, the reader is left to believe that these personal testimonies, along with other documented struggles and issues faced by these high school students of color as they grappled with issues related to the curriculum, were gathered through traditional research methods. This representation of the data was only partially correct. The graduate students who collected the data used the tenets of critical race theory; they used race—in this instance shared racial narratives—to negotiate a space for the development of the counterstories of these high school students. The question remains, "Who benefits?" As the black graduate students began to analyze the data, they were faced with a challenge rooted in the ancient Egyptian principle of Maat (reciprocity)—a principle that supports a mutual exchange between the server and the served (Alston, in press; Asante, 1987). They were torn between, on the one hand, their role as research assistants who had responsibilities within the existing questions and purposes that guided the study, and on the other hand, their assumed responsibilities to the students and to the community at large. As Carter (2003) states, "We [Black researchers] have a responsibility to resist the temptation to do 'hit and run' research that is unconcerned about the consequences of our work. Instead, as much as is possible, we must encourage a research sensibility and ethic that expresses and demonstrates concern for the collective good of our communities. We must facilitate a 'rearticulated consciousness' (Collins, 2000, p. 186) in the academy."

While the methodology was "traditional" on the surface, the research design, in concert with underpinnings of liberatory research, would have moved this into a different epistemological position. A liberatory research epistemology would have motivated the researcher to situate her "whiteness" and the participants' "otherness" in the research design and in her subsequent methodological moves. An epistemology of liberation would have helped the researcher understand that there is no total escape from racism and white privilege, for these are part of the very nature of being. An epistemology of liberation would not have conceived of a methodological approach that was outside of a "grounding" in the epistemological impact of what it means to embrace the cross-cultural relationship as another place to collect data. No doubt, data that involved black students sharing particular ideological positions to a white female researcher may have informed their teachers (predominately white and female) in ways that would increase engagement and lead to increased academic achievement. Was this the purpose of the study? No. The purpose was to inquire about students' understanding of knowledge related to social sciences. However, liberatory research demands that while we research we simultaneously co-negotiate the collection of data that has the possibility for "misinterpretation, abuse and ill-usage" (Carter, 2003), always asking the question, "Who will benefit?" This makes liberatory research methodologically and critically different.

As long as liberatory research can be interpreted as methodologically distinct, but not critically different in its ability to improve, challenge, and alter traditional forms of academic research in general—or social and cultural consequences specifically—then it will continue to be "tolerated" as a "variation" and an "alternative" research stance. It will continue to be an "other" within the larger educational research community. Liberatory or emancipatory research is likely to be viewed this way by researchers who tend to call into question all inquiry that provides researchers with the opportunity to use their own race-based reality as theoretical grounding for epistemological and methodological moves. Such questioning constitutes a paradigmatic "backlash" that leaves race-based research and scholarship in a proverbial abyss.

Conservative backlashes notwithstanding, emancipatory research has been accepted in educational circles—but only as a means to offer a sanitized and depoliticized "reading list" in graduate qualitative research courses and/or opening conversations to discuss epistemological considerations related to the intersections and/or conflicts with qualitative research methodology (see, e.g., Denzin & Lincoln, 1997). Too often, discussion of the role of race and racism becomes little more than a critique of traditional research epistemologies and never questions the "normality" of research forms. In essence, academic research that is situated in race-based, gender-based, social class-based, and postcolonial-based ways of knowing tends to be blocked by empiricisms, scientisms, and normalisms that remain methodologically oppressive.

EPISTEMOLOGIES OF EMANCIPATION

Research is formalized curiosity. It is poking and prying with a purpose. (Hurston, 1994, p. 687)

If social science educational researchers were to operate from epistemologies of emancipation—with frameworks that were transformative (as opposed to accommodative) in nature—and engage in methodologies that encouraged participants to challenge and change the world, then the purpose of data collection would be fundamentally different. Rather than collect data for data's sake, research would become a conscious political, economic, and personal conduit for empowerment. Educational research could then be a catalyst to support and complement larger struggles for liberation. Thus the very nature of radical thought and liberatory action has far-reaching effects, and it comes with a heightened sense of responsibility for researchers whose work is based on a commitment to defy historical and contemporary racial oppression. For scholars of color who have experienced the specificity of oppression their entire lives, such a move provides the basis for research that unapologetically places discussions of race, gender, class, and sexuality as part of a larger political and epistemological struggle for a better and just future.

Much of the research I have done has been in communities of color and has been influenced by these very tenets. My work with a group of urban middle school students and their social studies teacher was situated in a commitment to work to dismantle deficit models of approaching black students in educational research. Was this a research question? No, but taken holistically, the epistemology of emancipation forced me to incorporate ways of knowing that were rooted in the long history of a racialized discourse of deficit that the educational research community at large had institutionalized. In contrast to this narrative, as I sought to answer my questions related to civic participation and social action, I collected data that would highlight students of color not as failures, but as individuals who were engaged in civic participation with a view to social change, at the same time that they were faced with external and social factors such as media influences, drugs, peer pressure, and underprepared teachers.

As I conducted my research, I was not the "great emancipator." Rather, each student, the classroom teacher, and this researcher worked in concert to engage in research that simultaneously was committed to the tenets of education—from the time of Socrates to Du Bois—that embraced the work of new ways of thinking and being and of questioning in critical ways. Social science education and research rooted in the underpinnings of democratic thought and justice should be about the business of facilitating social change that is emancipatory.

THE EMANCIPATORY RESEARCHER

[We] have to think seriously about linkages between research and activism, about cross-racial and transnational coalitional strategies, and about the importance of linking our work to radical and social agenda. (Davis, 1998, p. 231)

Emancipatory research is generally recognized as most effective when undertaken by—or in concert with—the community, organizations, or peoples that are most affected by its analysis and dissemination. As such, research born at the intersections of the specificity of oppression can become a catalyst to fundamentally change the conditions of oppression (Davis, 1998; Freire, 1970). This can be a monumental task, and there are certain challenges that will continue to arise as we move forward with this effort. However, the intentional use of more broadly defined data sites will allow for complexities too often hidden by traditional data collection, analysis, and dissemination. A project in which I was able to use this approach involved work done in the creation of a Web-based interactive CD-ROM entitled, "Integrating New Teachers into Urban Communities: Developing Culturally Relevant Teaching with Technology" (Voithofer & Tyson, 2004).

We knew that 50% of new teachers in urban schools leave the profession in the first 5 years of teaching (Darling-Hammond & Schlan, 1996). Many have few life experiences to prepare them to relate to the realities of inner-city communities, and they receive minimal academic preparation or field experience that would support their work in these schools. High attrition rates and lack of cultural literacy complicate schools' ability to provide students with the quality, committed teachers essential to student learning (Brookhart & Loadman, 1999). In addition, the reality of the digital divide faced by urban schools and neighborhoods limits the ability of new teachers to expose students to the wide array of culturally relevant technologies.

We also knew that teachers who are most successful in urban schools tend to (1) be involved in the school's community and have an understanding of students' lives outside of school (Cook & Van Cleaf, 2000; Ladson-Billings, 1994); (2) be culturally competent and have a sociopolitical consciousness in the context of the school, community, and nation (Gay, 2000; Ladson-Billings, 2001); and (3) integrate technology into a student-centered classroom (Sandholtz, Ringstaff, & Dwyer, 1997).

Given the goal of our study—to work within the catchment area of a school to develop culturally relevant technology tools to prepare new teachers for urban school assignments—we knew that we needed a different epistemological approach to the research site. Our site became the community at large, and we developed a profile of the local community through teacher, student, parent, and administrator interviews. In addition, my colleague observed in the community, and I lived there myself. We included videotaped interviews from teachers, librarians, park and recreation center staff, parents and caregivers, novice teachers, seasoned teachers, students and more students, storeowners, and many others. It is key for teachers to know the community of the students they teach, and the CD-ROM we produced opened a window to the community so that myths and presuppositions could be challenged. It also facilitated a critique of teachers' understanding of academic achievement, cultural consciousness, and social-political consciousness, and this allowed new teachers in urban schools to (re)inform and disrupt a deficit approach to educating urban youth—and thus to begin envisioning their roles in larger movements for social justice. In this instance, from an epistemology of emancipation, we combined the efforts of educators, technologists, community schools, and professional organizations in order to provide a better understanding of the capabilities of technology in addressing teaching for social justice. This effort served new teachers in urban low-performing schools, school administrators and policymakers, and institutions of higher education that prepare teachers (Voithofer & Tyson, under review).

For researchers of color, the ability to do emancipatory research potentially creates an alienated life. Indeed, the trauma of independence exacts much from those who build their research agendas outside dominant educational research circles. My research has undergone extra review in the name of "rigor." Just recently, a research initiative has been called into question under the pretext and rhetoric of scholarly rigor and the requirements of the peer review process. Although rigor or peer review may be issues, the residuals of white privilege (McIntosh, 1988) as a part of my research experiences make me ask at every turn if issues related to race, gender, and sexuality are also integral parts of the critique of my work.

Each instance contributes to the "'cumulative racism,' or a convergence of all the subtle yet still prejudicial put-downs or actions" (Parker, 2004, p. 87) that marginalized groups (including researchers) experience. I, we, survive on the margins and take pride in the uniqueness of our marginality. Without a doubt, though, such a position also exacts a cost, as we often are caught in the middle of competing agendas (Tyson, 1998; see also Delgado Bernal, 1998; Villenas, 1996).

Moreover, as critical race theorists suggest, racism is a permanent fixture in our society. Therefore, it does not take long for us, researchers of color, to face the reality that no matter how hard we work, we will probably not see the end of racism in our lifetimes. Such a realization can discourage us from aggressively moving forward. Nevertheless, many of us hold on to the belief that all we can do in our lifetime is become agents for social change through our research practices. If we wait for racism to be obliterated before we begin to enact epistemologies of emancipation, then we will be wasting—and waiting—a long time.

Emancipatory research facilitates radical thought; radical thought supports radical action; and radical action can advance a transformative social agenda. In other words, research can provide a working model for resolving the problems of marginalized populations because it incorporates a more organic methodology, connects with the "grass roots," enhances data collection and collaborative analysis, and can result in a grounded theory that arises from the specificity of the day-to-day experiences of oppressed people and provides links with broader social and political solutions to educational problems. Its hope and promise lie in courageous action for change and the desire for critical understanding.

Historically, an increased desire for liberatory and courageous action has led to revolutions. Those of us in social education spend lots of time reading, researching, and reporting on revolutionary times. The time for change is now, and the time for educational research to lead such a change is at hand. Academia, on the other hand, is not a place for fomenting a revolution. Oppositionally speaking, academia is conservatively maintaining the status quo, a status quo that reinforces a context that confuses knowing and understanding. The next logical challenge to follow is facing our practice—the work done in the many social education classrooms each day. If these epistemological underpinnings can influence our methodological research moves, we should next ask, "Can these epistemological underpinnings influence pedagogical moves?" The lines become even more blurred when we examine this theoretical frame through the lens of action research, when pedagogy and methodology can be symbiotic, emergent, and murky. While outside the scope of this chapter, it leads to the question, "How can we bring these theoretical constructs to the curriculum and the classroom, expanding the work of pedagogues of critical theory and teachers for social justice?" As a researcher who shares in the intersections of specificity of institutional and historical oppression, as a researcher whose epistemologies and methodologies can set the stage for change, and as a researcher who wants to teach "liberating social sciences," I refuse to be marginalized or "othered" by choosing this epistemological stance. My grandmother always told me: If you stand up for what is right, don't look over your shoulder to see who is standing with you—just stand. Therefore, I stand, sometimes alone, sometimes shoulder-to-shoulder with others who are also empowered to do this work. Together we give support to each other and to those that wish to participate in a social science research revolution!

NOTE

1.   Dubois (1903) describes "double consciousness" as "a peculiar sensation.... One ever feels his two-ness—an American, a Negro; two souls, two thoughts, two unreconciled strivings, two warring ideals in one dark body, whose dogged strength alone keeps it from being torn asunder" (p. 3). Gays, lesbians, and individuals who are transgendered are not minority groups based on race. However, the historical oppression is analogous, in some ways, to racial oppression.

ACKNOWLEDGMENT

This chapter is a revision and extension of an earlier chapter (Tyson, 2003).

REFERENCES

Abu-Lughod, L. (1990). Can there be a feminist ethnography? *Women and Performance: A Journal of Feminist Theory, 5,* 7–27.
Alston, J. A. (in press). Tempered radicals and servant leaders: Black females persevering in the superintendency. *Educational Administration Quarterly.*
Asante, M. (1987). *The Afrocentric idea.* Philadelphia: Temple University.
Bankert, E., & Cooper, J. A. (n.d.). *CITI course in the protection of human research subjects: History and ethical principles.* Retrieved May 28, 2005, from https://www.citiprogram.org.
Behar, R. (1993). *Translated women: Crossing the border with Esperanza's story.* Boston: Beacon Press.
Behar, R., & Gordon, D. (Eds.) .(1995). *Women writing culture.* Berkeley: University of California Press.
Bell, D. (1995). Racial realism—After we're gone: Prudent speculations on America in a post-racial epoch. In R. Delgado (Ed.), *Critical race theory: The cutting edge* (pp. 2–8). Philadelphia: Temple University Press.

Brookhart, S. M., & Loadman, W. E. (1999). Realities of teaching in racially/ethnically diverse schools: Feedback from entry-level teachers. *Urban Education, 34,* 89–114.

Carter, M. (2003). Telling tales out of school: "What's the fate of a black story in a White world of White stories?" In G. R. López & L. Parker (Eds.), *Interrogating racism in qualitative research methodology* (pp. 29–48). New York: Peter Lang.

Cook, D. W., & Van Cleaf, V. W. (2000). Multicultural perceptions of 1st-year elementary teachers' urban, suburban, and rural student teaching placements. *Urban Education, 35,* 165–174.

Condron, L. (1997). *Tales of women in science and technology: How women computer scientists in engineering environments experience their profession.* Unpublished doctoral dissertation, Ohio State University.

Crenshaw, K., Gotanda, N., Peller, B., & Thomas, K. (Eds.). (1995). *Critical race theory: Key writings that formed the movement.* New York: New Press.

Darling-Hammond, L., & Sclan, E. (1996). Who teaches and why: Building a profession for 21st century schools. In J. Sikula, T. Buttery, & E. Guyton (Eds.), *The handbook of research on teacher education* (pp. 67–101). New York: Macmillan.

Davis, A. (1998). Black women in the academy. In J. James (Ed.), *The Angela Y. Davis reader* (pp. 222–231). Malden, MA: Blackwell.

Delgado, R. (Ed.). (1995). *Critical race theory: The cutting edge.* Philadelphia: Temple University Press.

Delgado Bernal, D. (1998). Using a Chicana feminist epistemology in educational research. *Harvard Educational Review, 68,* 555–582.

Denzin, N., & Lincoln, Y. (1997). *Handbook of qualitative research.* Thousand Oaks, CA: Sage.

DuBois, W. E. B. (1903). *The souls of Black folks.* Chicago: A.C. McClurg.

Erchick, D. B. (2001). Developing mathematical voice: Women reflecting on the adolescent years. In P. O'Reilly, E. M. Penn, & K. deMarrais (Eds.), *Educating young adolescent girls* (pp. 149–170). Mahwah, NJ: Erlbaum.

Erchick, D. B. (in review). Relationships among girls, content, and pedagogy in the Matherscize Summer Mathematics Camp. In D. B. Erchick, L. Condron, P. Appelbaum, & R. Klein (Eds.) *Gender and mathematics: Reflections upon and movement toward new spaces.*

Freire, P. (1970). *Pedagogy of the oppressed.* New York: Continuum.

Freire, P. (1985). *The politics of education: Culture, power, and liberation.* South Hadley, MA: Bergin & Garvey.

Gay, G. (2000). *Culturally responsive teaching: Theory, research, and practice.* New York: Teacher's College Press.

Hughes, L. (1990). *The ways of white folks.* New York: Vintage Books. (Original work published 1934)

Hurston, Z. N. (1994) *Folklore, memoirs, and other writings* (C. Wall, Ed.). New York: The Library of American Literary Classics.

Irvine, J. (1997). *Critical knowledge for diverse teachers and learners.* Washington, DC: American Association of Colleges for Teacher Education.

Ladson-Billings, G. (1994). *The dreamkeepers: Successful teachers of African American children.* San Francisco: Jossey Bass.

Ladson-Billings, G. (1998). Just what is critical race theory and what is it doing in a nice field like education? *International Journal of Qualitative Studies in Education, 11*, 7–24.

Ladson-Billings, G. (2001) *Crossing over to Canaan: The journey of new teachers in diverse classrooms.* San Francisco: Jossey Bass.

López, G. R. (1997). Reflections on epistemology and standpoint theories: A response to "An indigenous approach to creating knowledge." *International Journal of Qualitative Studies in Education, 11*, 225–231.

Lorde, A. (1984). The master's tools will never dismantle the master's house. In *Sister outsider: Essays and speeches.* Freedom, CA: Crossing Press.

Matsuda, M., Lawrence, C., Delgado, R., & Crenshaw, K. (Eds.). (1993). *Words that wound: Critical race theory, assaultive speech, and the first amendment.* Boulder, CO: Westview.

Mazzei, L. A. (2003). Inhabited silences: In pursuit of a muffled subtext. *Qualitative Inquiry, 9*, 355–368.

Mazzei, L. A. (2004). Silent listenings: Deconstructive practices in discourse-based research. *Educational Researcher, 33*(2), 26–34.

McIntosh, P. (1998) White privilege: Unpacking the invisible knapsack. In P. S. Rothenberg (Ed.), *Race, class, and gender in the United States: An integrated study* (pp. 165–169). New York: St. Martin's Press.

Narayan, K. (1993). How native is a "native" anthropologist? *American Anthropologist, 95*, 671–686.

Parker, L. (2004). Commentary: Can critical theories on or of race be used in evaluation research in education? *New Directions in Evaluation, 101*, 85–93.

Parker, L., Deyhle, D., Villenas, S., & Nebeker, K. C. (1998). Race is…race ain't: An exploration of the utility of critical race theory in qualitative research in education. *International Journal of Qualitative Studies in Education, 11*, 43–55.

Sargent, J. (Director). (1997). *Miss Evers' boys* [Motion picture]. New York: HBO Films.

Sandholtz, J. H., Dwyer, D. C., & Ringstaff, C. (1997). *Teaching with technology: Creating student-centered classrooms.* New York: Teachers College Press.

Scheurich, J. J., & Young, M. D. (1997). Coloring epistemologies: Are our research epistemologies racially based? *Educational Researcher, 26*(4), 4–17.

Subedi, B. (2002). *Diasporic maneuvers: Asian immigrant/American mediations of cultural identity and pedagogy.* Unpublished doctoral dissertation, Ohio State University.

Thomas, S. B. (1999, September). Anatomy of an apology: Reflections on the 1997 presidential apology for the syphilis study at Tuskegee. *The academic exchange: An online place for scholarly conversation at Emory.* Retrieved May 28, 2005, from http://www.emory.edu/ACAD_EXCHANGE/1999/sept99/anatomy.html

Trinh, T. M. (1990). Not you/like you: Post-colonial women and the interlocking questions of identity and difference. In G. Anzaldúa (Ed.), *Making face, making soul/Haciendo caras: Creative and critical perspectives by feminists of color* (pp. 371–375). San Francisco: Aunt Lute Books.

Tyson, C. A. (1998). A response to "Coloring epistemologies: Are our qualitative research epistemologies racially biased?" *Educational Researcher, 27*(9), 21–22.

Tyson, C. A. (2002). "Get up offa that thing": African American middle school students respond to literature to develop a framework for understanding social action. *Theory and Research in Social Education, 30,* 42–65.

Tyson, C. A. (2003). Research, race, and an epistemology of emancipation. In G. R. López and L. Parker (Eds.), *Interrogating racism in qualitative research methodology* (pp. 19–28). New York: Peter Lang.

Voithofer, R., & Tyson, C. A. (under review). *Integrating new teachers into urban communities: Developing culturally relevant pedagogy with technology.*

Voithofer, R., & Tyson, C. A. (2004). *Integrating new teachers into urban communities: Developing culturally relevant pedagogy with technology* [CD-ROM]. Columbus, OH: Authors.

Villenas, S. (1996). The colonizer/colonized Chicana ethnographer: Identity, marginalization, and co-optation in the field. *Harvard Educational Review, 66,* 711–731.

CHAPTER 4

THE LAMP AND THE MIRROR

Action Research and Self Studies
in the Social Studies

Marilyn Johnston

Action research and self-study have had little currency in social studies education. They have been important in other areas of educational research but are relatively underused in ours. Yet they have at least as much to offer the social studies as they do to other areas, because they are oriented to the improvement of teacher practice. In addition, these research approaches naturally raise questions about social structures and justice issues, which are important for social studies. I will argue that these approaches provide fertile inquiry strategies for both K–12 and university social studies educators.

Both action research and self-study are focused on the examination by teachers of their teaching practice. The two approaches overlap but they have different histories and somewhat different foci. Action research is like a lamp. It looks outward. It shines light on some aspect of teaching practice and helps us to see more clearly and carefully in order to promote change. Self-study looks inward and is like a mirror. We look systematically at the self as a way to understand who we are as teachers and how understanding the self can provide insights into our teaching. I use the lamp and mirror as images to suggest difference in the focus of action research and self-studies. In practice, however, they are not opposites. All inquiry on teaching

Research Methods in Social Studies Education, pages 57–83
Copyright © 2006 by Information Age Publishing

and learning involves shining a light on aspects of practice; action researchers both study their practice (the lamp) and are reflective on their learning (the mirror).

Various terms are used for these kinds of research. Sometimes *practitioner research* or *teacher researcher* are used to mean any kind of research done by teachers, but here I focus on two specific types of practitioner/teacher research—action research and self-study—in order to make some distinctions between them and to show how they are two viable options for social studies educators. One chapter cannot cover everything needed to carry out these kinds of research, but I hope to suggest that action and self-study research are viable and complementary modes of research that can enhance the teaching of social studies. I also discuss practical procedures and give examples of both approaches. Examples from my own and others' research are placed in italics for easy identification. These examples are used to connect definitions, purposes, and theoretical claims to practice.

For 5 years in my own research, I have been meeting separately with the students of color in our MEd program to talk about issues of equity and social justice related to my teaching of the social studies methods course and the program at large. The motivation for this project grew out of data collected as students exited the program. In these exit interviews, students of color had consistently suggested that the program did not meet their needs in one way or another. No matter how we tried to make changes, their responses were the same. Along with another colleague (Mike Thomas) and a doctoral student (Young Ah Lee), we invited the students of color to be our cultural consultants to help us better understand their perspectives. We met separately from the majority white students to talk. Our stated focus was on issues of equity and social justice in our teaching and the MEd program, but the students talked about many issues of concern to them. They worried about the prejudices and biases they saw in their fellow students. They shared racist incidents that happened in the program, in their school placements, and in their lives more generally. They discussed the pressure they felt as graduate students and supported each other in various ways. This study had elements of both self-study (as we were examining our teaching and personal biases) as well as action research (as we tried to change our teaching and aspects of the program based on our inquiry).

I begin by looking at action research, then self-studies, and then the commonalities between them.

ACTION RESEARCH

Action research typically consists of a cycle of activities focused on a question emerging from one's teaching practice. An action plan is formed and put into practice, and data collection, analysis, and interpretation of data occur simultaneously and interactively. From the analysis and interpretations, new questions typically arise, and the cycle may begin again. Action research can be done by a teacher in his or her classroom, by a group of teachers (e.g., a grade-level team), or by a whole staff looking at a school issue. Any aspect of classroom practice and learning is a viable subject for action research—including teaching strategies, curriculum, students, educational activities in the community, or social issues in the curriculum or classroom.

The cyclical nature of action research has been represented in many ways (see Figure 4.1 for a schematic diagram). While it typically begins with a question that arises from practice, a teacher researcher can enter the cycle at any point. For example, in the current political context of data-driven decision making, teachers often disaggregate test data and plan ways to respond to student needs. The data provides the starting point for an action research study. From this data analysis, some research questions are articulated and then an action plan is designed to address the issues identified in the research questions.

I recently worked with a group of teachers from an elementary school. In the process of disaggregating and analyzing their school test data, they found that a large percentage of their students had not done well on extended written responses. They discussed the many reasons and influences on this, and then made a schoolwide plan to help stu-

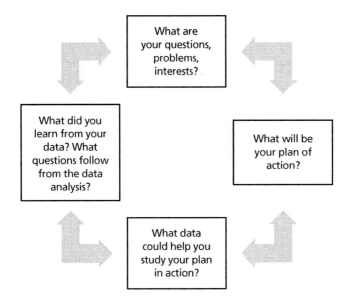

Figure 4.1.   Action research cycle.

dents learn how to respond better to these kinds of questions. They also discussed pressures of testing on teachers and students, varied sociocultural influences on their students' learning in an urban context, political and social justice issues related to testing, and ways in which they could make their research questions and action plans oriented to more than teaching to the test. They designed small, classroom-based inquiry projects to teach and plans for collecting data on student learning. They planned to share their research with each other and cumulate their findings across the school. Here, teachers entered the cycle at the data analysis point (i.e., analyzing the test data), which led to articulating questions/problems that emerged from their analysis. This led them to plan actions, and then they collected data to study how well their plan worked as they put it into practice.

During the action phase, the teacher-researcher collects data systematically, watching carefully the impact of the action on students' learning. This data is then interpreted to decide whether the new action is a desirable change in practice. At this point, new questions may arise and the cycle may begin again. Movement around the cycle can take a few days, a month, or a school year, depending on the question and the scope of the research.

Taking Action—Creating Change

The literature suggests various purposes and possibilities for action research.[1] For example, the purpose can be to change teaching practice (Burnaford, Fischer, & Hobson, 2001), reform teacher education (Clift, Veal, Johnson, & Holland, 1990), promote school reform (Hursh, 1995), create social change and justice (Carr & Kemmis, 1986; Kemmis & McTaggart, 1988), create a body of knowledge on teaching (Cochran-Smith & Lytle, 1993), make schools and society more democratic (Noffke & Stevenson, 1995), view teaching itself as a form of inquiry (Elliott, 1985), support collaborative conversations using feminist models (Hollingsworth & Sockett, 1994), and promote professional development (Oja & Smulyan, 1989). The distinguishing characteristic of action research, however, is its focus on *action*. Taking action and studying its consequences for student learning is the hallmark of action research. The action is intended to create change for the better and the study is intended to find out if it does.

Assumptions about change, however, need to be interrogated. Change is not always productive, and even when it looks good on the surface, the underlying attitudes and assumptions may need examination. Change initiated by a research plan can make things worse rather than better (e.g., enhance test scores but create less motivation to learn). Research findings can be used to support conventional practice and policies, rather than teacher autonomy, authentic student learning, and equitable and just schooling practices. Research can, but does not necessarily, support the ability of teachers to examine their purposes and change them in light of informed inquiry and interpretations. Asking critical questions, therefore, is necessary at all points in the action research cycle. Just as teachers in general should be critically reflective about their teaching, so action researchers need to be critically reflective about their research purposes, questions, plans, and interpretations. Many action researchers (e.g., Carr & Kemmis, 1986; Noffke & Stevenson, 1995) argue that social justice questions must be asked during all phases of the action research cycle because education is political and issues of equity and social justice are always a part of educational and research processes.

I tried to be continually critically reflective about my research purposes in the cultural consultant project. My initial question was about how to make my teaching and the MEd program more culturally relevant for students of color. But was I exploiting the students of color for my own purposes? Was I "using" them for my research purposes in ways that did not benefit their learning? Even though I couched this study as a self-study, was I situating the students as subjects of this study for my own purposes? Were students of color once again the object of study by white researchers? These were not easy questions to answer. We talked about them in the cultural consultant group. The students said they liked having a place to talk on their own. They felt supported by the other students in the group, and said they felt like we listened and tried to respond to their issues. Although all of the students who attended regularly reported that they felt positive about the group conversations, and although they encouraged students coming into the program to join the cultural consultant conversations, there was still a need for us as researchers to remain vigilant. Imposition and exploitation are always possibilities in cross-cultural research and teaching.

SELF-STUDY RESEARCH

A self-study is defined by the focus of research, not by its methods: In self-studies, the "self," the person, is at the center. Self-reflection is important in all research, and it is often an important part of action research, but in a self-study the focus is on the self who practices—the content, context, and nature of a teacher's activity (Loughran & Northfield, 1998). This focus does not isolate the researcher from others, nor does it rule out studying one's teaching practices; rather, it sees the research question and investigation through the perspective of the one who teaches. Analysis of the self as a teacher and learner is the centerpiece, but this self is also situated, and the context matters. Cole and Knowles (1998) identify two main purposes of self-study—self-understanding and professional development. They propose that self-study is "essentially being thoughtful (in a Deweyan sense) about one's work. It is reflective inquiry" (p. 225).

Because the self-study researcher is situated in a social context, issues related to relationships and power are involved. Self-study researchers must be critically reflective about how these influence their self-study and their reporting of research. Power relations and other people are always a part of self-studies, because the self lives in a social space. Self-studies have a tendency to become romanticized and self-indulgent if they are not situated in the struggles, politics, complexities, and tensions of the context and are not subjected to the questions, critique, and validation of others (Bullough & Pinnegar, 2004).

The self-study movement has a more recent history than action research.[2] Zeichner (1999) claims, "The birth of the self-study in teacher education movement around 1990 has been probably the single most significant development ever in the field of teacher education research" (p. 8). Although self-study in teacher research is relatively recent, the phrase itself is somewhat older, and Loughran (2004) identifies three historical uses of the term. The first was related to instructional approaches in which students worked individually through self-paced/self-evaluated curriculum. The focus was on the student learning at his or her own pace working through sequenced materials. Later, the term was used in psychological studies associated with exploring individuals' concept of self and the influence of self-image on learning (e.g., how concepts of the self influenced the learning or academic success of beginning teachers). The third use of the term is related to self-study of an institutional context, for example, a university or a school. This type of self-study was an institutional or programmatic evaluation. The goal was to align institutional beliefs/purposes and practices, and the self (whether the individual or the institution) was assumed to be responsible for this alignment.

Self-study, as it has developed within the current self-study research movement, is most closely aligned with the purposes of this third historical use of the term, but researchers work individually or in small groups to reflect on their selves as teachers rather than doing outward-focused institutional self-assessment. Self-study research is also related to psychological studies because studying the self necessarily includes reflection on the self as a psychological and developing person.

The current self-study movement is tied to the establishment of the Self-Study of Teacher Education Practice (S-STEP) special interest group (SIG) at AERA (American Educational Research Association) in 1992. It began with teacher educators who were interested in studying their own practices. In the ensuing years, this self-study group has become one of the largest SIGs in AERA, has hosted four international conferences, and has produced numerous books and articles in addition to the recent *International Handbook of Self-Study of Teaching and Teacher Education Practices* (Loughran, Hamilton, LaBoskey, & Russell, 2004). Notice in the handbook title that the scope of self studies has expanded beyond teacher education to include all teaching contexts. An ERIC search lists some 2,000 articles produced by teachers at all levels that use self-study as a descriptor (Loughran, 2004). This level of activity reflects a currently vibrant area of research activity.

COMMONALITIES IN ACTION RESEARCH AND SELF-STUDY

Action research and self-studies are similar in at least eight ways, including: (1) the bottom-up nature of research questions, (2) the importance of collaboration, (3) a focus on reflection, (4) a shared research paradigm, (5) the influence of teacher orientations, (6) teachers marginalized and/or empowered by research, (7) the influence of sociocultural contexts of schools, and (8) ethical issues.

It Starts from the Bottom Up

One common characteristic of action and self-study research is that questions and plans are initiated by the person doing the research and are rooted in the everyday practice of teaching. While consultants and research groups may be used to support one's research, it is nonetheless a bottom-up process in which the insider identifies questions and is responsible for interpretations and descriptions of his or her learning.

A classroom teacher (Mary Christenson) and a former student teacher (Sheila Serrao) conducted a collaborative action research in Mary's urban, second-grade classroom. Their question emerged from a shared frustration with students' lack of social skills. They decided to use action research to investigate potential benefits and burdens of cooperative learning even though many of their colleagues felt that "these students" would not be able to handle this approach to learning. Teaching in the neighborhood where she lived as a child, Mary's attitudes and expectations for students were not always shared by her colleagues. Sheila was substituting in Mary's classroom one day a week while Mary helped supervise student teachers for the Professional Development School project in which she was participating. As they put their action plan into practice, they systematically observed students in cooperative learning groups initiated during social studies instruction. While cooperative learning was challenging for both teachers and students, especially in the beginning, Mary and Sheila were heartened by the ways in which group work helped students learn social skills and academic content. Their research led to changes in their attitudes, expectations, and teaching practices, and they felt empowered as teachers and researchers, particularly when their research report was published (Christenson & Serrao, 1997).

Both action and self-study research grow from the questions that teachers have about their teaching practices and student learning.

The Importance of Collaboration

The use of collaborative partners while doing research is strongly suggested in both action research and self-studies. A research group provides critical friends for researchers; other people can ask questions to help clarify questions, plans, and interpretations. Moreover, reading together in a research group is a good way to begin one's journey as an action or self-study researcher. A collaborative group provides a place to learn about doing research, to solve problems that emerge in research, and to help maintain motivation. Other eyes are also helpful in the data analysis and interpretation phase: It is easy to miss things when researching in one's own classroom, because although a teacher may have the advantage of knowing the context and her students well, she may also be blinded in some ways by familiarity with her context and the data. Colleagues can help ask questions about things she may take for granted, provide another set of eyes as she analyzes her data, and help her deepen her interpretations.

I have personally found collaborative teaching contexts to be places where I can get help, support, and critique for my research. For example, several years ago I taught a newly designed course on classroom-based inquiry. I wanted to demonstrate the collaborative norms and characteristics of action research in the actual teaching of the course. I asked five doctoral students in the course to co-teach with me. We designed an action research project to study our teaching of this course (our action plan) as well as what we were learning. We shared our research with classroom teachers in the course throughout the quarter. From research proposal development through data analysis, we demonstrated how to do action research as we taught about it. Following the course we worked collaboratively to further analyze our data and interpret what we learned from doing this research (Christenson et al., 2002; Johnston et al., 2003). In this kind of collaborative research group, we could ask each other questions and utilize our different perspectives to add depth and critique to the inquiry process.

Reflection at the Heart of it All

There is also a more general assumption about reflection that underlies action and self-study research. Whether stated explicitly or not, it is assumed that the systematic reflection that results from doing teacher research leads to better action (Schön, 1987) and that reflective teachers are more effective teachers (Grant & Zeichner, 1984). Reflection happens at all stages of the research. It helps us critically evaluate our research purposes, plans, data analyses, and learning. As we complete our research project, reflection helps us identify new questions coming out of our study and leads us to our next research question.

There is an assumption underlying these research approaches that we benefit from a careful, reflective attitude that examines what we are doing as teachers and the consequences of our actions for students and student learning. This is a very Deweyan idea—that reflection and inquiry create and inform future purposes. For Dewey (1933), reflection is "an active, persistent, and consideration of any belief or supposed form of knowledge in the light of grounds that support it and the future conclusions to which it tends" (p. 9). Reflection on purposes is fluid and continually influences future purposes. On this view, it is important to critically assess the goals, processes, and outcomes of our research.

> *Critique and reflection are part of the cyclical and emergent character of both self-studies and action research. Reflection on the direction and issues within the research sometimes leads to mid-course changes in questions or design. For example, my initial purpose in the cultural consultant project was to study my own teaching. The scope of students' interests and concerns and the diversity in their points of view helped me reflect on my teaching, but it also broadened my purposes. I realized after a while that I could not just think about my own teaching. As a result of our conversations, I was trying new things in my teaching. This led me to think of my project as more of an action research study. I eventually came to see meetings with students of color as an action plan itself, because the most important thing we all learned was the significance of having time to talk about these issues in a safe space apart from the larger cohort of white students. My purposes changed as inquiry and reflection enlarged my understandings.*

Good teachers regularly reflect on their teaching. This reflection turns into "research" when systematic data collection and analysis are added to the mix. When problems are carefully articulated and data is systematically collected, reflection has turned into research. Intuitions ground most of the decisions that teachers make—hundreds of them in the course of a day. Inquiry into these intuitions through systematic data collection and analysis shines the light on particular aspects of our practice and gives us information about students and processes that we cannot see otherwise. Being systematic allows us to document actions and consequences in ways that support grounded interpretations and deeper understandings. It is rare to collect systematic data on teaching and not find surprises.

For some action researchers, especially in Australia and England, a critical social lens has been central to action research (e.g., Kemmis, 1985; Kemmis & McTaggart, 1988). On this view, we are encouraged to critique the social norms and practices that underlie our teaching practices and that may obstruct schooling for social justice. From this point of view, it is not enough to examine only teaching practice; teachers must also consider social and political influences on the teacher and students, as well as on schooling more generally. For social studies educators, this focus supports their teaching goals and this adds a research lens to further their understandings of their own teaching for social justice.

A Shared Research Paradigm

Both action research and self-studies typically work within a naturalistic or qualitative paradigm. Naturalistic researchers study "natural" settings— that is, social contexts and interactions among people. This research paradigm is well suited to classroom settings and self-studies, but not to positivist perspectives on research. Often the differences between research paradigms are not properly acknowledged, and thus naturalistic studies are judged by the requirements of a positivist paradigm. From a positivist position, action research and self-studies do not measure up to the "rigor" of controlled studies and statistical manipulation of large samples. Teacher researchers study their teaching by collecting primarily qualitative data (e.g., interviews, focus group conversations, student work samples, teacher and student journals, etc.). Typically these studies will not satisfy, nor are they intended to satisfy, the requirements of positivist research, particularly what the current federal government defines as "scientific," namely quasi-experimental control group studies (Erickson, 2005; see also http://www.ed.gov/nclb/methods/whatworks/research/index.html). Nor can we easily generalize the results of our research to other situations. We do case studies of particular practice to provide useable insights and accessibility primarily of our own practice, but not to generalize to all classrooms. This does not mean, however, that our studies have no relevance outside our own contexts: Donmoyer (1990) argues that the accessibility and rich descriptions of case studies take a reader where he or she could not have gone personally. As readers, we can vicariously experience complex situations and unique individuals, and we learn from these in-depth examples by comparing them to our own experience. We can ask ourselves whether and how far our situation and practices are similar to those in the study, and whether similar actions might be useful in our practice.

Positivist critiques may be most troublesome for teacher educators who have pressures to do research and publish, depending on the particular institutions' norms about what is "acceptable" research. Personally I have jumped through the promotion hoops, so I have the luxury of doing the kind of research I choose. However, for untenured faculty, action and self-study approaches may present real challenges. Mitigating these potential pressures is the increasingly receptive climate for publishing self-studies. There is even a new journal dedicated to publishing this research, Studying Teacher Education: A Journal of Self-Study of Teacher Educator Practices. *The increasing number of dissertations done with self-study approaches is also a sign that there is a burgeoning openness to this research, at least on some university campuses.*

Self-studies may be the most vulnerable to traditional positivist critiques. From a positivist research perspective, self-studies can appear to be unsystematic and narcissistic. Because positivist researchers attempt to keep the researcher out of the research, a focus on the self runs counter to traditional requirements for objectivity and validity. In education, however, if we claim that "we teach who we are" (Parker, 1998), than there is little about us as persons that doesn't impact our teaching in some way. It is challenging, nevertheless, to know which parts of our selves are relevant to the study at hand. Not everything matters. It is incumbent on the self-study researcher to walk this fine line between self-indulgence and analysis and to determine what does, and does not, promote a deeper understanding of the teacher and his or her teaching. Bullough and Pinnegar (2001) describe it this way:

> Quality self-study research requires that the researcher negotiate a particularly sensitive balance between biography and history…such study does not focus on the self per se but on the space between self and the practice engaged in. There is always a tension between those two elements, self and the arena of practice, between self in relation to practice and the others who share the practice setting. (p. 15)

Teacher Orientations Matter

The choice between action research and self-study will be influenced by the teacher's purposes and questions as well. If social studies teachers are focused primarily on subject-matter learning and/or the primary goal is to develop an informed future citizen, then action research may be the best choice. Likewise, if the teacher wants to change some aspect of his or her teaching or implement a new curriculum, then action research will be useful. The primary focus of action research is to support teachers in changing and improving their practice.

If the teacher's orientation is focused on reflective inquiry, then self-study research may be more appropriate. In self-studies, personal goals, experiences, and perspectives are the subject of inquiry. Who we are as teachers or students, what we do as we teach and learn, what we think about social justice issues in our lives and the world, who we are in relation to other people and learners is the stuff of self-studies.

My teaching purposes have been directly influenced by my research. For example, in my social studies methods courses I have my students develop cultural memoirs. They col-

lect and describe artifacts that symbolize who they are as cultural persons and how this will influence them as teachers. Their beliefs and perspectives on race, class, sexual orientation, disabilities, and so on are examined as they construct memoirs about themselves. They share these memoir projects with me and with each other. I introduce this assignment as a self-study and the goal is to support their preparation to become culturally sensitive teachers. In tandem, I am doing action research to study how this project influences their evolving understandings of themselves and their abilities to teach in culturally relevant ways.

For teachers with commitments to social justice issues, both action and self-studies are useful. In action research, we might study new ways of teaching about social justice concerns and social activism and what impact it has on students' learning. In self-studies, we could focus on our own teacher perspectives as we teach about social justice or we could engage students in critical self-studies of their biases, prejudices, and learning. We might look at our own biases and perspectives as they influence how and what we teach. For many social studies educators, these issues are at the heart of social studies. Conducting and publishing research in any of these areas will support social studies educators in general.

Marginalized and/or Empowered by Research

Teachers learning about action and self-study research for the first time are often hesitant. Research is not what teachers typically do in their classrooms. Doing something different in your classroom can lead to marginalization. Marginalization is something that occurs when a person or group is discriminated against. We could argue that teachers have traditionally been marginalized by researchers and policymakers. Teachers' voices have often been absent from research as outside "experts" studied classrooms and reported on their results. Both teachers and students were subjects to be studied rather than voices speaking about their own experience.

In policy contexts, teachers have also been silenced by the deafening discourses of accountability and "leave no child behind." One could argue that both children and teachers have been left behind in the rush to use test scores to label and categorize them. Action and self-study research are means to insert teacher and student voices into this discourse, and to claim a space for insider perspectives. These kinds of research studies capture the complexity of classrooms including the varied impact of political agendas on teachers and students. This complexity and first-person realism is often absent from research done by outsiders. Teacher voices and perspectives are silenced when test scores are the only description of a school offered to the public and policymakers.

There are frequent discussions in the action research literature about the empowerment that results from action research (Hubbard & Power, 2001; McLean, 1997). Understanding one's own teaching and context from a research perspective can create an enlightened consciousness that supports more articulate and grounded claims. Teacher researchers can speak with increased confidence. The authority that comes from basing one's arguments on research findings comes partly from a heightened knowledge of the situation; the systematicity of research provides a more solid ground for knowing than intuitions and self-reflection. This confidence is also supported by the perceived value of "research" in common parlance. Even though teacher research does not meet, or is intended to meet, positivist criteria for quantitative "scientific research," it nevertheless carries the weight of the social belief that research provides truth and guidance.

I regularly teach a course on action research at my university and I can't remember how many times teachers have later told me how doing research made them feel "more professional," positively changed the way their parents perceived them, helped them argue a case with the principal to influence change in their school, or revitalized their teaching. Of course, there are also reports of marginalization, difficulty finding collaborative partners, and negative consequences in schools for doing research.

Mary Christenson's cooperative learning project had a similar effect. Although she didn't get much encouragement within her school for conducting or publishing her research, doing this project gave her the confidence she needed to go forward with her desire to get a PhD. Not that we want teachers to leave their classrooms, but empowerment means that teachers feel confident to pursue their goals for professional growth, wherever that might take them. Nevertheless, Mary's dissertation study was a collaborative self-study and action research project that looked at controversial issue discussions with young children about environmental issues. Mary is currently an assistant professor at Ohio State–Lima teaching science and social studies.

The Influence of Sociocultural Contexts in Schools

Sociocultural contexts of schools vary widely and determine the norms, policies, and relationships within a particular school. Many teachers find these norms challenging as they do action research and self-studies. Some teachers report feeling alienated because their enthusiasm for research is not supported by their peers. Their colleagues may feel coerced to do research themselves but resist because of the time demands, lack of interest, or because they don't see research as a part of what teachers should be doing. They may feel threatened by the investigative thrust of the research—by what might be uncovered. Or they may feel intimidated by colleagues who become more articulate about teaching as a consequence of having "research" to back up their teaching practices.

Likewise, principals may not support teachers doing research. They may not understand the purposes, they may fear it will detract from a focus on teaching, or they may fear the empowerment that often ensues as teachers become more confident about their teaching. Teachers with research to back up their claims may oppose what principals or school districts have set as goals and strategies.

The culture of the school was a critical factor in Mary's research project. Mary was criticized by some of her colleagues because they felt that the published report of her research cast their school, and the traditional teaching and attitudes prevalent in the school, in a negative light. This was not her intent. Mary gave her principal a copy of her publication and he returned it to her mailbox later without comment. These kinds of interactions are not supportive of teacher research. In a more supportive school context, doing her action research project might have felt more positive. Mary's support came from Sheila and other teachers in the Professional Development School—persons outside her school context.

Ethical Issues

Ethical issues permeate all aspects of teaching and research. Attention to these issues is critical for all researchers, not just action and self-study practitioners. Yet, it is interesting to note that ethical issues often get short-changed in the literature on teacher research in general. Zeni's (2000) book-length discussion makes a significant contribution. She shows how current ethical guides, even those within qualitative research, often fail to address important aspects of insider research issues. Action research and self-studies do raise important ethical issues that are connected to discussions of naturalistic/qualitative research in general, but these issues are infrequently applied to action research and self-studies specifically. I'll focus here on just two issues—representation and power—as examples of the importance of thinking about ethical issues in research.

Issues of Representation

Questions about representation in research are closely tied to issues of difference and otherness, issues that are always of concern to social studies educators, particularly in relation to cross-cultural content and pedagogy. A person who represents another has the power to describe, to interpret, and to control what is said about the other. In the process of doing our research, we should question the authority we claim as we speak about others. We should interrogate how "others" are represented in our research, curricula, and instruction and we should examine what happens to difference and otherness in this representation. Qualitative research methodologists in education in general have borrowed heavily from anthropology (Clifford & Marcus, 1986; Marcus & Fischer, 1986) to raise questions about representing others and, in particular, the effects of those in power (teachers/professors/researchers) on those in subordinate positions (subjects/participants/students).

Anzaldua (1987), Lorde (1984), Mohanty (2003), Spivak (1999), and West (1993) have all critiqued the tendency of representations to reduce and appropriate the identities of those living "on the margins" (hooks, 1989). Discussions of representation converge at the intersections of race, class, gender, culture, and colonialism and have consequences for both those who represent and those represented. An African American using postmodern feminist theories, bell hooks argues that she is positioned as the "other" located in the "margins" and silenced by the representations made by those at the "center"—those with the power to do the representing. Often this speech about the "other" annihilates, erases:

> No need to hear your voice when I can talk about you better than you can speak about yourself. No need to hear your voice. Only tell me about your pain. I want to know your story. And then I will tell it back to you in a new way. Tell it back to you in such a way that it has become mine, my own. Rewriting you, I write myself anew. I am still author, authority. I am still the colonizer, the speaking subject, and you are now at the center of my talk." (hooks, 1990, pp. 151–152)

The person who represents here is the colonizer, the one with the authority to describe the other as different, as exotic, as "other" (Said, 1979). It is here that post-colonial theorists, such as Said (1979), Bhabha (1994), and Spivak (1999), offer insights into the dangers of constructing the "other" in ways that maintain power for those in authority. Authority is established by seeing the "other" as exotic, intellectually inferior, child-like, culturally strange, or lacking in the cultural values and norms of those in power. The list of ways in which those who are different have been "othered" is long. This construction can be supported by politicians, policymakers, researchers, educators, or anyone who has the power to control and/or educate and it is often built into school policies. It thus becomes an integral aspect of our research in schools, whether acknowledged or not. Power issues become particularly acute when researchers study persons who are already marginalized because of some social difference that sets them apart from the dominant culture—for example, when students from cultures and races are different from the teacher-researchers.

Representation in the social studies

In social studies this "othering" is often done by exoticizing other cultures in order to make them "interesting" to students or trivializing cultural rituals expecting that eating some foreign food or dancing a folk dance will lead to culture understanding. However, developing stereotypes is more likely the outcome. In urban schools, "othering" occurs when teachers use the phrase, "these children can't…" Such statements imply that students have deficits—related to their culture, language, home contexts—and thus need special treatment, which usually translates into less of what majority children would be expected to have or accomplish. In this process the children lose rights and freedoms; their identity is constructed by outsiders, rather than by those inside their culture/group.

Action and self-study researchers must be wary of "othering" students in ways that perpetuate the colonization of those who are different. The power to support stereotypes through research is as real as the power to critique and enlighten our understandings of how best to educate all children. Some of these issues of representation are powerfully captured in artwork by Barbara Kruger entitled *Your Gaze Hits the Side of My Face* (see Figure 4.2). Kruger is an American artist who deals with issues of sexism, power, and identity. I use this photograph in my social studies methods course to talk about social issues; I use it in my action research course to talk about representation.

In this image you see a profile of a woman that is carved in stone. To the left of the face, the words from the title are spaced down the side of the photograph. The gaze in this case is the male gaze on a woman's face. "Gaze" implies power, the power to create the "other." It is not reciprocal; it is the power to look and not be looked at and it positions the person who is looked at as the less powerful. The choice of the stone face of a woman suggests the metaphor of the male gaze turning women to stone. Women are objects to be looked at, not agents who look. The gaze here can be read as parallel to the researcher who gazes at the subjects of the research and does not allow them to represent themselves. Researchers have power over their participants as they document, interpret, and represent "others." It is the researcher's gaze on others that is too often evident in a typical research account.

Research in school contexts is always about power and representation because students are in a less powerful position than teachers and the potential for simply confirming prejudices is ever present. As researchers, we need others, including our students, to enter our projects with critical questions in order to guard against such exploitation.

Dealing with ethical issues in our research

Action and self-study researchers and others have tried to mitigate this power differential by becoming a "participant observer," a collaborator, co-

Figure 4.2.   Barbara Kruger, "Untitled" (Your gaze hits the side of my face),
55" × 41" photograph, 1981. Courtesy of Mary Boone Gallery, New York.

researcher, or dialogue partner (Glesne, 1999, Hubbard & Power, 2001,
Mills, 2000).

> *Collaboration during the research process is one way to address issues of representa-
> tion and power. Two times during the 5-year cultural consultant project, my co-
> researcher and I worked collaboratively with students to do the actual research analy-
> sis and writing. At the end of the first year, we jointly analyzed data from the first
> year's conversations, constructing themes and scoring data to them. We wrote stories
> about our experiences together and made presentations at two national conferences
> (Johnston & Lee, 2004; Johnston, Ramos, & Thomas, 2000; Johnston, Summers-
> Eskridge, Wyatt, & Thomas, 2000). In the third year we wrote collaborative case
> studies to emphasize differences in the life experiences and perspectives of four of the
> cultural consultant participants. Collaborative data analysis and writing allows for
> multiple voices and this can somewhat mitigate the power differential between
> researchers and participants. This varies depending on the person, but it sends a
> powerful message that their voices matter and that researchers are willing to listen
> and integrate their points of view.*

The goal is to be collaborative and critical during all phases of the research, particularly in constructing interpretations. Collaboration can be with participants or with others in a research group. Self-study research takes this effort one step further and deliberately reverses the focus. The goal is to look at the self, rather than to study the other. On the surface this might make it seem that ethical issues are of less consequence. Yet the contexts within which self-studies are conducted are fraught with power issues, so representation of the self and others is still a central question. When students' perspectives about our teaching are part of the self-study, as in my cultural consultant project example, issues of power are obviously an important aspect of ethical research issues.

USES OF ACTION AND SELF-STUDY RESEARCH IN THE SOCIAL STUDIES

There are many ways in which action and self-study research could be useful to us as social studies educators. Whatever issues and challenges we have as teachers can be supported by doing research and studying our teaching. Here I look at three areas in which such research can be particularly useful: (1) looking at social justice issues in social studies, (2) using inquiry as a mode of professional development, and (3) connecting democratic research processes and social studies aims.

Research to Address Social Justice Issues

Action and self-study research can be used to assist social studies teachers in addressing social justice issues. Aspects of difference, including race, culture, social class, sexual orientations, or disabilities, are inherent in all educational contexts. They are less apparent in some school contexts and subjects than others, yet all educational contexts reflect values, including deeply racist, sexist, or homophobic tendencies of our society. Many students, especially in urban contexts, experience inequities and lack of social justice in direct ways. Other students, given the homogeneous contexts in which they live and learn, have less awareness of these issues.

Social studies education provides the opportunity, and some would argue the obligation, to address these issues in culturally sensitive ways. In social studies, social justice issues are deeply embedded in the very content that we teach, whether we choose to make them explicit or not. Social justice concerns pervade interpretations of history; sociological analyses of race, class, and gender; geographical representations of the distribution of the world's resources; and political analyses of influence and inequities in national policies. Textbooks, of course, mask most of these kinds of issues, but teachers have opportunities to uncover them and to initiate critical analyses with students.

Action and self-study research can aid in these efforts. They help us unmask our prejudices and biases, study our own social justice agendas in practice, and learn from what students can tell us about their points of view and their learning. If we want students to become critical, culturally sensitive citizens, we must model this for them. Studying our teaching contexts and practices (action research) and our own perspectives and learning about our practices (self-study) is one way to do this.

In a review of self-studies in teacher education for the recent handbook of self-study research, Clift (2004) concludes: "The language of social activism and societal critique or cultural critique has seldom been employed [in self-study research]; the goals of change are limited to the individual teacher educator or teacher education student" (p. 1362). While individual teacher educators are conducting self-studies in increasing numbers, there is little evidence yet that social justice language has penetrated self-study research in teacher education.

Using Inquiry as a Model of Professional Development

Teacher researchers are participating in and modeling inquiry as professional development. Research helps us develop as professionals because we become more knowledgeable about our craft as well as ourselves as teachers. This is professional development, not training. As classroom teachers do inquiry, we are not relying on outside experts to tell us how to improve our teaching. We are working on our own self-defined goals to solve self-identified problems. This kind of professional development typically is more engrossing and meaningful than the sporadic, no-choice imposition of training sessions provided by school districts. Professionals know what they need and what their questions are. Teacher research is a way to address these.

Teacher educators and classroom teachers working with student teachers directly demonstrate the value of inquiry for professional development by doing research. If we want future teachers to be critically reflective practitioners, then we must model what that looks like in our own teacher education programs and classroom teaching. When mentor teachers do research in their classrooms, their student teachers benefit from seeing a model of professional development in action. Inquiry also affords mentor teachers a way to make their goals and purposes more visible for their mentees. Future teachers are unlikely to develop habits of critical self-reflection in a context where their instructors or mentor teachers do not demonstrate such an orientation. Doing action and self-study research is one way to model this kind of self-reflection and on-going professional development.

Integrating Democratic Research Processes and Social Studies Aims

Educating future citizens for a democratic society is a central role of the social studies. We could argue that our teaching, as well as our research methodologies, ought to put democratic norms and processes to practice. Action research and self-studies are inherently democratic because they support the articulation of multiple points of view, in which teacher researchers can learn from a wider discussion of differences. Ansley and Gaventa (1997), speaking of a variety of qualitative research approaches, write:

> Fortunately, we are witnessing the emergence of models that promote more democratic methods of inquiry, more reciprocal relationships between researchers and their subjects [participants], and new collaborations between research institutions and communities. (p. 45)

Noffke and Stevenson (1995) ask whether we can claim that "democracy exists when voices of many are excluded and the pressures to conform exceed those of dissidence and difference" (p. 8). The full idea of democracy requires dissidence and difference. In short, action and self-study research provide a means for increasing participation and learning through democratic means.

A REVIEW OF ACTION AND SELF-STUDY RESEARCH IN THE SOCIAL STUDIES

While action and self-study research is limited in social studies, there are some good examples, and although most are written by teacher educators, they are useful for social studies educators at all levels. (The potential for improving the teaching of social studies from research done by school-based teachers is a field waiting to be cultivated.) Some of these studies are framed explicitly as action research or self-studies; others are not identified directly as such, but they meet the criteria of planning action and studying the process and the results.[3]

Wilson (1990), for example, conducted an action research study of her own teaching in a third-grade social studies class. Her focus was the role of subject-matter knowledge in elementary school teaching. Her study included a close examination of her teaching, including her planning, decision making, and classroom instruction, as well as her understanding of the comments and learning of the students. Based on her research, she asserts that subject matter is important and can expand what a teacher hears in students' comments but that it is not sufficient for creating powerful instructional representations. She concludes that teachers need pedagogical content knowledge as well as knowledge of their subject matter. Similarly, VanSledright (2002) provides a book-length description of his study of fifth-graders' learning as he taught several history units focused on exploring and analyzing history. He gives detailed accounts of his teaching and the students' reactions, his research methodology, and his analysis of student learning.

Most instances of action research in social studies have focused on methods courses and field experiences. Dinkelman (1999), for example, conducted an action research study in which he followed three students from his secondary social studies methods course, interviewing them at the beginning, middle, and end of the semester. He also looked at their assignments, checking for evidence of critical reflection. He developed three case studies of these students and a cross-case analysis. He found evidence in all three cases of critical reflection and critically reflective teaching, but no connection to critical democratic citizenship or any change in their views concerning the purposes for teaching social studies. In a follow-up study of these case study students during their student teaching, Dinkelman (2000) found limited but significant evidence of critical reflection and critical reflective teaching. This study supports the view that critical reflection is a viable practical aim for preservice teacher education. Based on this work, Dinkelman (2003) also has developed a five-part theoretical rationale to support the use of self-study to promote reflective instruction.

Similarly, Noffke and her colleagues have published a series of articles on her social studies methods course teaching (e.g., Buednai, Meacham, & Noffke, 2000; Hyland & Noffke, 2001). These are action research projects that consider how community and social inquiry assignments can be used to develop concepts of marginalization and privilege, including a critical analysis of teaching from this perspective. Noffke and her colleagues study their students' learning as they cross cultural boundaries to learn about historically marginalized groups. They study their own teaching within institutional contexts and constraints. Throughout they raise hard, critical questions about their teaching and discuss both the intended and possibly unintended consequences.

Brice and Hartzler-Miller (2004) conducted a self-study using autoethnographic and feminist methodology. They used narrative analysis of their own life stories with secondary and university teachers to document pivotal experiences, pedagogical practices, and points of conflict or tension within themselves or with others. Through this process, they unearthed elements of a critical ethic for social studies education that has guided their pedagogical decisions. This critical ethic consists of a commitment to selecting controversial and complex content, inviting students to dissent, and encouraging students to recognize their participation in systemic patterns of injustice. In addition, they included the idea of generosity, which refers to a commitment to honoring the interpretations others make of their experiences. They articulate a social studies approach that focuses on social critique, concern for justice, and democratic forms of discourse.

CONCLUSIONS

We can enhance teaching through action and self-study research by studying our practices and/or the self that teaches. Shining a light on either our actions or on our selves enhances our ability to learn and thus to grow as educators. While the metaphors of the lamp and mirror emphasize differences between action research and self-studies, in the life of a teacher researcher, these distinctions may be less obvious. Action researchers often include a study of themselves in order to examine their influences in the classrooms; self-study research often leads to developing action plans in the classroom. Both approaches have the potential to enhance our understandings, our teaching, and our students' learning. These teacher research approaches hold particular potential for social studies educators to grow as teachers, to uncover and examine our prejudices and teaching purposes, and to help our students become critically reflective and socially active citizens. These are not research studies from which we can generalize "findings"; rather, these studies provide opportunities for critical reflection, adaptations, and personal and professional insights for both the researchers and other teachers.

Inside the social studies profession, we continue our debates on the nature of social studies, while the larger political context clamps down on what is taught by defining what is tested. Most teachers I know are burdened by these accountability measures that restrict teaching goals and methods, though they are meant to enhance learning. This is not a context that empowers teachers or supports experimentation. The emancipatory potential of practitioner research runs counter to current restricted educational reform policies. Action and self-study research have the potential to help educators both study and critique the impact of these policies on teaching, as well as better understand how we can proceed in ways that support our professional goals and enhance our insights. As we educate the citizens of tomorrow, we need tools to sustain and nurture the critical purposes of social studies education. Action and self-study research are tools that can support teachers and enhance teaching and learning for a democratic society.

NOTES

1. There are numerous books that describe the planning and implementation of action research (Cochran-Smith & Lytle, 1993; Hubbard & Power, 2001; Kemmis & McTaggart, 1988; Mills, 2000; Noffke & Stevenson, 1995; Sagor, 1992; Stringer, 1996) and many books and articles describing teacher research projects (Bisplinghoff & Allen, 1998; Burnaford et al., 2001; Clift et al., 1990; Hohenbrink, Johnston, & Westhoven, 1997; McCutcheon, 1987; McNiff, Lomax, & Whitehead, 1996; Nath & Tellez, 1995; Nias, 1988; Wells, 1993).

2. There are many accounts of the early history of action research in the United States and internationally, including Boud, Keogh, and Walker (1985); Clift, Houston, and Pugach (1990); Foshay (1994); Kemmis (1982); Kyle and Hovda (1987); Noffke (1997); and Wallace (1987).

3. For additional examples of action and self-study research in social studies, particularly in methods courses, see Boyle-Baise (2003); Crocco, Faithfull, and Schwartz (2003); DeWitt and Freie (2004); Gerwin (2003); Hohenbrink et al. (1997); Hollingsworth, Gallego, and Standerford (1995); Jacobs and Marino (2004); and Johnston (1990).

REFERENCES

Anzaldua, G. (1987). *La frontera/borderlands.* San Francisco: Spinsters/Aunt Lute.

Ansley, F., & Gaventa, J. (1997). Researching for democracy and democratizing research. *Change, 29,* 46–53.

Bisplinghoff, B., Allen, J., & Shockley-Bisplinghoff, B. (1998). *Engaging teachers: Creating teaching and researching relationships.* Portsmouth, NH: Heinemann

Bhabha, H. (1994). *The location of culture.* New York: Routledge.

Boud, D., Keogh, R., & Walker, D. (1985). *Reflection: Turning experience into learning.* New York: Nichols.

Boyle-Baise, M. (2003). Doing democracy in social studies methods. *Theory and Research in Social Education, 31,* 51–71.

Brice, L., & Hartzler-Miller, C. (2004). *Holding ourselves to a critical ethic as social studies educators.* Paper presented at the College and University Faculty Assembly of the National Council for the Social Studies, Baltimore.

Buednai, E., S. Meacham, & Noffke. S. E. (2000). Community, displacement, and inquiry: Living social justice in a social studies methods course. In D. Hursh & E. W. Ross (Eds.), *Democratic social education: Social studies for social change* (pp. 73–84). New York: Falmer Press.

Bullough, R., & Pinnegar, S. (2001). Guidelines for quality in autobiographical forms of self-study research. *Educational Researcher, 30*(3), 13–21.

Bullough, R., Jr., & Pinnegar, S. (2004). Thinking about the thinking about self-study: An analysis of eight chapters. In J. J. Loughran, M. L. Hamilton, V. K. LaBoskey, & T. Russell (Eds.), *The international handbook of self-study of teaching and teacher education practices* (pp. 313–342). London, Kluwer Academic.

Burnaford, G. E., Fischer, J., & Hobson, D. (Eds.). (2001). *Teachers doing research: The power of action through inquiry.* New York: Erlbaum.

Carr, W., & Kemmis, S. (1986). *Becoming critical: Education, knowledge, and action research.* London: Falmer.

Christenson, M., & Serrao, S. (1997). Cooperative learning in a hostile environment. *Teaching and Change, 4*, 137–156.

Christenson, M., Slutsky, R., Bendau, S., Covert, J., Dyer, J., Risko, G., & Johnston, M. (2002). The rocky road of teachers becoming action researchers. *Teaching and Teacher Education, 18*, 259–272.

Clifford, J., & Marcus, G. (1986). *Writing cultures.* Berkeley: University of California Press.

Clift, R. T. (2004). Self-study research in the context of teacher education programs. In J. J. Loughran, M. L. Hamilton, V. K. LaBoskey, & T. Russell (Eds.), *International handbook of self-study of teaching and teacher education practices* (pp. 1333–1366). Dordrecht, The Netherlands: Kluwer Academic.

Clift, R., Houston, W. R., & Pugach, M. (Eds.). (1990). *Encouraging reflective practice in education: An analysis of issues and program.* New York: Teachers College Press.

Clift, R., Veal, M. L., Johnson, M., & Holland, P. (1990). Restructuring teacher education through collaborative action research. *Journal of Teacher Education, 41*(2), 52–62.

Cochran-Smith, M., & Lytle, S. (1993). *Inside/outside: Teacher research and knowledge.* New York: Teachers College Press.

Cole, A. L., & Knowles, J. G. (1998). The self-study of teacher education practices and the reform of teacher education. In M. L. Hamilton (Ed.), *Reconceptualizing teaching practice: Self-study in teacher education* (pp. 224–234). London: Falmer Press.

Crocco, M. S., Faithfull, B., & Schwartz, S. (2003). Inquiring minds want to know: Action research at a New York City professional development school. *Journal of Teacher Education, 54*, 19–30.

Dewey, J. (1933). *How we think: A restatement of the relation of reflective thinking to the educative process.* Chicago: Henry Regnery.

DeWitt, S. W., & Freie, C. (2004). *Switching hats: Reflections on purposes and practice in a social studies methods classroom.* Paper presented at the College and University Faculty Assembly of the National Council for the Social Studies, Baltimore.

Dinkelman, T. (1999). Critical reflection in a social studies methods semester. *Theory and Research in Social Education, 27*, 329–357.

Dinkelman, T. (2000). An inquiry into the development of critical reflection in secondary student teachers. *Teaching and Teacher Education 16*,195–122.

Dinkelman, T. (2003). Self-study in teacher education: A means and ends tool for promoting reflective teaching. *Journal of Teacher Education 54*, 6–18.

Donmoyer, R. (1990). Generalizability and the single case study. In E. W. Eisner & A. Peshkin (Eds.), *Qualitative inquiry in education: The continuing debate* (pp. 175–200). New York: Teachers College Press.

Elliott, J. (1985). Educational action research. In J. Nisbet & S. Nisbet (Eds.), *Research, policy and practice: World yearbook of education* (pp. 231–250). London: Logan Page.

Erickson, F. (2005). Arts, humanities, and sciences in educational research and social engineering in federal education policy. *Teachers College Record, 107*, 4–9.

Foshay, A. W. (1994). Action research: An early history in the United States. *Journal of Curriculum and Supervision, 9*, 317–325.

Gerwin, D. (2003). A relevant lesson: Hitler goes to the mall. *Theory and Research in Social Education 31*, 435–365.

Glesne, C. (1999). *Becoming qualitative researchers: An introduction.* New York: Longman

Grant, C., & Zeichner, K. (1984). On becoming a reflective teacher. In C. Grant (Ed.), *Preparing for reflective teaching* (pp. 1–18). Boston: Allyn & Bacon.

Hohenbrink, J., Johnston, M., & Westhoven, L. (1997). Collaborative teaching of a social studies methods course: Intimidation and change. *Journal of Teacher Education, 48*, 293–300.

Hollingsworth, S., & Sockett, H. (Eds.). (1994). *Teacher research and educational reform.* Chicago: University of Chicago Press.

Hollingsworth, S., Gallego, M., & Standerford, N. (1995). Integrative social studies for urban middle schools: A case for multiple literacies. *Theory and Research in Social Education 23*, 204–233.

hooks, b. (1989). *Talking back: Thinking feminist, thinking black.* Boston: South End Press.

hooks, b. (1990). *Yearning: Race, gender, and cultural politics.* Boston: South End Press.

Hubbard, R., & Power, B. (2001). *Living the questions: A guide for teacher-researchers.* Portsmouth, NH: Heinemann.

Hursh, D. (1995). Developing discourses and structures to support action research for educational reform. In S. E. Noffke & R. B. Stevenson (Eds.), *Educational action research: Becoming practically critical* (pp. 141–153). New York: Teachers College Press.

Hyland, N. E., & Noffke, S. E. (2001). *Understanding diversity through social and community inquiry: An action research study.* Paper presented to the College and University Faculty Assembly of the National Council for the Social Studies, Washington, DC.

Jacobs, B. M., & Marino, M. P. (2004). *"Is this high school?": The question of instruction in a social studies methods course.* Paper presented at the College and University Faculty Assembly of the National Council for the Social Studies, Baltimore.

Johnston, M. (1990). Teachers' backgrounds and beliefs: Influences on learning to teach in the social studies. *Theory and Research in Social Education, 21*, 14–26.

Johnston, M., Bendau, S., Covert, J., Christenson, M., Dyer, J., Risko, G., & Slutsky, R. (2003). Conducting action research while teaching about it. *Action in Teacher Education, 25*(2), 9–15.

Johnston, M., & Lee, Y. A. (2004). *A self-study informed by our students of color:Talking about race and social justice in an M.Ed. program.* Paper presented at the College and University Faculty Assembly of the National Council of the Social Studies, Baltimore.

Johnston, M., Ramos, M., & Thomas, M. (2000). *Students of color as cultural consultants: An action research study of a social studies and science methods course.* Paper presented at the College and University Faculty Assembly of the National Council for the Social Studies, San Antonio, TX.

Johnston, M., Summers-Eskridge, L., Wyatt, T., & Thomas, M. (2000). *Action research to raise questions about race in teacher education.* Paper presented at the Journal of Curriculum Theory Conference on Curriculum Theory and Classroom Practice, Bergamo Conference, Dayton, OH.

Kemmis, S. (1982). Action research in retrospect and prospect. In S. Kemmis (Ed.), *The action research reader,* (2nd ed., pp. 11–31). Geelong, Australia: Deakin University Press.

Kemmis, S. (1985). Action research. In T. Husen & T. Postlethwaite (Eds.), *International encyclopedia of education: Research and studies* (pp. 35–42). Oxford: Pergamon.

Kemmis, S., & McTaggart, R. (Eds.). (1988). *The action research planner* (3rd ed.). Geelong, Australia: Deakin University Press.

Kyle, D. W., & Hovda, R. A. (1987). The potential and practice of action research. *Peabody Journal of Education, 64*(2), 1–127.

Loughran, J., & Northfield, J. (1998). A framework for the development of self-study practice. In M. L. Hamilton (Ed.), *Reconceptualizing teaching practice: Self-study in teacher education* (pp. 7–18). London: Falmer Press.

Loughran, J. J. (2004). A history and context of self-study of teaching and teacher education practices. In J. Loughran, M. L. Hamilton, V. LaBoskey, & T. Russell (Eds.), *The international handbook of self-study of teaching and teacher education practices* (pp. 7–39). Dordrecht, The Netherlands: Kluwer Academic.

Loughran, J., Hamilton, M. L., LaBoskey, V., & Russell, T. (Eds.). (2004). *The international handbook of self-study of teaching and teacher education practices.* Dordrecht, The Netherlands: Kluwer Academic.

Lorde, A. (1984). *Sister outsider.* New York: The Crossing Press.

Marcus, G. E., & Fischer, M. (1986). *Anthropology as cultural critique: An experimental moment in the human sciences.* Chicago: University of Chicago Press.

McCutcheon, G. (1987). Teachers' experience doing action research. *Peabody Journal of Education, 64*(2), 115–127.

McLean, J. (1997). Teacher empowerment through action research. *Kappa Delta Pi Record, 34,* 34–38.

McNiff, J., Lomax, P., & Whitehead, J. (1996). *You and your action research project.* New York: Routledge.

Mills, G. E. (2000). *Action research: A guide for the teacher research.* Columbus, OH: Prentice Hall.

Mohanty, C. T. (2003). *Feminism without borders: Decolonizing theory, practicing solidarity.* Durham, NC: Duke University Press.

Nath, J. M., & Tellez, K. (1995). A room of one's own: Teaching and learning to teach through inquiry. *Action in Teacher Education, 16,* 1–13.

Nias, J. (1988). How practitioners are silenced, how practitioners are empowered. In J. Nias & S. Groundwater-Smith (Eds.), *The inquiring teacher: Supporting and sustaining teacher research* (pp. 19–36). London: Falmer Press.

Noffke, S. E., & Stevenson, R. B. (1995). *Educational action research: Becoming practically critical.* New York: Teachers College Press.

Noffke, S. E. (1997). Themes and tension in US action research: Towards historical analysis. In S. Hollingsworth (Ed.), *International action research: A casebook for educational reform* (pp. 2–16). London: Falmer Press.

Oja, S. N., & Smulyan, L. (1989). *Collaborative action research: A developmental approach*. Basingstoke, UK: The Falmer Press.

Palmer, P. (1998). *The courage to teach: Exploring the inner landscape of a teacher's life*. San Francisco: Jossey-Bass.

Sagor, R. (1992). *How to conduct collaborative action research*. Alexandria, VA: Association for Supervision and Curriculum Development.

Said, E. (1979). *Orientalism*. New York: Vintage.

Schön, D. (1987). *Educating the reflective practitioner: Toward a new design for teaching and learning in the professions*. San Francisco: Jossey-Bass.

Spivak, G. C. (1999). *A critique of postcolonial reason: Toward a history of the vanishing present*. Cambridge, MA: Harvard University Press.

Stringer, E. (1996). *Action research: A handbook for practitioners*. Thousand Oaks, CA: Sage.

VanSledright, B. (2002). *In search of America's past: Learning to read history in elementary school*. New York: Teachers College Press.

Wallace, M. (1987). A historical review of action research: Some implications for the education of teachers in their managerial role. *Journal of Education for Teaching, 13*, 97–115.

Wells, G. (1993). *Changing schools from within: Creating communities of inquiry*. Portsmouth, NH: Heinemann.

West, C. (1993). *Race matters*. Boston: Beacon Press.

Wilson, S. M. (1990). *Mastodons, maps, and Michigan: Exploring uncharted territory while teaching elementary school social studies* (Elementary Subjects Center Series No. 24). East Lansing, MI: Michigan State University, Institute for Research on Teaching. (ERIC Document Reproduction Service No. ED326470)

Zeichner, K. (1999). The new scholarship in teacher education. *Educational Researcher, 28*(9), 4–15.

Zeni, J. (2000). *Ethical issues in practitioner research*. New York: Teachers College Press.

CHAPTER 5

CHILDREN AS CO-RESEARCHERS

Developing a Democratic Research Practice with Children

Fionnuala Waldron

In recent years, there has been a burgeoning of interest in how we conduct research with children. The traditional model of research that views children as, at best, subjects of research with no active role to play beyond the provision of data is being increasingly challenged by methodologies that see research as a collaboration between researcher and subjects. Involving children in the process as co-researchers is an evolving practice that is informed by respect for children as social agents and recognition of the value of children's voices. It is supported by a wider questioning within the broader research community around the role of the researcher and the nature of the research relationship (Thorne, 2002). The traditional view of research as an inquiry conducted by a disinterested and professional researcher, producing data that is objective, replicable, and verifiable, has been questioned by the idea of knowledge as political, situated, and contextualized, and by the realization that researchers bring with them their own preconceptions, assumptions, and experiences. Where childhood research is concerned, it can be argued that research in the past told us more about adults' concepts of childhood than how children

Research Methods in Social Studies Education, pages 85–109
Copyright © 2006 by Information Age Publishing
All rights of reproduction in any form reserved.

experienced their childhoods, because it focused on child development and socialization, "the study of what children will become" (Morrow & Richards, 1996, p. 92), rather than how children live their lives as children. The growth in interest in looking at childhood *qua* childhood, rather than focusing on it as the journey toward adulthood, married with changing views of children and of children's capacities, has led to new approaches in research, and these bring with them their own ethical and methodological issues and concerns.

Research models are inevitably influenced by the researchers' views of childhood and of children (Punch, 2002). One would expect very different research to emanate from the researcher who sees childhood as a protected space and children as vulnerable and incompetent than from the researcher who sees children as both competent and actively engaged with their environment. Christensen and Prout (2002) identify four main perspectives in child research—the child as object, the child as subject, the child as social actor, and an emerging view of the child as participant and co-researcher. Although these perspectives are premised on different conceptions of the child, they co-exist in contemporary research. Indeed, Christensen and Prout argue that a range of perspectives can be present within a single piece of research when insufficient thought is given to the ethical implications of new methodologies. What this chapter seeks to do is to provide some space for that reflection by suggesting areas of tension within this developing praxis that need to be explored in an honest and critical way. I will begin by examining the roots from which the impulse toward a democratic practice in research with children has grown. I will then consider the methodological and ethical implications of such a practice. I will posit the idea of a continuum of participation as a working model (see Figure 5.1) for research with children and present a case study, based on a research project recently completed (Pike & Waldron, 2004), in which the methodology used will be subjected to critical reflection.[1]

CHILDREN AND CHILDHOOD: FROM DEPENDENCE TO AGENCY

Since the late 1980s, a new paradigm of childhood has emerged that provides a radical challenge to the conceptualization of children as passive recipients of socialization and of childhood as primarily a preparation for adulthood. The traditional view of children, as adults-in-the-making, saw the child as moving, in developmental stages, from immaturity to adulthood, from dependence to independence, from incompetence to competence, their value "not in *being* but in *becoming*" (Oakley, 1994, p. 23). Influenced by Piagetian theory, the progress from childhood to adulthood was deemed to follow a predetermined and age-related chronological path that viewed the experience of being a child as relatively fixed and universal, ignoring, to a large extent, the impact of culture, class, gender, race, or disability on children's realities. This monolithic view of childhood was questioned by work such as that of Ariès (1962), whose seminal investigation of the social history of family life indicated its specificity in relation to time and the recent provenance of modern conceptions of childhood. Theorists such as Vygotsky (1986) and Donaldson (1978) challenged the extent to which children's capacities were determined by age and revealed the impact of social context on children's understanding. Throughout the 1970s and 1980s, developments within sociological theory, where a more interactive relationship between the individual and social structures was being posited, contributed to the ongoing questioning of developmentalism as the dominant model of childhood. By 1990, the idea of childhood as a social construction was identified as an "emergent paradigm" within the sociology of childhood (Prout & James, 1990, p. 3).[2] The myth of the "generic" or universal child was again challenged by the international project, Childhood as a Social Phenomenon (Bardy, Qvortrup, Sgritta, & Wintersberger, 1990–1994), which brought together analyses of the status of children in 16 countries. What that project, and many subsequent studies of children in different contexts (e.g., Begley, 2000; Mayall, 2001b; Punch, 2001), reveals is a multiplicity of childhoods, affected by a wide range of intersecting influences, such as gender, class, ethnicity, religion, and disability. This body of work has led to an idea of the socially constructed child as a local and particularistic phenomenon (Jenks, 2000). Moreover, the new paradigm sees children "as social actors and participants in the social world, and also participants in the formation of their own childhood" (Alanen, 2001, p.12).

This recognition of children's agency is coupled with a view of childhood as a social category and its structural position within the wider social order as a focus for analysis and critique (Prout & James, 1990; Qvortrup, 1993). In this context, the idea of "generation" has been suggested as a tool, akin to "class" and "gender," for the analysis of structural relations (Mayall, 2000; Mayall & Zeiher, 2003). Alanen (2001) for example, maintains that, as well as being a social phenomenon, childhood is also a generational phenomenon. Going beyond the idea of generation as a means of analyzing the external structural relationship between childhood and society, Alanen argues for a research focus on the practices through which the generational categories of child and adult are constructed and reconstructed on a daily basis, a focus that includes the recognition of both children and adults as social agents. The problematizing of concepts such as adult and child and the exploration of generational relations at both a macro and a micro level suggest the need to engage more directly with the experience of childhood in a way that recognizes both the agency of the child in the construction of her or his childhood and the child's position as the primary holder of knowledge about her or his life.

New ideas within the sociology of childhood have been paralleled by developments in the area of children's rights and conceptions of citizenship. The inclusion of participation rights in the United Nations Convention on the Rights of the Child (UNCROC; 1989) has broadened the platform for children's rights beyond those of provision and protection to include some recognition of autonomy (Alderson, 2000; Sinclair Taylor, 2000). This marks an important shift away from the idea of the child as simply in need of protection toward a recognition of the child as a social agent with the right to hold and express an opinion (Article 12), the right to freedom of expression (Article 13), freedom of thought, conscience, and religion (Article 14), and freedom of association and peaceful assembly (Article 15). While the convention includes qualifications relating to age and maturity, national resources, and the requirements of national law, by giving children the right to an opinion and the right to participate in decisions about their lives, it has provided an instrument that can be used to create spaces where children's knowledge and perspectives are given an active voice.

The inclusion of participation rights in the UNCROC has also encouraged debate around the idea of the child as citizen and a renewal of interest in the role of citizenship education. The traditional view of citizenship education is to see it as a preparation for adult citizenship. While more recent models emphasize the importance of developing in children the skills, attitudes, and dispositions of participative citizenship and support the involvement of children in democratic initiatives and structures within the school, such initiatives are generally framed within an educational context, becoming "training grounds for children" rather than exercises in actual citizenship (Jans, 2004, p. 31). The idea of the child as a social agent, acting on and in the world, offers the possibility of an emerging model of child citizenry. Positing the idea of citizenship as a process rather than a finished state, Jans argues that, if citizenship is construed as "social involvement and participation," then children's interaction with their environment already confers on them the status of citizen (p. 40). Translating the right to participation and to a voice in issues that concern them from well-meaning rhetoric to lived reality is dependent on the extent to which child participation is construed as the exercise of citizenship rather than a rehearsal for adult life. The requirement for countries that have ratified the UNCROC to report periodically on their progress in institutionalizing those rights (Article 44) provides some impetus toward their actualization.[3] Moreover, the obligation to realize children's rights to have their views taken into account and to participate in decision making provides a practical imperative for participating countries to re-envision the research process at a national level (Alderson, 2000).

RETHINKING RESEARCH: FROM RESEARCH OBJECT TO CO-RESEARCHER

Collaborative research with children can be seen as part of a wider movement within the research community toward a practice that recognizes the subjectivity of the other and confronts the unequal relationship between researchers and the researched. Much of the impetus for this re-envisioning of the research process has come from the feminist movement. Providing a compelling critique of traditional research, the development of feminist methodologies has challenged the power relations of the research industry at several levels and put women's voices and agency at the center of research about women (Truman, 1994). Research, in this conception, is seen as a political activity with an emancipatory project (Byrne & Lentin, 2000; Klein, 1983; Smith, 1987). The idea of emancipatory research—that is, research with a transformative intent—is also theoretically rooted in critical theory and has relevance beyond gender-related research to include class, ethnicity, sexuality, and disability (Lynch, 2000; see also Tyson, Chapter 3, this volume). Parallels have been drawn between the ways in which children and women have traditionally been constituted as objects rather than subjects of academic research (Alanen, 1994; Oakley, 1994), "muted" by the absence of their voices from the dominant discourse (Prout & James, 1990, p. 7). Providing space for children's voices within the research process, then, can also be seen as a political act, one that seeks to redress their "muted" status and acknowledge them as authentic generators of knowledge about their lives.

The view of children as active constructors of meaning is located within a broader epistemology that sees knowledge as socially constructed through collaboration and interaction. As well as providing a theoretical framework for the understanding of children's roles as meaning makers, social constructivism provides the epistemological basis for collaborative research and for the methodological approaches used. It is pertinent in this context to ask whether there is something about doing research with children that requires distinct methodologies. Do researchers need, for example, to develop special child-centered approaches? Punch (2002) suggests that differences between research with adults and children may arise more from the structural positioning of childhood in society and adults' perceptions of children's competencies and reliability, as well as their belief in the superiority of adult knowledge, than from any inherent differences between adults and children as research subjects. Given that adults themselves are not a homogeneous grouping, it is arguable that it is diversity itself that needs to be taken into account rather than generational differences. There may be no essential difference between research with adults and children that necessitates an explicitly child-centered methodology, over and above the need for *all* research, to take account of the specific requirements of particular contexts and subjects (Christensen & James, 2000; Christensen & Prout, 2002). The issue becomes one of "research participant-centred" (Punch, 2002, p. 337) rather than child-centered research.

Research with children, then, can draw on a wide range of methodologies, which includes more traditional approaches such as questionnaires, interviews, and observation as well as newer approaches that allow for individual and contextual differences and recognize the diverse ways in which children construct meaning. Prosser (1998) identifies a wide range of image-based approaches—films, photographs, drawings, cartoons, graffiti, maps, diagrams, signs, and symbols—that can be used in research to provide access to different modes of constructing and expressing meaning. Moreover, the use of activity-based and participant-oriented techniques, many of which include the creation of visual images, can help to address the power differential in the research context by offering opportunities to children for increased participation and decision making. Participatory Rural Appraisal (PRA) is often cited as the forerunner of activity-based research techniques with children. PRA refers to a research approach with adults, one that was developed with the aim of empowering participants and legitimizing local knowledge in the context of marginalized and/or illiterate communities in developing countries. With roots in Freirean philosophy, it belongs to a constructivist rather than positivist or post-positivist paradigm (O'Kane, 2000) and values local knowledge and capabilities. It includes within its methodologies activities such as focus group discussions, ranking exercises, mapping, and decision tables. The researcher and participants are seen as co-workers, engaged in a dialogical process directed toward change. Although many of the techniques would be similar to those used to promote thinking skills and dialogue in education, the provenance of participatory methodologies used in research with children is frequently given as PRA, thus locating them within a particular motivational and conceptual framework.

Acknowledging children's capacity to generate worthwhile and meaningful data through participative research methodologies is, perhaps, the least challenging and most generally accepted aspect of democratizing research with children. Issues relating to the status and ownership of the knowledge generated by children during the research process, and decisions around what happens to it, are more problematic. Control of the knowledge created and of the interpretation and presentation of that knowledge brings with it the power of definition. Indeed, the construction of researchers and academics as "experts" who know more about the lives of the researched group than the group themselves has been described as a form of colonization, which is ultimately disempowering; as Lynch (2000) puts it, "There are experts there to interpret your world and to speak on your behalf. They take away your voice by speaking about you and for you" (p. 80; see also Johnston, Chapter 4, this volume). Is it all, then, a question of power? How can a researcher, intent on providing an authentic space for children's voices and perspectives, resolve the power difference that Lynch identifies as the greatest problem in the research relationship?

ETHICAL ISSUES IN RESEARCH WITH CHILDREN: A QUESTION OF POWER?

Christensen and Prout (2002) argue that research with children must begin from a position of "ethical symmetry" (p. 478) in which the principles applied to research with adults become the starting point from which an ethical perspective on child research develops. Indeed, there is a strong argument that, where ethics is concerned, research with children poses the same questions as those posed by research in general (Lindsay, 2000), particularly research that is conducted with marginalized or oppressed groups. The idea of power is central to a consideration of those questions. There is an obvious imbalance between the researcher and the researched across all stages of the process—planning, implementation, analysis/interpretation, and dissemination. The imbalance includes, but is not confined to, the power to make decisions about the focus of the research, how that research will be conducted and interpreted, and what reality will be represented in the public domain. In the case of children, one enters a complex matrix of power relationships: that between adult and child, between researcher and researched, and, depending on the context, between the child and the school community or family. That these relationships are intersected by considerations of class, ethnicity, and disability (among others) increases the complexity. While there may not be a difference in kind between the ethical issues that arise in relation to research with adults and research with children, the extent of the power difference, allied with the increased vulnerability that arises from lack of experience, would suggest that a number of issues can be identified that have a particular resonance where the participating group is children. These are the ideas of purpose, beneficence, and informed consent and authenticity.

It may seem self-evident that all research should have purpose and meaning. It is arguable, however, that, given the control adults generally exert on children's everyday lives and routines, there is a greater onus on the researcher working with children to ensure that the research is meaningful in the context of the children's lives. As children constitute "one of the most governed groups by both state and civic society" (Hill, Davis, Prout, & Tisdall, 2004, p. 77), they represent a research population that is open to exploitation. This vulnerability increases the responsibility on researchers to ensure that their work is both purposeful and necessary. It is arguable that the general caution not to do harm to one's research subjects does not go far enough in the case of children and that the principle of beneficence should be interpreted to mean that the research be of positive benefit to them. One could argue that research that benefits children in a general sense meets this ethical obligation. However, given that the negative caution is specific to the group partaking in the research—one must ensure that the research does not harm that particular group of children—it is difficult to argue that a general, diffused benefit to children is sufficient to meet our obligations as researchers in this instance. In any case, the idea that engagement in a research project would bring with it some positive benefits for the participants is surely desirable.

From the perspective of the researcher, learning about the research topic has always been a primary aim of the research. Improvements in research skills, the development of new methodological approaches, and a deeper understanding of the role of the researcher are other possible and desirable learning outcomes. For children also, there is an established link between the idea of research and engagement with the world. Most school-based social studies programs, for example, would include at least some element of research as a means of learning. The idea that children, as research participants, should learn and grow from that experience would be one that few would disagree with, and for many research projects such learning would be embedded in the process in any case. It may well be, for example, that the very act of expressing an opinion, and being listened to, contributes both to the self-esteem of the child and offers an opportunity for the development of her or his thinking on the research topic. If the research is planned as a participatory and/or collaborative project, the learning outcomes for the children could be quite significant in terms of developing children's abilities to pose questions, develop ideas, and make decisions and judgments, as well as contributing to skills of analysis, interpretation, and critique. Such outcomes are more likely if children's learning is made an explicit aim of the research—planned for rather than incidental to it.

The most frequently addressed ethical issue in relation to research with children is the idea of informed consent. While the practice of seeking the consent of parents and other gatekeepers to grant access to children's lives is well established, the idea that children themselves should have the right to grant or deny access is less so, at least in some countries (Alderson,

2000). The issue of informed consent is a complex one that has relevance beyond the initial point of access. Researchers need to be aware that it may be difficult for children to refuse consent; they may feel intimidated by the adult presence of the researcher; their reluctance may be overridden by a general desire to please or to do the right thing; they may be reluctant to stand out from the crowd. The responsibility of the researcher, therefore, is to ensure that the opportunities to give or refuse consent provided for the children are genuine and that they are assured that a refusal to take part will have no negative consequences for them. This will require, at the very least, that children understand the purpose of the research and the roles of both the researcher and the research subjects in the proposed project. It is arguable, however, that they need to be given sufficient information at all stages of the process, as well as opportunities to affirm their willingness to continue or to withdraw consent at strategic points in the research, up to and including the final analysis and publication. This can be problematic for the adult researchers in that it raises the possibility of consent being withdrawn at a late stage in the project after a considerable investment of time and resources. Yet, the corollary of denying this opportunity to children is the prospect of revealing children's lives without their consent.

Although the promise of confidentiality and anonymity offers some protection and reassurance to children, it might not be sufficient to secure their agreement. There may be no easy answer to this. The idea of research subjects having the right of veto over the product of research about their lives can itself raise ethical dilemmas if, for example, the research reveals knowledge that society needs, perhaps for the protection of a third party or the research subjects themselves. Research into adolescent drinking or drug taking, for example, could be a case in point. Moreover, the rights of the researcher to professional credibility and academic independence should also be taken into account. The idea of a collaborative research model, which invites the research subjects, as co-researchers, to participate in decision making about the research process, could offer *one* approach to solving this dilemma. Within such a model, children may feel more in control of the knowledge they have generated about their lives and less reluctant to share it. It could be that offering the research subjects a right of reply, or an opportunity to incorporate into the final research report an alternative perspective, may resolve consent issues in some cases. If the presentation of research findings is done at an early stage in the analysis, it can give children the opportunity to engage with the researcher's ideas in a critical way, and offering their own interpretations of the data could also promote a greater investment by the children in the final research outcomes.

It can be argued, however, that there are projects where the reporting of research findings to the research group is impractical (Mayall, 2001a). If the group, for example, is large and/or dispersed over time or place, the idea of involving them in the final analysis or of presenting the findings to them may not be possible to implement. It is possible that there is no clear-cut response that fits all situations here and that this is an issue that is not amenable to an unambiguous answer. Perhaps the best approach is to adopt an ethical perspective that is rooted in a commitment to children's rights to full information and informed consent and is responsive to the situation of the particular research group and/or project. The nature of the research activity, the degree of intrusiveness, and the level of exposure for the individual child are relevant considerations in this context (Lindsay, 2000). The danger with such an approach, however, is that children's rights to full information, and, by implication, informed consent, are held hostage by the constraints of the research situation and agenda. Informed consent becomes a luxury that can be dispensed with if it becomes a problem. It may be that the best way of resolving this dilemma is to adopt the idea of informed consent as an ethical baseline in research with children from which any deviation would have to be justified on a case-by-case basis.

It is reasonable to suppose that the presentation of research findings to children should be part of any research model as a matter of course, yet the evidence of it in the literature is relatively scarce. For reasons of courtesy, respect, and appreciation, child subjects of research should have access to any research findings arising from projects in which they have engaged. Providing opportunities for children to contribute to the analysis of the knowledge they have produced, however, or to provide an alternative perspective to the researcher, goes far beyond the idea of informed consent. A concern for the integrity and ownership of the knowledge produced by children about their lives raises questions that go right to the heart of the interpretation and analysis of research data. How can a researcher draw meaning from research data while respecting children's rights of self-definition? Grover (2004) argues that the ability to exercise some control over how one is portrayed by others is "related to issues of human dignity" (p. 82). She argues the need for a phenomenological approach where children can communicate their experience without having their meaning transformed or manipulated by the researcher. Fearful of the premature imposition of categories of analysis, she warns of the need to preserve the "authentic voice of the child," adding that it is "time that children are regarded as experts on their own subjective experience" (p. 91). Others suggest a grounded theory approach to analysis (Strauss & Corbin, 1997) that allows meaning to emerge from the data as a way of preserving the authenticity of children's voices and respecting their role as meaning-makers (France, Bendelow, & Williams, 2000). Involving children in the interpretation and analysis of research data provides the most radical solution to this dilemma (Alderson, 2000).

In terms of children's involvement as research subjects in a participative model of research, then, one could posit a continuum beginning with full access to information and progressing to include consultation, participation, and collaboration. The schema presented in Figure 5.1 offers one representation of that process. Developed as a response to what I feared were inconsistencies in my own research practice, it identifies access to decision making as the key indicator of an evolving collaborative practice. Although presented as a continuum, it is important to be clear about the main characteristics of each of the four levels described. There is a difference (which is one of kind rather than degree) between giving children the opportunity to express their opinions and giving them a voice in the research process. Implicit in the idea of voice is some control over decision making and a consultative process, whereas allowing children's views to be heard does not in itself give children any such role (Hill et al., 2004). A distinction can equally be made between participation and the idea of collaborative research with children. While participation can include the idea of shared decision-making, it may not include collaboration in the overall design of the project or in decisions around the final research output. A model that included participatory task-based methodologies, for example, without inviting involvement in broader aspects of the research, would be an example of this (see, e.g., Punch, 2001, 2002).

In practice, the lines between the four levels suggested—information, consultation, participation, and collaboration—can be somewhat blurred, with two or more levels present in a single research project. O'Kane (2000) provides a good example of this, giving children considerable power around agenda setting and organization while retaining control of the overall design.[1] As Christensen and Prout (2002) suggest, this could be problematic if contradictory perspectives on children and childhood informed the approaches taken. Research, for example, that claimed to use participatory methodologies acknowledging the child as meaning-maker and social actor would sit uneasily with a disregard for the principle of informed consent on the part of the child. However, if one takes children's right to full information as the ethical baseline in research with children, the idea of a continuum of participation, such as that presented in the schema, offers a progressive and ethically consistent approach.

While it is simplistic and misleading to think of the dynamics of power as a zero-sum phenomenon, maximizing children's participation in research along the continuum does necessitate a parallel development in the role of the researcher as indicated in the schema. This begins with a commitment to respect children's views and abilities (Alderson, 2000) as well as their right to be informed and to make choices, and ends with the researcher working with children as research partners. Such development is dependent on the readiness of the researcher to challenge traditional models of

Child

Research characteristics

Researcher

Child	Research characteristics	Researcher
As co-researcher... Collaborating in every stage of the research, from planning to publication of outcomes Critical reflection on process of research and identity as researcher	Collaboration in the framing and in the planning of the research process Participating in gathering and interpretation of data Participating in decisions about outcomes	**As co-researcher...** Collaborating in every stage of the research, from planning to publication of outcomes Critical reflection on process of research and identity as researcher
As participant... Participating in decision making and/or agenda setting through task-oriented and/or problematizing methodologies	Use of methodologies that provide opportunities for children to create meaningful data Providing opportunities for engaging in decisions around the research and the research agenda	**As facilitator...** Creating opportunities for children to participate in creating meaningful data and in decision making around research process
As contributor... Consulted about the process and product but with no decision-making role	Use of methodologies that allow children to share their views and opinions Children consulted about their experience of the research and their views of the research outcomes	**As active listener...** Providing authentic opportunities for children to give their views on research topic and process Listening to children's views on the research outcomes
As research subject... Informed about the process and outcomes	Informed about the purpose and process of the research and their role within it. Informed about each stage in the research including outcomes Given right to withdraw from process at any stage	**As respectful researcher...** Ensuring that children are in a position to give informed consent Valuing children's time and contribution

Access to decision making

Participation in decision making

Sharing of decision making

Figure 5.1.   Continuum of children's participation in research. © Fionnuala Waldron. Reprinted courtesy of Fionnuala Waldron.

adult–child relationships, building one that is reciprocal and honest. Reciprocity presumes that the researcher is willing to disclose to children who she or he is and to engage with them in an authentic way. For this reason, conceptions of the researcher as "least adult" (Mandell 1991) or as "a different kind of adult" (Christensen, 2004) seem self-defeating, obscuring rather than revealing the dynamics of intergenerational relationships. As Mayall (2000) points out, children recognize the relations of power between adults and children. Rather than seeking to circumvent generational issues, she suggests an approach that acknowledges them and asks children to help the researcher, as an adult, to understand childhood.

To sum up then, developing a democratic research practice with children implies a research relationship that is reciprocal and honest and a research process that maximizes children's access to decision making. Articulated through the use of methodological approaches that actively empower children, the creation of a democratic practice implies, at its most developed, the involvement of children in all stages of the research process, from design to dissemination. A critical measure of such an approach, however, is the idea of authenticity. How can one be certain that the opportunities being offered to children to take control of the research process go beyond the superficial? Ensuring that one's practice, as a researcher, is consistent with the underlying principles of this approach requires critical vigilance and honest reflection. The following case study grew out of such a reflexive process and does not claim to offer a model of collaborative research with children. Rather, it indicates an emerging praxis that hopes to build on the lessons learned and the questions raised.

CASE STUDY: A COLLABORATIVE METHODOLOGY IN THE MAKING

In the Spring of 2003, my colleague Susan Pike and I began a process of inquiry (which is ongoing) into children's ideas about national identity. While the original research project involved three urban and socially differentiated primary schools with 79 11- to 12-year-old child participants, the issues raised resulted in an extension of the research to rural schools and the identification of further research questions. It also resulted in critical engagement with the methodology we had used and with the underlying principles of our research approach. The research project arose out of our discussions around child citizenship and the need to take seriously the idea of children's voices. Given our self-identities as teachers as well as researchers, we were concerned to develop a pedagogy within citizenship education that engaged with children's own ideas about concepts such as citizenship, democracy, nationality, and identity, rather than one that saw itself as educating children toward a preconceived model of the good citizen. With that concern came the recognition that we had no real knowledge of how Irish children thought about these issues. What was their understanding of Irishness and how was that understanding created? What did the idea of citizen mean to them and how did it relate to their ideas about identity? We wanted to focus particularly on whether they saw Irish identity as fixed and bounded or open to change and outside influences.

At the planning stage, a number of issues relating to the choice of methodologies presented themselves. First, while the children participating in the research were drawn from the same age cohort, they were not a homogeneous grouping. Beginning from a standpoint of respect for children's competencies (Morrow & Richards, 1996), we needed to allow for both the plurality and specificity of the childhoods we would encounter and to take account of the different sociocultural and educational contexts of each class group. In order to maximize the opportunities for individual children to participate and have their voices heard, we were keen to use a range of approaches. Moreover, drawing on our identities as both teachers and researchers, we were conscious that the use of a variety of methodologies within a single research project might help to prevent boredom (Punch, 2002), as well as controlling for bias and allowing for the triangulation of data (Morrow & Richards, 1996). Second, given that the project itself had its provenance in a concern for the child as citizen, and taking account of the power problematic identified earlier, we were intent that the methodology and research relations should as far as possible be true to the underlying philosophy of participative citizenship and offer the possibility of dispersing power and control within the research relationship. However, constraints around resources and time (both personal and school-based) meant that the development of research relationships and methodologies over an extended time period was not an option. We decided to focus on identifying strategic moments in the research and maximizing children's participation and contribution at those points. In taking this approach, we recognized that the first strategic moment had already passed—namely, the initial framing and planning of the project. Subsequent moments identified were the introduction of the research to the children, the use of participatory activities, the semi-structured interviews, and the preliminary analysis and presentation of research outcomes.

The project began with a general discussion about research in which children described different topics they had researched in social studies and explained how they had gone about it. The children spoke about examples of research and researchers they had come across in their daily lives (e.g., market research, phone-in radio and television polls) and the reasons people might do research were discussed. Having identified ourselves as researchers, the children questioned us about our lives and our work. Although the discussions varied from school to school, a number of themes emerged from children's questions. First, they were interested in us as individuals, in what our work entailed and why we did it. Second, they asked penetrating questions about the purpose of the research and why we would be interested in their opinions. Third, they wanted to know what would happen to the data, who would see it, and whether or not they would be identified. When the children were satisfied they had enough information, they were asked if they wanted to participate and assured that they could withdraw at a later stage if they wanted to.

The children then engaged in a participatory group activity. As noted earlier, participatory or task-oriented approaches are frequently linked within the research literature to Participatory Rural Appraisal. The impulse in this case, however, was also located in our experience as teachers and our interest in developing critical thinking in children. The purpose of the activity was to break the ice with the children and to allow them to think about the issue of identity in a nonthreatening way. Groups were self-selecting and, in the main, were single gender groups based on personal friendships. Each group was given a page with an outline drawing of a spaceship. This was Spaceship Ireland and their task was to fill it with everything they would need to reconstruct Ireland on another planet in the event of an evacuation of Earth due to an imminent disaster. The decision to use a dramatic frame for the first activity arose from the desire to provide a safe space within which to begin the exploration of Irishness in a nonintrusive way. This was felt by us to be particularly important as we anticipated a degree of ethnic diversity in our research groups and were anxious to develop a model that would allow for full participation while not requiring children to label themselves as Irish. Drama-based approaches or imaginative stimuli can be good ways of providing spaces that, by distancing the problem from the child's personal experience, allow potentially controversial topics to be explored. In this case, it provided the children with a stimulus for discussion and debate. This was sufficiently open to allow for a variety of opinions, yet constrained enough to encourage the children to focus on what they saw as important. As a warm-up activity, it worked well and generated a high level of participation and enjoyment. As a research tool, it surprised us in its capacity to capture the emblematic and iconic elements of children's sense of national identity.

The second activity the children engaged in was the writing of a personal response to the question "What does it mean to be Irish?" The question itself was piloted with both children and young adults and chosen for its capacity to go beyond the cognitive to the affective dimensions of identity as well as allowing for alternative perspectives from children with other national backgrounds. The use of children's writings as a research tool has obvious limitations. First, the extent to which a piece of writing will inform the researcher about how a child is thinking is dependant, to a large extent, on the child's ability to write. It excludes those who have difficulties with writing and is age dependent. Second, the meaning of a piece of writing is not always self-evident and may need to be interpreted by the writer at a follow-up discussion/interview. In the case of this research, that was not part of the process, and indeed there were some written comments whose meanings remained ambiguous. However, it is easy to underestimate children's abilities to express themselves through writing, and children's spontaneous writings can give great insight into their understanding of the world (Waldron, 2003). Moreover, writing can allow children more control over their responses than an interview setting. They can decide how much to write or whether to write at all (indeed, a small number of children did decide not to write anything), whereas in an interview they may feel pressure to contribute. Writing can also be a more reflective process, providing the children with the time to think about their responses. In the case of this research, the preliminary activity had ensured that children came to the writing actively thinking about Irish identity and their subsequent writing showed the benefit of this.

It was decided during the planning of the research that, in order to provide the children with access to different means of expression, children's drawings would also be used as a source from which to draw some insight into their construction of national identity. Children were invited to draw two images, one a drawing of an Irish person from their perspective and the other a drawing of an Irish person from the perspective of someone from another country. While we were convinced of the value of getting both perspectives and, through them, illuminating something of children's sense of Ireland's place in the world, we were concerned that the juxtaposition of both drawings would be confusing. However, this was not the source of difficulty in relation to this activity. Rather, it was the idea of creating an image itself that proved problematic for some. While drawings might appear to offer a way of researching children's views that is nonthreatening and open to all children, the reality is more complex. As an activity children voluntarily engage in for enjoyment, drawing can offer a creative way of exploring issues with children. However, not all children perceive themselves as competent drawers. There can also be cultural, economic, and physical barriers to children's opportunities to practice drawing or to engage with visual images. Moreover, it cannot be assumed that children's drawings are self-explanatory or easily interpreted by adults (Punch, 2002). Prosser (1998, p. 98) argues that theorists are too ready to catalogue the perceived drawbacks of image-based research, while less ready to recognize its strengths. Indeed, many of the reservations expressed above apply equally to children's writings. However, it is easy to underestimate the complexity of children's drawings, to see them as recorded reality rather than interpretations of that reality. Children's drawings can include a range of drawing conventions and stereotypes (Wetton & McWhirter, 1998) and be open to peer influence (Punch, 2002). They can also be humorous, ironic, and idiosyncratic and include symbolic elements, the interpretation of which require knowledge of the "local cultures of communication among children" (Christensen & Prout, 2002, p. 483), making them more amenable to peer interpreters than adult researchers. The images the children created in our project were interesting, ambiguous, and provocative, providing some valuable insights as well as moments of frustration and incomprehension on our part.

The next stage of the research involved semi-structured interviews of a representative group from each cohort. This was discussed beforehand with the children, the majority of whom were eager to be interviewed. If we had been working with fewer time constraints, it would have been preferable for all children to have the opportunity to participate in the interviews. In the event, five children were chosen for each interview based on their written pieces. Children were selected to give a range of perspectives and to promote discussion. When planning the research, we were interested in developing an approach that allowed the children, as far as possible, to set the agenda for the interview. We were also conscious that, because we were unable to do follow-up interviews with each of the children, we needed to develop a way of linking the writing experience to the interviews in a way that extended our understanding of what the children had written. For each class grouping, the children's writings were analyzed and 10 representative or commonly made statements were chosen and placed on card strips. At the start of the interview, the children were asked to consider the statements, to decide whether or not they agreed with them, and to rank those they agreed with according to the importance they accorded them. The activity generated quite a lot of debate and in each group raised a number of significant issues that were subsequently discussed.

As well as allowing the children to set the agenda for the remainder of the interview, the activity encouraged them to critique their own ideas, or at least those ideas produced by their class grouping. The extent to which the children engaged in a process of critique varied from group to group and in one case the presence of a dominant voice threatened to circumvent the best efforts of the researcher to provide a reflexive space for the children.[5] However, while some intervention in the management of the discussion in this case was necessary, all of the children did participate and the pace and progress of the discussion was, to a large extent, determined by the children. Apart from the ideas and arguments aired, what came across was a high level of engagement with the topic and a real attempt to think through the issues raised by their own writings in the initial phase. Allowing the children to set the discussion agenda did limit, to some extent, our freedom to raise issues we were interested in pursuing. This is a limitation also noted by O'Kane (2000) in a similar context. While she sees the opportunities offered to the research participants to "set the agenda" as helping to transform the traditional power relations of the research process, and to promote a sense of ownership and autonomy, she notes that the corollary of this is that that it may limit the field of inquiry to those issues identified by the children as significant and, consequently, "the opportunity to gather information in a uniform way is forfeited" (pp. 152–155). However, the idea of engaging in a shared process of inquiry with children was not interpreted by us to mean that we had no voice, and we felt free to raise questions that grew out of the children's discussions or contributed to a fuller exploration of their ideas. Although the group discussions overlapped in the topics raised and the questions pursued, there were significant differences between them. Given the different social contexts of the schools and the specificity of children's experiences, this was not surprising and, indeed, added to the interest and complexity of the final analysis.

The final stage of the research, from the children's perspective, came when we returned to their schools and presented to them our preliminary analysis of their ideas. Having listened to our presentation, the children were invited to comment both on their own ideas and on the preliminary categorization. While the response varied from school to school, in all cases some level of critique was evident. Children were particularly insightful in identifying outside influences on their thinking, particularly those that were media- and school-based. From our point of view, this was very useful, as it both confirmed and validated our own interpretation of the children's ideas and allowed for misinterpretations to be revisited. Moreover, it provided a real opportunity to build into the research a positive benefit for the children involved in the study, over and above those inherent in the process itself. As well as recognizing and identifying how they had been influenced, the representation of the children's ideas allowed them to reflect on stereotyping, bias, and racism. Given the sensitive issues that emerged around national identity during the project, there was a danger that for some children (particularly those who did not engage in the level of debate generated during the interviews), the experience of participating might leave prejudices or overgeneralizations unchallenged or even reinforce them. This possibility was ethically unacceptable to us. It was essential, then, that the research project included the opportunity for the children to challenge and develop their own thinking on identity through a process of reflection and critique. The representation of the data to the children at this stage also brought with it a sense of closure and accomplishment. Not only had they contributed, in a serious and worthwhile way, to a debate that had a recognized contemporary relevance, they could also see that their views had been listened to, taken seriously, and fairly represented.[6] Moreover, the process of representation allowed the children to take collective ownership of the knowledge they had produced. They had the opportunity to challenge its authenticity and accuracy as a representation of their views as well as to contribute to the analysis of data. Furthermore, it provided a context for the children to discuss issues around the release of data into the public domain.

We had embarked on this inquiry aware of its limitations as a model of democratic practice. It was not, however, until its final stages that a more critical evaluation of the process was possible. To what extent had our project, both in its conception and in its implementation, embodied the idea of research with children as a process of collaboration? It is arguable that, given the lack of involvement of the children at the design stage, all subsequent participation was on our terms, with little opportunity for the children to engage in decision making in a meaningful way. While I have some sympathy with that perspective, it is ultimately self-defeating, positing an all-or-nothing approach to a process characterized by negotiation and construction. Although the initial activity, the writing process, and the creation of images allowed the children to explore their ideas of Irish identity in a varied and creative way, the extent to which they were involved in decision making was limited. Collaboratively (in the case of the spaceship activity) and individually, the children made choices about their representations of Irishness and about their level of engagement with the process. The decision to use their writings as a stimulus for the interviews, however, allowed children to participate in setting the agenda for further inquiry at a collective level.

Again, our overall model limited the extent to which the children were enabled to control the interviews. The establishment of the process required decisions and choices on our part. We designed the activity and chose both the representative statements and the interview participants. There was a considerable ceding of power in the context of the group interviews, however, and this should not be underestimated. The children controlled the agenda to a large extent, and our participation as adult researchers was in terms of their articulated concerns and views. The questions we asked arose out of the issues they identified rather than out of our own research agenda.

In our analysis of the data generated by different activities, we used a grounded theory approach and allowed the categories of analysis to arise out of the data rather than imposing on it our own interpretative framework. Moreover, the representation of the research data to children in the form of a preliminary analysis allowed them to participate, at an early stage, in the generation of theory. The form chosen for this representation (i.e., in a whole class environment) could have been made more responsive to the children's views through the inclusion of group discussions and activities around emerging themes. The biggest danger, I would suggest, is allowing a superficial engagement by the children with the research findings to become the basis for an exaggerated claim around collaborative theory building. In the case of this project, while the engagement was limited both by the process used and the time allowed, it contributed in a meaningful way to our overall analysis and we hope to continue to develop this approach in future research.

Could the research have been conceived of differently in a way that involved children more closely in the initial stages of the project? While the resolution of this question awaits a future synergy of theory and practice, I would like to offer some tentative reflections. It is arguable that involving the children in the design of the research question and process would have required from them a level of reflexivity that would be difficult to achieve even if the research participants were adult, because it would have demanded an ability to gain a critical distance from their constructions of themselves in order to interrogate them. The model of the child as co-researcher presented in the schema outlined in Figure 5.1 includes the idea of such reflexivity, but can it be achieved in practice? Warren (2000) was confronted by a similar dilemma in his efforts to involve children as co-researchers in investigating the construction of gender identities in the primary school context in which he worked as a teacher. His analysis of his methodology suggests that the problem lay in the positioning of the child researchers within the insider/outsider model associated with participant observation, "passionately engaged in the precarious business of securing a gender identity" while, at the same time, required to disengage from that "gendered world" in order to observe and catalogue its processes. Warren notes, "The research activity cannot itself be disengaged from the children's own projects of 'self-making'" (p. 130). Rather than seeing this as an argument for abandoning the possibility of co-research with children, Warren suggests the idea, already an accepted one for adult researchers, of bringing to the foreground the assumptions and interpretative frameworks of child researchers through a process of critique and reflection that would focus also on "how their different identities, including that of researcher, are always in the process of 'becoming'" (p. 134).[7]

The application of the outsider/insider phenomenon to children's participation in research deserves further consideration. While the responsibility of the researcher to interrogate her or his own *a priori* assumptions and interpretative frameworks is well established, the idea that the child researcher should or could assume that responsibility is not. Are children able to shoulder this level of responsibility? If not, how can they participate in the generation of authentic knowledge about their lives, going beyond a "false perception" to a critical engagement with that reality (Freire, 1996,

p. 34)? Is it, perhaps, the case that, while children might be capable of full engagement in research that is focused on the social relations of childhood (e.g., research into children's access to resources), they may be less able to engage with research focusing on their own constructions of the world? A number of responses suggest themselves. It is not the case that children can be considered as either competent or incompetent in relation to their ability to interrogate their own worldviews and assumptions. Children's competence is always in the making. Moreover, recognition of the role that perspective plays in research, and an understanding of the need to make such perspectives explicit, is already part of children's educational experience, particularly in the area of social studies. Indeed, it could be argued that the idea of providing opportunities within research for children to engage in reflexive practices is part of a broader debate about the relationship between research and education and the positioning of the research process within the wider framework of lifelong learning. It may well be that there are research areas that are more open to children's involvement as co-researchers than others, particularly where such involvement extends to the choice of research question and the design of the research process. That does not mean, however, that children's participation and access to decision making should not be maximized in all research contexts.

CONCLUSION

The idea of children's participation in research is premised on a perspective that recognizes children's agency and their competence to construct valid and worthwhile knowledge about the world and that is informed by a commitment to children's right to have their voices heard particularly, though not exclusively, on issues related to their lives. As an approach to research, it has the capability to engage the researcher and the child in a process of critical reflection leading to individual and professional growth. Developing a research practice consistent with this idea, however, requires an honest engagement with its limitations and constraints as well as its possibilities. It may be unhelpful and unnecessary, for example, to think of children as co-researchers in an absolutist sense. There are constraints around age that can limit the extent of children's involvement. There may be research questions or contexts that are less amenable to collaboration than others. Aspects of the research may require skills and knowledge that are not yet available to children (Mayall, 1994). The danger in this approach, however, is that children's participation could either become a luxury to be enjoyed whenever the research demands were deemed not to be too serious or, alternatively, their participation could be reduced to its most superficial aspects. The idea, then, of a continuum of participation (as outlined in Figure 5.1), which is responsive to the research context, needs to be rooted in a professional commitment to plan for the maximum level of participation possible in each context.

Participation in itself, however, even if it includes access to decision making, may not be enough to ensure a collaborative process. Providing opportunities for children to problematize their worlds and to critically reflect on their own identities and their relations with the world is also necessary. Smith and Taylor (2000) make the point that the "missing piece of the puzzle in understanding childhood has been the voice of the child." It may be that, in order to complete the puzzle, we need to ensure that children's voices have the opportunity to interrogate, rather than simply reflect their reality.

NOTES

1. While the term "child" is generally taken to mean anyone under the age of 18, this chapter focuses on children between the ages of 4 and 12, which, in Ireland, would approximately cover the years of primary schooling. This chapter does not discuss issues around age-related competencies but rather takes the view posited by Solberg (1996) that decisions around research should be based on "the situational contexts within which children act" (p. 54) rather than assumptions about age.

2. For a comprehensive account of the emergence of this new paradigm, see Prout and James (1990).

3. At the time of writing, the UNCROC has been ratified by all UN member states, except the United States and Somalia.

4. O'Kane's research offers a model that is highly participatory, in which the children involved were engaged in active meaning-making and agenda setting. The use of participatory techniques enabled "children's voices, needs and interests to be articulated and to take precedence over adults' research agenda" (O'Kane, 2000, p. 152). While they had no obvious input into the design of the research, they were fully informed, free to participate or not, and partook in decisions around organization. Furthermore, the research included an action phase focused on "the inclusion of children in decision-making processes" (p. 138).

5. It would be naïve to think that the only relevant power relationship in the research process is that between the children and the adult researcher or that children do not exert power in relationships whether with adults or other children. Children can both silence and be silenced when opinions and ideas are being shared. In the context of group interviews, agreement of ground rules before the interview and a working model (such as that developed around circle time) that allows all participants the opportunity to contribute can minimize such silencing.

6. The fieldwork for this study was conducted during a national debate on citizenship, in the lead up to a referendum (which was held on June 11, 2004)

on the constitutional right to citizenship, which brought in qualifications around parentage and residency.

7. See Christensen and James (2000) for other research-based examples of the involvement of children in a reflexive process.

REFERENCES

Alanen, L. (1994). Gender and generation: Feminism and the "child question." In J. Qvortrup, M. Bardy, G. Sgritta, & H. Wintersberger (Eds.), *Childhood matters: social theory, practice and politics* (pp. 27–42). Aldershot, UK: Avebury Press.

Alanen, L. (2001). Explorations in generational analysis. In L. Alanen & B. Mayall (Eds.), *Conceptualizing child-adult relations* (pp. 11–22). London: Routledge Falmer.

Alderson, P. (2000). Children as researchers: The effects of participation rights on research methodology. In P. Christensen & A. James (Eds.), *Research with children: Perspectives and practices* (pp. 241–257). London: Falmer Press.

Ariès, P. (1962). *Centuries of childhood: A social history of family life.* New York: Vintage Books.

Bardy M., Qvortrup, J., Sgritta G., & Wintersberger, H. (Eds.) (1990-4). *Childhood as a social phenomenon: A series of national reports* (Eurosocial Reports 1-16). Vienna, Austria: European Centre.

Begley, A. (2000). The educational self-perceptions of children with Down Syndrome. In A. Lewis & G. Lindsay (Eds.), *Researching children's perspectives* (pp. 98–111). Buckingham, UK: Open University Press.

Byrne, A., & Lentin, R. (2000). *(Re)searching women: Feminist research methodologies in the social sciences in Ireland.* Dublin, Ireland: Institute of Public Administration.

Christensen, P. H. (2004). Children's participation in ethnographic research: Issues of power and representation. *Children and Society, 18,* 165–176.

Christensen, P., & James, A. (Eds.). (2000). *Research with children: Perspectives and practices.* London: Falmer Press.

Christensen, P., & Prout, A. (2002). Working with ethical symmetry in social research with children. *Childhood, 9,* 477–497.

Donaldson, M. (1978). *Children's Minds.* London: Fontana.

France, A., Bendelow, G., & Williams, S. (2000). A "risky" business: Researching the health beliefs of children and young people. In A. Lewis & G. Lindsay (Eds.), *Researching children's perspectives* (pp. 150–162). Buckingham, UK: Open University Press.

Freire, P. (1996). *Pedagogy of the oppressed,* London: Penguin.

Grover, S. (2004). Why won't they listen to us? On giving power and voice to children participating in social research. *Childhood, 11,* 81–93.

Hill, M., Davis, J., Prout, A., & Tisdall, K. (2004). Moving the participation agenda forward. *Children and Society, 18,* 77–96.

Jans, M. (2004). Children as citizens: Towards a contemporary notion of child participation. *Childhood, 11,* 27–44.

Jenks, C. (2000). Zeitgeist research on childhood. In P. Christensen & A. James (Eds.), *Research with children: Perspectives and practices* (pp. 62–76). London: Falmer Press.

Klein, R. D. (1983). How to do what we want to do: Thoughts about feminist methodology. In G. Bowles & R.D. Klein (Eds.), *Theories of women's studies* (pp. 88–104). London: Routledge & Kegan Paul.

Lindsay, G. (2000). Researching children's perspectives: Ethical issues. In A. Lewis & G. Lindsay (Eds.), *Researching children's perspectives* (pp. 3–20). Buckingham, UK: Open University Press.

Lynch, K. (2000). The role of emancipatory research in the academy. In A. Byrne & R. Lentin (Eds.), *(Re)searching women: Feminist research methodologies in the Social Sciences in Ireland* (pp. 73–104). Dublin, Ireland: Institute of Public Administration.

Mandell, N. (1991). The least adult role in studying children. In F. C. Waksler (Ed.), *Studying the social worlds of children: Sociological readings* (pp. 38–59). London: Falmer Press.

Mayall, B. (Ed.). (1994). *Children's childhoods: Observed and experienced.* London: Falmer Press.

Mayall, B. (2000). Conversations with children: Working with generational issues. In P. Christensen & A. James (Eds.), *Research with children: Perspectives and Practices* (pp. 120–135). London: Falmer Press.

Mayall, B. (2001a). Introduction. In L. Alanen & B. Mayall (Eds.), *Conceptualizing child–adult relations* (pp. 1–10). London: Routledge Falmer.

Mayall, B. (2001b). Understanding childhoods: A London study. In L. Alanen & B. Mayall (Eds.), *Conceptualizing child-adult relations* (pp. 114–128). London: Routledge Falmer.

Mayall, B., & Zeiher, H. (Eds.).(2003). *Childhood in generational perspective.* London: Institute of Education.

Morrow, V., & Richards, M. (1996). The ethics of social research with children: An overview. *Children and Society, 10,* 90–105.

O'Kane, C. (2000). The development of participatory techniques: Facilitating children's views about decisions which affect them. In P. Christensen & A. James (Eds.), *Research with children: Perspectives and practices* (pp. 136–159). London: Falmer Press.

Oakley, A. (1994). Women and children first and last: Parallels and differences between children's and women's studies. In B. Mayall (Ed.), *Children's childhoods observed and experienced* (pp. 13–32). London: The Falmer Press.

Pike, S., & Waldron, F. (2004, October). *"A cup of tea with your friends": Irish Primary children's ideas on national identity.* Paper presented to Voices and Images of Childhood and Adolescence: Rethinking Young Peoples' Identities Conference, St. Patrick's College, Dublin.

Prosser, J. (1998). The status of image-based research. In J. Prosser (Ed.), *Image-based research: A sourcebook for qualitative researchers* (pp. 97–112). London: Falmer Press.

Prout, A., & James, A. (1990). A new paradigm for the sociology of childhood? Provenance, promise and problems. In A. James & A. Prout (Eds.), *Construct-

ing and reconstructing childhood: Contemporary issues in the sociological study of childhood (pp. 7–33). London: Falmer Press.

Punch, S. (2001). Negotiating autonomy: Childhoods in rural Bolivia. In L. Alanen & B. Mayall (Eds.), *Conceptualizing child-adult relations* (pp. 23–36). London: Routledge Falmer.

Punch, S. (2002). Research with children: The same or different from research with adults? *Childhood, 9*, 321–341.

Qvortrup, J. (Ed.). (1993). *Childhood as a social phenomenon: Lessons from an international project* (Eurosocial Report 47). Vienna, Austria: European Centre.

Sinclair Taylor, A. (2000). The UN Convention on the Rights of the Child: Giving children a voice. In A. Lewis & G. Lindsay (Eds.), *Researching children's perspectives* (pp. 21–33). Buckingham, UK: Open University Press.

Smith, A. B., & Taylor, N. J. (2000). Introduction. In A. B. Smith, N. J. Taylor, & M. M. Gollop (Eds.), *Children's voices: Research, policy and practice* (pp. ix–xiii). Auckland, New Zealand: Pearson Education.

Smith, D. E. (1987). Women's perspective as a radical critique of sociology. In S. Harding (Ed.), *Feminism and methodology.* Milton Keynes, UK: Open University Press.

Solberg, A. (1996). The challenge in child research: From "being" to "doing." In J. Brannen & M. O'Brien (Eds.), *Children in families: Research and policy* (pp. 53–65). London: Falmer Press.

Strauss, A., & Corbin, J. (1997). *Grounded theory in practice.* London: Sage.

Thorne, B. (2002). From silence to voice: Bringing children more fully into knowledge. *Childhood, 9*, 251–254.

Truman, C. (1994). Feminist challenges to traditional research: Have they gone far enough? In B. Humphries & C. Truman (Eds.), *Re-thinking social research: Anti-discriminatory approaches in research methodology* (pp. 21–36). Aldershot, UK: Avebury.

Vygotsky, L. (1986). *Thought and Language.* Cambridge, MA: Massachusetts Institute of Technology.

Waldron, F. (2003). Irish Primary children's perceptions of history. *Irish Educational Studies, 22*, 63–90.

Warren, S. (2000). Let's do it properly: Inviting children to be researchers. In A. Lewis & G. Lindsay (Eds.), *Researching children's perspectives.* (pp. 122–134). Buckingham, UK: Open University Press.

Wetton, N. M., & McWhirter, J, (1998). Images and curriculum development in health education. In J. Prosser (Ed.), *Image-based research: A sourcebook for qualitative researchers* (pp. 263–283). London: Falmer Press.

CHAPTER 6

DONNING WIGS, DIVINING FEELINGS, AND OTHER DILEMMAS OF DOING RESEARCH IN DEVOUTLY RELIGIOUS CONTEXTS

Simone A. Schweber

I am driving my car in a small Midwestern city that I do not know well. I have spent the morning explaining my research interests to various members of the administrative body of an ultra-orthodox Jewish religious school for girls, a process called "negotiating access." I think I have been successful, but I am unsure. I am wearing a long, black skirt that covers my knees, tights that cover my legs below, a long-sleeved blouse with a light sweater over it and a scarf that hides my neck. My usually wild hair is tucked neatly into a hat that covers almost all of it; only a few curls on my forehead and at the base of my neck are obstinately poking out. Proof of my transformation: my small children almost didn't recognize me when I was leaving the house in the morning. My daughter, who was 3 years old at the time, cried bitterly when she saw me dressed this way, every part of me shrouded. She howled at me to take off my hat and would only hug me goodbye when I complied.

At the school, by contrast, I am underdressed, or at least dressed as an obvious outsider. Unlike the women moving in and around the office, my

Research Methods in Social Studies Education, pages 111–137
Copyright © 2006 by Information Age Publishing

get-up is too dark and too fancy, implying that I don't dress this way every day. My shoes are too hip with their thick, platform bases. My face is overeager. Moreover, I am incapable of moving casually in the outfit I have on. I feel vaguely Victorian and puritanical simultaneously; I'm layered in clothes and anxious about being immodest. Most of all, my hat betrays me. The married women in the school are wearing wigs, not hats. Not a single strand of their real hair is showing.[1] Had I chosen to wear a wig rather than a hat that morning, I think later, maybe I would have been granted access to the school. Though I was later granted access to a different ultra-orthodox Jewish school, I regretted that I had not worn the wig, that school having been a preferable site.

For me, though, the choice between hat and wig had been difficult to make. I come from a long line of traditionally orthodox Jews, and I am close to my female cousins who cover their hair and knees and ankles and elbows. There is much I love about their lives: the grandeur of their families (one first cousin has 13 children), the clear-headedness endowed by their sense of purpose, the close-knittedness of their communities, the ease with which they pray. My grandmother would have been overjoyed to see me wearing a long skirt and a wig. Before she died, she used to write long letters entreating me to give up studying for a PhD in favor of learning the Torah (the Hebrew Bible). I myself like the wigs traditionally orthodox women wear. They're easy to clean and easier to style than my own hair. Tempting as they are, though, I am ultimately my parents' daughter as well, and both my parents would have been scandalized by such a choice. My father, a scientist turned historian, was the first in that long line of Jews to chart a new course religiously, defining his life as deeply Jewish in value, if also increasingly secular in practice. My mother was a proud and avowed feminist who earned a PhD in genetics in the 1950s, one of a few lone females in a world dominated by men. She would roll over in her grave to think of me covering my hair. Because my father has always been somewhat more inclined toward respectability, he would understand the need for a head covering but might consider a wig excessive, the trappings of petty mimicry. Choosing between hat and wig thus felt like a heavily symbolic act to me; more than a decision between self-representations, it was a test of familial loyalties, a competition between personal identities.

Dressing for classroom observations at the Charismatic, evangelical, fundamentalist Christian school I researched at a year later was significantly less psychically cumbersome. Not only was the dress code at the Christian school simpler, but my investment in it was emotionally cleaner. I dressed appropriately there for the sake of appropriateness; I didn't want to offend those who had agreed to be studied. Period. The choice between pants or a skirt wasn't freighted with notions of personal integrity. Neither my mother's nor my grandmother's ghosts weighed in during my internal dialogues about what to wear.

This contrast between the messiness of my decision making for the Jewish school versus its relative tidiness at the Christian one remained a constant throughout my research, causing me unnecessary missteps at the former while smoothing my path at the latter.[2] With regards to the Jewish school, I was flooded by the emotions of shared ethnicity, common peoplehood. My thinking was constantly interrupted by the voices of ghosts, the seductiveness of assumption, and the competing attractions of nostalgia and disdain, desire and shame, certainty and ambivalence, relentless ambivalence. Enmeshed in "webs of significance"[3] at the Jewish school, my critical facilities were gummed up and sticky, slowed by the molasses of attachment; my intellectual work there was always laborious, my research process, fumbling, though both were at times joyful, too. At the Christian school, I felt intellectually freer, if emotionally flatter. I reeked professionalism; though not aloof, I was detached, interested of course, dedicated absolutely, but basically detached.

I preferred my work at the Christian school for that reason. Ethnographically, I prefer detachment and the illusions of scientism it propagates. Much as I believe that both attachment and detachment pose intellectual and emotional trade-offs, that neither is inherently superior as a tool of the trade,[4] detachment is easier on the soul. Moreover, I like to imagine my researcher persona as the cinematic equivalent of Grace Kelly, and at the Jewish school, I felt much more like Woody Allen, or even Elmer Fudd. I lacked the kind of elegance I so admire.

ACCESS

It took 3 years for me to negotiate access to an ultra-orthodox Jewish school. The school-community I had had my heart set on was exceedingly insular, which is to say that it was not only my choice of hat that denied me access. Naively, though, I had thought that by virtue of my Jewishness, I would be welcomed to such a school. By virtue of my family background, I would be considered if not an "insider," at least an eligible outsider, someone worth educating and possibly converting to greater Jewish observance. Two years in a row, I was granted access by the rabbi who served as head of school, permission slips were sent to students' parents, and then a week before observations were set to begin, the rabbinic board that oversaw the head rabbi foreclosed the research. Though I was disappointed, I didn't take these refusals personally. I understood their inherent distrust of me. Moreover, I could imagine that, whether wearing a hat or a wig, I was exactly the kind of woman their insularity was meant to hide from view; most in that community would not want their daughters growing up to become educational researchers, and they would definitely not want their daughters growing up to become less observant Jews. In the third year, when I knew that my funding would expire, I switched tacks for gaining access and switched schools as well. I asked a personal friend who was a member of a different ultra-orthodox community to introduce me to the personnel at the school her children attended. I can't say that this made all the difference in my being accepted since the two ultra-orthodox communities were ideologically disparate in ways that mattered, the second community being committed to the notion of proselytizing to Jews and therefore much more positively disposed to accept a Jewish outsider. Nonetheless, I'm sure that it helped to have a liaison who was considered trustworthy.

I expected it to be much harder to negotiate access to a fundamentalist Christian school. I was, after all, a complete outsider to that system, in Peshkin's (1986) phrasing, "a perpetual outsider" (p. 22). As a Jew, I was unsaved; as a woman, I lacked traditional authority; as a professor, I could be perceived to uphold liberal, humanist notions that fundamentalist Christianity eschews. It had taken Peshkin multiple tries to negotiate access to a similar school, which he called "Bethany Baptist Academy." As he recounted in the introduction to his seminal ethnography of that school:

> In the course of [a] pilot year, we [his research assistants and he] were allowed entry to one [school] only to be asked later to leave; allowed entry to another for "two weeks only, that's all, no bargaining"; and absolutely refused entry to a third.
>
> The refusing pastor spurned me with a flourish. To my innocent statement that we wanted merely to learn about the world of a Christian day school, he replied:
>
>> You're like a Russian who says he wants to attend meetings at the Pentagon—just to learn…. No matter how good a person you are, you will misrepresent my school because you don't have the Holy Spirit in you. First, become a child of the King, and then you can pursue your study of Christian schools. (p. 12)

While the study I was proposing was far less invasive and much less ambitious than was Peshkin's, I expected to encounter philosophically similar responses. There was certainly no reason for me to think that I would gain access more easily than had he.[5] And yet, it took exactly three phone calls on the same day to gain entry to the fundamentalist Christian school of my dreams: one to the principal, one to the head of school, a third to the teacher. In good form, I met with each in person, describing in detail my research, its goals and methodology, my working style and hoped-for results. The administrators were careful, and the teacher was cautious, rightfully so, but from the moment I walked in, I was welcomed, and warmly. Once they felt they knew what I would do—inasmuch as I knew it—I was granted access.

It's easy enough to draw facile conclusions from the comparison of my entry to these schools. (As examples: Jews are more paranoid than Christians; suburban Christians are friendlier than urban Jews; Christian proselytizing communities are easier to access than Jewish proselytizing ones, etc.) I consider the difference to be mostly a reflection of the counterintuitive nature of my status as insider/outsider in both contexts. Within fundamentalist movements generally, Antoun (2001) has categorized two types of "others": internal and external "enemies" against which fundamentalists define themselves (p. 56). For fundamentalist Christians, "the internal…enemies are the non-fundamentalist Christians who claim to be followers of Jesus but accept the norms laid down by the state and other nonreligious institutions…and [who] cavort with members of the secular society" (p. 56). External enemies, by contrast, are non-Christians, "particularly the communist, the atheist, and the secular humanist—and often members of other faiths" (p. 56). For ultra-orthodox Jews, Antoun describes the internal enemy as secular Jews, Jews called "*maskilim*" (p. 56), literally those who enlighten, who question the sanctity of the Hebrew Bible or the imperatives to observe Jewish law in strictly traditional forms. Heilman (1992), whose writings on the *haredim* (or ultra-orthodox Jews) formed the basis for Antoun's theorizing, stipulates that internal enemies include anyone who follows "*chukos hagoyim* (the laws [ways] of the Gentiles [i.e., other nations]), [a culture which] is at worst anathema and at best a disappointment" (p. 198). External enemies consist of those outside the religion who actually or imaginatively oppose the continuation of the Jewish people; they are the goyim who create the *chukos hagoyim*, and they range from the harmless to the murderous.

According to Antoun (2001), religious fundamentalists typically perceive internal enemies as more threatening than external ones, and though such a claim hardly seems ahistorically applicable, it certainly seems sufficient to explaining my story of negotiating entry. At the first Jewish school site I approached, I was an internal "enemy," redeemed at the second Jewish school both by an evangelical ideology and by my friendship with a true insider. At the Christian school, I was something between outsider and insider. I may have felt myself to be fully an outsider, but by virtue of being Jewish, I occupied a liminal status, simultaneously insider and outsider, Jews being considered God's first chosen, the forebears of Jesus and thus insiders, and yet having rejected Jesus as the messiah and being outcast as God's chosen, doomed to being "perpetual outsiders" (Peshkin, 1986, p. 22) in fundamentalist Christian theology. Put differently, I wonder whether and how a Muslim or Hindu researcher would have been welcomed into the same fundamentalist Christian school, for I am sure that my Jewishness afforded special privileges and extracted certain costs in that context, just as it did at the Jewish school.

RITUALS

The Jewish school has only one entrance. It's a side door to the building, angled inauspiciously and mostly obscured by bushes. A video camera is perched blatantly over the door so that visitors can be electronically screened. In accordance with traditional Jewish law, a *mezuzah* adorns the doorpost of the entryway. It's a small, nondescript case that contains a parchment rolled up within it, and it serves as a reminder of God's presence and authority. An observant Jew, upon being buzzed in to the school, will touch her hand to the mezuzah, raising her hand to her lips and kissing it without breaking stride. Observant Jews repeat this motion each time they enter a doorway with a mezuzah, which in Jewish buildings often includes bedroom doors, kitchen doors, and house doors. At the school, the main entrance, every schoolroom door, and the cafeteria entryway were all adorned with mezuzahs. Moreover, the tradition of kissing the mezuzah holds whether one is entering or leaving. Repeated so frequently, the gesture can seem mechanical, soulless, obligatory even. Some of the eighth-grade girls in the class that I observed articulated the motion of kissing the mezuzah with just a hint of rebellion, an understated playfulness that, whether intended or not, poked fun at the ritual.

During class, if a girl had to use the restroom, she silently approached the front of the room, stood by the doorway, and waited until a nod from the teacher signaled her excusal. All eyes in the class would thereafter follow this girl out of the room as the obligatory mezuzah kissing transpired. The more observant girls, the ones Levine (2003) has identified as *chassidishe*, always kissed the mezuzah plainly, modestly, in earnest. These girls, in accordance with the strictest dictates of Hasidism, didn't "call undue attention to [their] bodie[ies]" (p. 50) and would never compromise the integrity of ritual commandments. These were the girls whose skirts exceeded regulation length, who never wore long socks instead of tights and who tended not to have pierced ears or flashy glasses. The "normal" girls, however—a self-designated descriptor—make up the majority of the Lubavitch population of girls, and they are prone to "lively, impish" (p. 51) behavior. To these girls, "the thrill of social popularity is more immediate and tangible than the subtle rewards of spiritual refinement" (p. 51). It was a subgroup of these "normal girls," who, when requesting permission to go to the bathroom, would kiss the mezuzah with two rigidly stretched fingers, gracefully sweeping their whole hand so that the still-straight fingers arced over their lips and extended out into the air in a continuous motion. It may be hard to picture the gesture, but had it included the right prop between the stiff pointer and middle fingers, it would have looked suspiciously like a Virginia Slims ad from the 1950s. The cigarette flourish, for the girls, marked a boundary between cliques and between social and religious camps. Importantly, though, neither group of girls would have considered not kissing the mezuzah.

For me, the mezuzah posed a test of Jewish observance, of insider/outsider status, and again of loyalties, every time I entered and exited the building or the classroom. At the building entryway, the stakes were lower. I never felt really compelled to kiss the mezuzah, proof in a way that an electronic device doesn't hold the power of interpersonal interaction.[6] As I entered the classroom, though, I sometimes wished to perform the ritual, hoping to show the girls in the room that I was like them, of them, if at a different point on the continuum of Jewish practice, not to mention a different stage of life. And yet, simultaneously, I didn't want, even symbolically, to seem beholden to the myth that greater observance of ritual promotes a more authentic Judaism. I felt that if I kissed the mezuzah, I might be seen as someone whose ritual observance was increasing, a sign of the Hegelian "progress" that this Jewish sect promotes. In short, I didn't want to appear as the researcher "going native," the seemingly secular Jew sliding toward Lubavitch. The internal arguments trumped behavioral risk-taking, and my philosophical objections won out over my social impulses. I can remember more than one day during the months of observations when I probably should have excused myself in order to use the washroom, but the anxiety associated with a public performance of the mezuzah-kissing ritual kept me glued in my seat instead, desperately longing for class to conclude. In the end, I never kissed the mezuzah. Ironically, now, months after the study ended, I wish that I had—not every time, not even often, but occasionally, or even just once, and not for the girls, for in the end it hardly mattered to them, not even for the sake of research, though it may well have bought me credibility among the *chassidishe* group, but for myself—the grand-daughter in me, maybe.

While I never kissed the mezuzah, I did occasionally exchange greetings in Hasidic terms used by the girls I studied. When ultra-orthodox Jews hear the question, "How are you?" (most frequently asked by outsiders), they respond by saying, "Blessed is God" in Hebrew (*"Baruch HaShem"*), or, its loose English equivalent inflected by Yiddish, "Thanks God." By this they mean to thank God for their good health or continued life. Asking after someone's health in a Hasidic school is thus not a great way to begin a conversation; it is, instead, an invitation to this ritual, the quotidian reminder of God's presence in all human realms. I knew this before entering the Jewish school. I knew it from interactions with my own cousins. And, yet, I am compulsively friendly when uncomfortable and overly nervous about seeming impolite. Following my mother's Midwestern example, I'm a smiler and a greeter as overcompensation for inbred awkwardness. As a result, over and over again, I would ask the girls in the class and the smaller girls who stared at me as I passed them in the halls, "How are you?" as though I didn't know what answer would follow. Repeatedly, in other words, I proclaimed my outsider status loudly and obviously, feeling foolish each time the habitual question escaped my lips. I knew of course that my version of politeness wasn't theirs and that my greetings were unnecessary.[7] But what I knew intellectually didn't transform me behaviorally. I simply couldn't stop myself from asking, and in turn, having the query lobbed right back at me.

"How are you?" I'd say, smiling, already cursing myself inside.

"Thanks God, and you?" (The school insider would reply.)

"Fine, thanks," I'd say, out of habit, thinking instead, "Actually, right now I'm annoyed with myself for having begun this exchange. Why can't I keep my mouth shut?"

I'm not sure when I started replying in the Hasidic style. Because it wasn't an object of study for me, I didn't note in my field notes when I used which greeting. I'm also not sure why uttering the phrase "Thanks God" eluded my internal censors more skillfully than did the mezuzah kissing impulse. What I do know is that after some point, occasionally, rather than responding as an outsider, I'd answer "Thanks God" when greeted, if only to curtail the cycle of self-recrimination and to quell the questions the transaction raised about my own Jewishness. "How is your little one today?" I was often asked after missing a day of observations at the school. "Thanks God," I could easily reply. Now, months after ending my observations, when people ask how I am, I reply "normally," "Fine, thanks," but internally, I hear the faint echo of the *chassidishe* response, as if it's the "right" answer haunting my secular life.

At the Christian school, ritual observance didn't punctuate informal social relations, at least not in ways I understood. The school personnel and the students greeted each other "normally." They entered and exited the building plainly. Because neither special dress nor unusual behaviors were demanded of insiders, ironically perhaps, I could pass as a fundamentalist Christian more easily than I could as an ultra-orthodox Jew. Excepting those who had been introduced to me, I think most of the students, parents, and teachers who passed me in the halls assumed I was a fundamentalist Christian like them. I was appropriately dressed, well-washed, and white-skinned, as were almost all of the school's population. Moreover, the insularity of such schools worked to my advantage, as it was quite rare for non-Christians to enter the school in the first place. Thus, while I felt myself to be an outsider, my status as such was only blatantly obvious in isolated moments, as opposed to my experience at the Jewish school, where the tango of insider/outsider dynamics played a kind of ever-present background music.

At the Christian school, prayers often opened class sessions. After the students bustled into their seats and the bell rang, the teacher I observed would sometimes solicit topics of concern from the students, asking if there were particular events or desires they'd like that morning's prayer to address. In the following excerpt, for example, her students raised their hands to provide the pseudonymous Mrs. Barrett with various "prayer requests":

> Student: My mom is trying to get a new job. She really hates her job. She always comes home super mad. She got diagnosed with depression because she worked there. She really hates it.
>
> Teacher: We'll pray about this. Beatrice?[8]
>
> Student: My mom has a couple of friends and they're both trying to find a new job.
>
> Teacher: Do you want me to just put down two friends or do you want me to put down their names?
>
> Beatrice: Mr. and Mrs. Brown.
>
> Teacher: (Writes on the board as she explains) By the way, what I'd like to do when we take these prayer requests, I'd like you to jot them down in a notebook. We're going to see how God works in these situations. (Calls on next student)
>
> Student: My Dad's car that he was going to get this month just got sold and that he could find a new one just like it.

Mrs. Barrett would then weave a prayer, threading together the disparate wishes of her students, only a few of which appear above. (The full class session from which the excerpt above was taken includes no fewer than 14 "prayer requests," ranging from curing a touch of flu to eliminating West Nile Virus.) Mrs. Barrett herself would have her head bowed, eyes closed, and hands clasped together as she spoke a prayer on behalf of her students, her school, her religious community, and the country.[9]

To me, these prayer sessions were understandable—they were in English, after all—and they were also truly strange. Before entering Mrs. Barrett's classroom, I had never heard Christian prayers in person, and the televangelists I had watched in preparation for doing this research didn't hold a candle to this teacher's eloquence or gentleness. I had never before heard spontaneously spun prayers, as the wording of prayers I was accustomed to reciting had been formalized mostly in centuries past. But in contrast to the prayer sessions I observed at the Jewish school, I felt utterly at ease as I listened in on Mrs. Barrett's prayers. Because they were a formal part of her class sessions, by the time her praying began, I was already seated quietly at the back of the room, my notebook open, my hand furiously writing, and my tape-recorder running. In other words, I was already comfortably lodged in my role as researcher.[10] In addition, I was sheltered by invisibility. As Mrs. Barrett prayed, no one could see me not praying, no matter that no one expected me to. The privacy afforded me by the closed eyes of my participants was blessedly complete, releasing me from the guilty dilemmas I experienced at the Jewish school—should I pray with the students when I know the prayers? Should I be praying as a researcher? When Mrs. Barrett prayed, I felt perched on the edge of her world, looking in from a safe distance rather than swayed by a worldview, swimming against the riptides of emotional currents.

INTERVIEWS

If the specificity of my Jewish attachments complicated the process of doing research at the Jewish school, I know that it also aided that research, at least on occasion. And while my lack of connection to the Christian school should, inversely, have compromised the research I conducted there, I know that not to be the case. A perfect point of comparison rests on the student interviews I conducted at both sites.

As background, I should mention that I have been doing the same kind of research now for about 8 years, a period not quite long enough for me to have become jaded, but too long for me to consider myself a novice. Though I am still excited when interviewing someone new, I am no longer nervous about it. Typically, I trust in my ability to build rapport, to pose questions or clarify them, to follow interesting tangents, and to keep to a rough time frame—the main attributes of a successful interview procedure. I have also had enough odd experiences that I trust in my abilities to handle the unpredictable outliers, both the run-of-the-mill and extreme varieties—the taciturn young child who is afraid to speak (run-of-the-mill), the parent who believed that aliens had birthed her child and were going to return and abduct him one day (extreme), or the teenager who wanted our interview to last 3 days out of desperate loneliness (somewhere in between). I tend to rely on semi-structured interviews (Fontana & Frey, 2000), as they provide a framework that makes the comparison of results easier and the flexibility to pursue elaborations when they seem fruitful. I usually interview youth individually unless they are very young and very nervous about being interviewed, and I usually schedule interviews only after having observed in the classroom for enough time that the students know my face, know something about me, and have interacted with me, at least superficially.

Amidst the small but impressive group of researchers in history education who investigate the "doing of history" (Levstik & Barton, 2001), the challenges and practices of learning to think historically (e.g., Ashby & Lee, 1987; Barton & Levstik, 1996; Brophy, 1990; Epstein, 1998; Grant, 2001; Levstik & Barton, 1996; Seixas, 1993; VanSledright, 1995; Wineburg, 2001), my research is concerned with how students experience the history curriculum and what they think they learn from it. As a result, I typically interview using straightforward questions, questions meant to assess students' knowledge, learning, enjoyment, and interests. And while I recognize the inevitable influences of researcher-pleasing behavior, adult-defying lying, and other common interview skews, I tend, despite them, to trust what teenagers tell me during interviews. For the most part, I have worked with adolescents who have never before participated in studies and who have been excited about being interviewed, are happy to share what they know, think, and feel. It's rare for young people to have opportunities to be heard, as individuals, by adults who have no direct authority over them, and I have found that, typically at least, most students enjoy the interaction, the chance to talk, be listened to and taken seriously.

The protocol in Figure 6.1 formed the basis for my first interviews with students at the Christian school,[11] and I had planned to use it when talking to the girls at the Jewish yeshivah as well.

At the Christian school, the protocol worked; that is, the questions generated talk, the students had no difficulties answering them, and their answers illuminated the issues I was studying. I attribute the protocol's success at the Christian school to a host of factors, chief among them, the fortunate coincidence of my blithe naiveté and the lack of specialized knowledge necessary for interviewing fundamentalist Christian kids. At the Christian school, there was no need for a specialized language to get at what I hoped to learn, no need to know Yiddish or Hebrew or to interpret English heavily inflected with Yiddish. (Chassidic English is sometimes referred to glibly as Yenglish.) While I'm sure that using language "coded" to fundamentalist Christians would have helped in garnering different answers, possibly deeper ones, I'm also sure that my lack of understanding enabled me to push along, obliviously sometimes, but productively so. My identity as unsaved, non-Christian, in other words, enabled me to ask naive, but informative questions, like, "How can you imagine what Jesus would have done when he didn't live in this era?" Even simplistic questions, such as "How do you like school?" provided unexpected insights at the Christian school, as the excerpt below from an interview transcript shows.

Demographic information

1. Please describe yourself to someone who doesn't know you—what would you say they should know about you to get a good sense of who you are (age/gender/race/religion/family size/interests/activities/hopes for the future)?
2. How did you end up being enrolled at this school? (Parents' choice? Yours?)
3. How long have you attended this school?
4. Do you like school? What do you like most about it? What do you like least?

Holocaust, prior exposure

5. Why do you think you are going to learn about the Holocaust in this class?
6. Have you ever learned about the Holocaust before?
7. Where/when: What do you remember learning then?
8. Have you seen any movies about the Holocaust? (If so, which?)
9. Do you have a family connection to the Holocaust?
10. What do you think you are going to learn about the Holocaust in this class?

Prior knowledge

11. What would you say the Holocaust is to someone who hadn't heard of it?
12. What are the main reasons the Holocaust occurred?
13. Do you know what groups were persecuted during the Holocaust? (Why for each?)
14. Why do you think Jews were targeted?
15. Are there any events that you think of as being comparable to the Holocaust?
16. How do you explain the behavior of the perpetrators?
17. What role do you think God played during the Holocaust? (Is God's role during the Holocaust similar or different from God's role in history more generally? Is this history unique in that regard?)
18. Do you think the Holocaust could have been prevented?
19. What can be learned from the Holocaust, if anything?

Closing questions

20. Do you have any questions about this history that you'd like answered, things you'd like to know or understand that you've wondered about?
21. Do you have any questions for me?

Figure 6.1.   Interview protocol.

Simone: How would you describe yourself to someone who didn't know you?

Reba[12]: I go to EGCS. I've gone there since kindergarten. I am a Christian. I'm 13 years old; I'll be 14 next July. My parents enrolled me here since I was 1 week old. Umm, what else?

Simone: What kind of Christian are you? In other words, is there a particular denomination you belong to?

Reba: I guess, Charismatic. I've never been to a different church.

Simone: And, what kinds of things do you like to do when you're not in school?

Reba: I like to ice skate, but I don't do it as much as I'd like. I like to read books.

Simone: Oh yeah? What kind?

Reba: A lot of stuff, mysteries, fiction.

Simone: How do you like school?

Reba: School is really nice. The people are really nice. They care how you're doing. They know how you are. I mean, I've never been to public school, so I don't really know, but I have friends who go to public school, and I don't think that that's how it is there. You know, at public school, the teachers wouldn't pray with you or take time to explain stuff.

Though I hadn't been planning to ask the students at the Christian school what they thought of their public school counterparts, in fact, it was useful or "useable" (Lagemann, 2002) attitudinal information, especially as I was concerned with the Christian students' understandings of "others" communicated through their Holocaust units.[13]

At the Jewish school, it became readily apparent to me that while some of the items on the first protocol "worked," others were obviously flawed; the girls answered them uniformly, as though speaking in the same voice. When asked, "Do you like school?" and "What do you like most about it?" the girls had no difficulty supplying answers, and their answers ranged, as one would expect (even at an exceedingly insular community of which this school was an outgrowth). It was in response to the question, "What don't you like?" that a few of the girls cringed, sometimes pausing awkwardly or visibly wincing to display their discomfort. When not made visibly uncomfortable by the question, the girls simply answered with what I soon realized was the religiously appropriate response:

Simone: Hennie, my first question is how would you describe yourself to people who don't know you?

Hennie: I'm very outgoing. I'm very studious, I love learning.

Simone: How old are you?

Hennie: 13

Simone: How would you describe yourself religiously?

Hennie: I'm Jewish, Orthodox, Lubavitch. I'm very serious about it, very proud of it. I'm proud of who I am.

Simone: Did you grow up "Orthodox Lubavitch"?

Hennie: Yes.

Simone: Did your parents?

Hennie: They both grew up in nonreligious homes. They kept *shab-bes* [the Yiddish term for the Sabbath] and everything. My aunt first was interested, and then my mother, and then their whole families did it together. And my father, I don't really know, I just know he became *frum* [Yiddish for Jewishly observant] somewhere...

Simone: And how long have you been going to this school?

Hennie: Since I was 2.

Simone: And do you know why your parents sent you here?

Hennie: This was the only Lubavitch school in [this area].

Simone: Do you like this school?

Hennie: I love it.

Simone: Is there anything you don't love about it?

Hennie: No school is perfect.

My biases prescribed disbelief at the constancy of this answer; no school is or can be perfect. To me, the purpose of the question was to help gauge students' interest in school, their comfort levels there, sometimes their critical capacities. I soon realized, though, that the question itself posed a religious conflict for the girls to whom it was being posed. To answer the question necessitated expressing negative sentiments about their school, or by implication, their school head, teachers, or peers. At the very least, it posed that potential, which the girls considered "*lashon hara,*" which literally means an "evil tongue," but colloquially refers to the spreading of gossip, a religiously forbidden act. In other words, the girls couldn't answer the question I had posed without breaking a commandment, one of the hundreds that orchestrated their lives. Within Lubavitch circles, observance of such *mitzvot,* good deeds or commandments, is thought to unleash the holy sparks that will hasten the arrival of the Messiah (Wellen Levine, 2003) such that observing *mitzvot* is a serious obligation.

I had no choice but to rethink the formulation of my question. I arrived at the following—not a perfect substitute, but a close cousin to the original: "If you were describing your school to someone who had never been here or heard of it, what would you say to prepare them for becoming a student here?" I also asked the proxy, "If you became principal of this school, what changes would you make (since principals almost always do that)?" The same kind of verbal acrobatics characterized my questions to the girls throughout the research since I had to rule out the whole class of questions that might lead one to commit an *avera* (a sin) such as *lashon hara* (disseminating gossip). While I wanted to probe and sometimes to push, it was simply ineffectual to pose religious dilemmas in the very questions I asked.

I also had to be careful about the wording I used to describe God. The girls at the yeshiva don't use God's name in common parlance, reserving it for prayer alone. Instead, they call God by a nickname, "*HaShem*," which literally means, "the name." Had I called God by the Hebrew terms that are recognized as God's name, I'm not sure how the girls would have reacted. I do know that they would not have answered in kind. Interestingly perhaps, it didn't bother me to use their term for God during interviews. Unlike the experience of avoiding the wig or wanting to kiss the mezuzah, for me, inexplicably maybe, using the girls' term for God simply seemed respectful, akin to translating specific terms for audiences who don't share the language. It didn't feel like a choice that implicated me religiously in any way or that I ought to have ethical reservations about as a researcher. Thus, in the excerpt below, I simply used the term, "*HaShem*," to mean God. I know it indicated to the girls, perhaps, that I shared their language. Whether my usage implied to them that I shared their worldview, however, I doubt, especially given the nature of my questioning:

Simone: This is a really hard question, but this is what I'm trying to learn. How do you think of *HaShem* in relation to the Holocaust?

Henya: I mean we know that *HaShem* controls everything and there are a lot of things we don't understand. So we can't question *HaShem* because that's just the way it is. But just to have that faith, even though I don't understand why such a bad thing could have happened and why *HaShem* didn't stop it, I still have a lot of questions, this is one of my questions, I just have to believe that this is what happened and I can't give up hope and my faith in *HaShem*.

Simone: So it's not like *HaShem*—

Henya: It's hard to say. When we believe in *HaShem*, it's hard to say that He made all these Jews murdered.... We know that even though everything is caused by *HaShem*, people still have free choice to do right and wrong.

Simone: So some people would say the Holocaust isn't about *HaShem*, it's about people doing this to other people, and not *HaShem* doing this.

Henya: Right, like you could say, why did I do something bad? Well, everything is from *HaShem*, so I did something bad, so it's not my fault, it's *HaShem's* fault. But we know that we do have, we call it *bechira*—[which means choice, free will] *HaShem* knows what we're going to choose, but He still gives us the choice to choose between right and wrong and what we're going to do.... He's on top of it.

As a side note, perhaps, despite the differences in language, the lack of Yiddish-inflected terminology, and my distinct lack of insider status, some of the Christian students I interviewed expressed ideas about God's role in the Holocaust and God's role more generally that were very similar, in spirit, to Henya's. The contours of the exchange below with Betty, for example, echoed the lines of Henya's thinking:

> Simone: Last question. Do you think the Holocaust could have been prevented?
>
> Betty: [3 second pause] Hmm...[another pause] I don't know how to answer that. It could have been, but I think that it was the way God wanted it.... I mean he didn't really want it that way, but you know, God knew it was going to happen, so it happened. But God gave us free will, but you know, God knew it was going to happen. I mean, like, yeah, it could have been prevented if people weren't so hateful to each other, you know, really hate each other, but could it have been prevented? I don't know.
>
> Simone: You said it could have been that God wanted it, well, "not really wanted it" but he knew it was going to happen. And you said something about we have free will...
>
> Betty: Yeah, God gave us free will. We make our own decisions; we can choose to fight.... We can do things, and choose to do things, but God knows what we are going to choose before we do. It's not like, "Oh my gosh, I can't believe I just did that." It's kind of mind boggling, but he knows what's going to happen, but we have free will, but he knows what is going to happen. So, we can make a choice, but he knows what is going to happen. It's kind of weird, he does, he knows everything, millions and billions of years ahead of time, or he knows just a thousand years ahead of time, a hundred years, you never know how much he knows...
>
> Simone: So he knew about all of the choices that everyone was making...
>
> Betty: He knew like the whole thing about Gore and Bush, when we had the election. It wasn't like he was sitting up there thinking, "Oh my gosh, what are we going to do? Now there's a recount? Oh no!" He knew about that, but it's like you don't know how far back he knew. He usually has a purpose for things, he always has a purpose for things, but you just can't see the purpose until later on.

Simone: So what was the purpose for the Holocaust? Is it "later on" enough to know?

Betty: I don't know. To show people in the world that God has the world under control and that He will take care of us if we just trust in Him.

This juxtaposition of interview excerpts highlights a paradox that my positions as a researcher evokes. On the face of it, the substance of the interviews themselves are comparably rich; that is, not only is the content of the students' comments similar, but the depth of the interview excerpts is, implying that my insider-ness at the Jewish school doesn't reap richer rewards than does my outsider-ness at the Christian school. On the face of it, the fact that I spoke the language of my participants at the Jewish school (using "*HaShem*" easily, for example) and that I had to echo the remarks of my participants at the Christian one ("You said...") didn't ultimately matter in terms of the information I garnered at both sites. That said, I'd be a fool to think that my positionality didn't matter. Precisely because I don't speak the language of fundamentalist Christians, I can't know what I was missing as a researcher, the communally specific images, references, background narratives (Mosborg, 2002), mythological stories, and communal discourse that I might have accessed had I been a true, or at least near, insider.[14]

TRUST

It would be unfair, to say the least, to compare the levels of trust that I earned at the two schools. I was, after all, situated completely differently at both, and the schools themselves were so different as to accord different kinds of relationships. As I have mentioned above, the Jewish school was insular and single-sexed, affording a kind of intimacy, maybe, that the Christian school perhaps couldn't approximate. Some of the girls at the Jewish school boarded as well, which meant that, for some, the school functioned as their home in a very real sense. Furthermore, I was alone in my research activities at the Jewish school, but aided by two research assistants at the Christian one. Thus, my interactions were diffused at the Christian school, intensified at the Jewish one. And the norms of classroom discourse—the quiet of the Christian classroom, the volubility of the Jewish one—both played into my possibilities for interaction as well, lessening the opportunities at the Christian one, increasing them at the Jewish one, all allowing for trust to build much more easily at the Jewish school.

With these qualifiers in place, it's worth noting that at the Jewish school, while I was more uncomfortable as a researcher, more vexed by the marionette-like strings of attachment, I was also more at home as a person. The girls trusted me, almost immediately, but eventually fully. They knew, of course, that I was an outsider, but I think they understood, too, that I was trying for insider status, and they were eager to help me along that pathway, mistaking my methodological proclivities perhaps for religious ones. When I forgot my hat one day, my hair showing brazenly, the girls didn't seem to mind, though I'm sure that they discussed it once I had left the room. Another day, weeks later, I mistakenly wore short socks under a long, black skirt whose slit up the back revealed a shocking length of calf. The girls in the class treated me no differently than they had on other days. (One girl, a *chassidishe* girl, commented gently to me that one could easily sew up such a slit. This was the same girl who, when asked what she would change about the school were she the principal, said that she would make sure that everyone followed the dress code fully. She thought the school should be "more strict" that way, "no TV, no movies, stuff like that.") I only realized the depth of my dress code infraction when I walked out to my car during recess that day. As I strode across the parking lot that doubled as the playground, the younger girls in the school grew quiet as I passed, averting their eyes as though ashamed of my clothing. I knew then that the girls must either like or trust me, or some ineffable combination of the two. They had acted as though the infraction hadn't mattered. I knew that they trusted me for sure when, near the end of the year, they asked if I could accompany them on their graduation trip to New York, a pilgrimage to the U.S. center of Lubavitch life, the place where their Rebbe had taught and was buried. I was flattered by the request, but I knew, too, that the school administrators would never approve of such a tag-along. The girls thought for sure it would be all right despite my protestations and went ahead and asked the head of school to allow me to come. The disappointment on their faces the next day was heartening. Months later, I am in e-mail contact with some of these girls who occasionally write about high school or send me pictures of their summer camping trips.

At the Christian school, I grew close to the teacher in the study. While I liked the students a lot, the combination of factors that constellated my research there didn't enable us to become friends. The teacher and I have, in the years since I completed the research there, had lunch, exchanged phone calls, and kept in touch. I have tremendous respect for her as a person, and I have valued coming to know her.

Despite both sets of attachments, complicated and clean, and despite the kind of trust I attempted to garner at both sites, successfully and not, it's fair to say that I would have preferred to commit "hit and run" research rather than sharing my results. I would have much preferred to do exactly the kind of ethically challenged research I discourage my students from doing, since sharing my results poses multiple challenges in both sites. Notwithstanding my promises to share with both schools' administrators, teachers, and interested parents and kids, I felt, upon the completion of my research, that what

I had found held potential interest for educational researchers and some subset of readers (family members and coerced friends), but none really for the members of the school communities themselves. In fact, for a while, given that conviction, I flirted with the idea of not following through on the promise of shared research. I am not particularly proud of that moment, and simultaneously, I don't believe it shows a lack of courage. I would share the results of my study, I believed, if I thought it would provide useful information to its participants. Instead, though, in ways I couldn't have anticipated, my research simply turned out to seem like it would not be meaningful to the participants I depended on to create it. While on the one hand, it has to be the right of the school members to judge the work's usefulness for themselves and it's an act of supreme hubris for me to make that call without their consent, on the other hand, it also seemed like my obligation not to waste their time, not to exploit their generosity further by having them engage in "member checks" that would ultimately only serve me and my interests. My work on Mrs. Barrett's classroom ended up critiquing the kind of insularity that both school communities treasure and the resulting "reflexive affirmation"[15] that both classrooms cultivate.[16] The narratives I produced, I suspected, simply elaborated points of disagreement between my worldview and those of the worlds I studied rather than providing pathways through the constellations that separate us. In short, it is still hard for me to imagine what the participants in my study stand to gain from the analysis I proffer. In the end, though, I couldn't comfortably ignore the commitments I made, the trust I would compromise forever by not reporting back. While I still worry about the potential for exploitation even in reporting back, and I would still prefer to respectfully avoid hammering (or yammering) at the walls of insulated worlds, I have, after a prolonged period of procrastination, scheduled times to share my findings officially.

In approaching these events with considerable trepidation, I am heartened by the story Alan Peshkin once told me[17] about what it was like to share the results of his study with the community at Bethany Baptist Academy. While his analysis had soundly critiqued the "total world" of a fundamentalist Christian school community, his readers there loved the book, so much so that they sold copies at the church's gift shop and consistently breached the anonymity he so delicately guarded. What Peshkin had lambasted in his account of the school were the very features of their lives that the school's authorities loved.

SUBJECTIVITY

In an oft-quoted article he wrote a few years after finishing his ethnography, Peshkin (1988) describes the shock of "stumbl[ing] upon [his] own subjectivity" (p. 18) as he constructed its narrative. While writing, he had realized that his account was hewn of personal judgments sharpened by their contact with a fundamentalist Christian school. Whereas he had studied similar community dynamics in a nonfundamentalist world and wrote about them in glowing terms, he found his praise restrained when describing Bethany Baptist Academy. In response, he devised a methodology for "taming" his subjectivity, a "formal, systematic monitoring of self" (p. 20) that heightened his awareness of when his emotions were engaged or his personal proclivities called forth. At such moments, which he elaborates as "the warm and the cool spots, the emergence of positive and negative feelings, the experiences [he] wanted more of or wanted to avoid, and when [he] felt moved to act in roles beyond those necessary to fulfill [his] research needs" (p. 18), Peshkin filled out a small card, noting the event and the feelings it evoked, later sorting the cards to find patterns that characterized competing "I"s. His goal was thus to "escape the thwarting biases that subjectivity engenders, while [simultaneously] attaining the singular perspective its special persuasions promise" (p. 21).

As articulated in this writing, Peshkin's version of subjectivity is decidedly post-positivistic; his subjectivity, though avowedly inescapable, can nonetheless be "tamed," shorn of the wooly biases that impinge on its clear-sightedness. For Peshkin, subjectivity has a core or center, a solid mass as well as rough edges that the rigors of a rational process of noticing and note-taking can smooth down. At base, his was a modernist project, wherein subject and object could be disentangled, if only temporarily, and reflexivity could be rationalized, if only narratively. In fact, his methodology for subjectivity-taming, in its heightened attention to particular moments of attachment as disjunctures, assumes that emotional disengagement or narrative distance is normative. The self, for Peshkin, *contains* competing "I"s; it encompasses them and bounds them into a wholeness; the competitions among identities do not construct the self.

Numerous qualitative researchers, writing after Peshkin, have critiqued the epistemological stance that positions subjectivity as unitary, "an essence at the heart of the individual which is unique, fixed and coherent" (Weedon, 1987, p. 32). Such writers (Bloom & Munro, 1995; Davies, 1992; Heshusius, 1994; Hollway, 1989; Jacobs, Munro, & Adams, 1995; Richardson, 1994; Roman, 1993; Walkerdine, 1990) describe subjectivity instead as fractured, fractious, fragmenting, unstable (but not pejoratively so), and continuously in process. Profoundly postmodern, many of these authors invoke subjectivity as part and parcel of a political project aimed at destabilizing the oppressiveness of individualist, masculinist, heterosexist, racist, and patriarchal discourses that inscribe subject positions (Ellsworth, 1997) with permanence and fixedness. Briefly summarized, their notions of subjectivity enable multiple selves to conflict and co-exist, to transform and transpire, not simply in the world, but in the process of world-making (Goodman, 1978; but see Goodman, 1955).

The clash between post-positivistic and postmodern notions of subjectivity is hardly new or even noteworthy (in Peshkin's sense). It is instead intractable and most likely enduring, even as the categories themselves interpenetrate. In reflecting on the experience of doing research at two religious schools, it seems to me that the dynamics of subjectivity itself are contextually dependent, that there are times/places/moments when, as a researcher, one's subjectivity feels as though it may be tamed, rationalized, contained, and domesticated. My experience in the Christian school afforded just such opportunities. While it may have felt slightly awkward for me, as a Jew, to sit in a group of devout students praying to Jesus, my assuredness as an educational researcher trumped my discomfort as a Jew; thus my subjectivity, or my experience of it, was "successfully" repressed. Of course the failing in this framing is that my subjectivity is limited to my ethnic identity rather than additionally encompassing my professional identity, and to pretend that subjective fissures don't vex my professional identity is laughable. For the sake of argument, though, there are also times/places/moments when the fracturing of subjectivity, its blossoming fury and ludicrous unravelings, its hybridity and multiplicity are unarguably uncontainable. While I may have felt myself to be "a Jew," individually and unitarily so in the Christian school,[18] I knew myself to be complicatedly Jewish, multiply and messily so, at the Jewish school. Above and beyond my familial heritages, I am inclined toward Jewish orthodoxy in terms of its communitarian promise, liturgically conservative in my Jewish practices, theologically Reconstructionist in my belief system, and politically Reform in my commitments, all features of my identity—or, competing identities—that the Jewish context itself invoked. Perhaps when there is no clear winner (professional researcher over complicated Jew), but rather multiple players (grand-daughter, daughter, mother, complicated Jew, researcher), perhaps in such cases, postmodern paradigms of subjectivity necessarily prevail.

Ian Hacking, in an essay (1986) entitled "Making Up People,[19] brilliantly bridges postmoderns and post-positivists, or, in his wording, nominalists and realists. Spinning his argument deftly, suspended in historical webs, Hacking claims that certain kinds of categories are obviously constituted socially, conjured into existence through language or traditions—this being the argument of nominalists or postmoderns. Likewise, however, other kinds of categories exist outside of their discursive properties; that is, they are categories not because we named them as such but because they are inherently so—this being the argument of realists or post-positivists. To showcase this claim, Hacking provides a few categorical examples, "horse, planet, [and] glove"[20] (p. 229):

It would be preposterous to suggest that the only thing horses have in common is that we call them horses. We may draw the boundaries to admit or to exclude Shetland ponies, but the similarities and differences are real enough. The planets furnish one of T.S. Kuhn's examples of conceptual change. Arguably the heavens looked different after we grouped Earth with the other planets and excluded Moon and Sun, but I am sure that acute thinkers had discovered a real difference. I hold (most of the time) that strict nominalism is unintelligible for horses and the planets. How could horses and planets be so obedient to our minds? Gloves are something else: we manufacture them. I know not which came first, the thought or the mitten, but they have evolved hand in hand. That the concept "glove" fits gloves so well is no surprise; we made them that way.

Put differently, while horses may be the darlings of the moderns, and gloves, the adored artifact among the postmoderns, I am arguing that subjectivity, as an extension of Hacking's bridge between warring paradigms, may sometimes run like a horse and at other times fit like a glove. The real questions, then, are not whether subjectivity is unitary or multiple, but when, and not whether the research itself is impacted by the single-seeding or cross-pollination of theory metaphors, but how.[21]

AN ENDING

I am traveling from the first Jewish site, the one that did not grant me access, and I am heading home. It is a hot day, maybe 90 degrees outside. The air-conditioning in my car doesn't work, and the windows are wide open. I have a few hours of driving ahead of me, and I am only a few miles from the school. I am still in an ultra-orthodox Jewish neighborhood, but I have worn a tank top under my long-sleeved shirt so that I can peel off my top layer to drive home in relative comfort. My mouth is brick-dry. I pull in to a 7-Eleven, and I'm planning to buy a slushy. As I walk into the store, I catch sight of myself in the glass windows. I can simultaneously see my reflection, me dressed up as an ultra-orthodox Jewish woman, and the sales clerk's wonderment, her looking out at me, maybe a little baffled.[22] There's nothing kosher in the store, and probably, not many ultra-orthodox Jews from the surrounding neighborhood frequent it. I suddenly realize that slushies aren't kosher (to the best of my knowledge) either. I feel terribly awkward for a moment. Do I buy a bottle of water instead of the desired slushy? What if someone from the school community sees me here, committing an *avera*?[23] (I have not as yet found out that my negotiations for access were unsuccessful at that school, and such a calculation seems professionally prudent.) I buy the bottle of water. As I'm about to leave, though, I pull off the hat that fits like a glove, run back inside to buy the slushy, and speed out of the parking lot like a galloping horse.

ACKNOWLEDGMENT

This chapter originally appeared in *Qualitative Inquiry*, and is reprinted courtesy of Sage Publications.

NOTES

1. For the women at the school, their dress and hair-covering is a reflection of their *tznius*, the religious dictates governing modesty (Wellen Levine, 2003). For more on the traditions of Jewish women's covering their hair, see Bronner (1993), Shapiro (1990), and Broyde, Krakowski, and Shapiro (1991).

2. For the sake of brevity, I have abbreviated my references to the two schools I did research at in the remainder of this chapter. In particular, I refer to the specific Charismatic, evangelical fundamentalist Christian school at which I conducted research as simply "the Christian school," and similarly, I refer to the Chasidic, ultra-orthodox girls yeshiva at which I conducted research as simply, "the Jewish school." By this shorthand, I don't in any way mean to imply that these schools are paradigmatic, representative, or even typical of all Christian or Jewish schools or of the Christian and Jewish schools that characterize their particular sects.

3. The full sentence in which the famous Weberian phrase appears in Geertz's (1973) writings states the following: "Believing, with Max Weber, that man is an animal suspended in webs of significance he himself has spun, I take culture to be those webs, and the analysis of it to be therefore not an experimental science in search of law but an interpretive one in search of meaning" (p. 5).

4. For a gorgeous articulation of these trade-offs, see Myerhoff's (1978) ethnography of a community center in Southern California catering to aged Jews, *Number Our Days*. Throughout the book, Myerhoff poignantly refers to the complexities of her position as ethnographer, Jew, substitute-daughter, and female researcher.

5. Since the time that Peshkin studied Bethany Baptist Academy, fundamentalist Christians have become much more overtly politicized, an act that has included a coordinated incursion into the public sphere. That said, it could not be assumed that such an incursion would translate into a willingness to have their private spheres (private schools) "invaded" by a member of the nonbelieving public.

6. The example harkens back to Milgram's (1978) famous experiments on obedience, whereby the greater the distance of the authority, the lesser the rates of obedience to it.

7. Geertz (1973) famously amplified the nature of "thick description" by describing the import of the researcher being able to interpret the distinctions between blinks, winks, and twitches. While I understood the distinc-

tions well enough to know that my version of etiquette didn't hold in their world, I was simply too inflexible to be able to change my behavior in light of that understanding. This instance complicates Geertz's claim somewhat, given that knowledge, while important for the written account, is only one part of the "doing" of research.

8. Beatrice, like all the names used in this chapter, is a pseudonym used to protect the anonymity of the student, school, and community.

9. The events of 9/11 intruded during the course of this fieldwork, which prompted more nationalistic prayers than she might have spoken otherwise. For an analysis of how Mrs. Barrett and her students interpreted the events of 9/11 on that day and in subsequent weeks, see Schweber (in press).

10. Though it is mistaken on my part to have considered myself only as a "researcher" once in the classroom, this is in large part a reflection of the fact that my research focused on classroom-based teaching and learning. Thus, while I was a researcher even as I drove to the school, I only felt myself to be actively "doing research" while in the classroom or while engaged in "research activities" outside of it, such as interviewing participants.

11. My research at the Christian school was aided immeasurably by two research assistants, Rebekah Irwin and Susan Gevelber, who helped in crafting this interview protocol.

12. Reba's name, like many of the students' names in this chapter, was a self-styled pseudonym.

13. For one account of this study, see Schweber and Irwin (2003).

14. A good example of a usage of specific or coded discourse (which leads to the syndrome of "if you have to ask, you won't get it,") includes George W. Bush's incorporation of religiously loaded phrases that his millions of evangelical Christian supporters would recognize and understand as conveying political messages. For both an example from the 2004 campaign trail and an analysis of its reverberations, see Cooperman (2004).

15. For more on "reflexive affirmation," see Schweber (under review).

16. I have not had as much trepidation about presenting my research at the Jewish school since I have not as yet completed the analysis there, which allows me to feel that I'm not yet procrastinating on fulfilling that obligation.

17. While Buddy Peshkin, as he liked to be called, held an appointment as a scholar at the Institute for Advanced Study of the Social Sciences, he led a seminar for Stanford graduate students that I was fortunate enough to participate in.

18. Peshkin may well have felt similarly while doing his research at Bethany Baptist Academy. As the lone Jew there, he may have felt unitarily subjective, the very kind of experience that would enable him to come up with a methodology that posits a unitary self. Sadly, his early death disallows the possibility to discuss this with him.

19. I am indebted to Connie North for pointing me to this article and for suggesting classroom-based uses of it.

20. In this essay, Hacking was writing not only about horse, planet, and glove, but also, and pointedly, about multiple personality. I fully suggest reading

the entirety of the chapter to access its nuance, but for the purposes of brevity, I focused here mainly on horse and glove.

21. As a side note, perhaps, this conclusion warrants a methodological rumination. For if I reject Peshkin's rationalization of subjectivity and resist "member checks" of my research findings, then I am beholden especially to reviewers, who, as part of the submission process, guard my work from the dual pitfalls of egregious narcissism and participant overidentification. And yet, unless the reviewers are insiders in the world I describe, unless they understand the language of my participants, they, like me at the Christian school, can fall prey to exoticizing the unknown. This possibility substantiates the argument for not only inviting more fundamentalist Christians into the academy, but for having greater diversity shown among those chosen as reviewers generally.

22. In an odd turn of the cycle of life imitating art imitating life, etc., I was conscious in that very moment of the similar image from Kondo's (1990) wonderful book, *Crafting Selves*, in which Kondo almost doesn't recognize her own reflection in a butcher's display case while doing ethnographic research in Japan. As she eloquently writes,

> Promptly at four p.m., the hour when most Japanese housewives do their shopping for the evening meal, I lifted the baby into her stroller and pushed her along ahead of me as I inspected the fish, selected the freshest looking vegetables, and mentally planned the meal for the evening. As I glanced into the shiny metal surface of the butcher's display case, I noticed someone who looked terribly familiar: a typical young housewife, clad in slip-on sandals and the loose, cotton shift called "home wear" (*homu wea*), a woman walking with a characteristically Japanese bend to the knees and a sliding of the feet. Suddenly, I clutched the handle of the stroller to stay myself as a wave of dizziness washed over me, for I realized I had caught a glimpse of nothing less than my own reflection.... In order to reconstitute myself as an American researcher, I felt I had to extricate myself from the conspiracy to rewrite my identity as Japanese. (p. 17)

23. While consuming an unkosher food would be one sin I engaged in, another would be the sin of *maras ayin*, which literally translates as embittering the eye, but which refers to the possibility of being seen to commit a sin, which could unintentionally lead others astray.

REFERENCES

Anderson, B. (1991). *Imagined communities.* New York: Verso Books.

Antoun, R. (2001). *Understanding fundamentalism: Christian, Islamic, and Jewish movements.* Lanham, MD: Rowman & Littlefield.

Apple, M. W. (2001). *Educating the "right" way: Markets, standards, god, and inequality.* New York: Routledge Falmer.

Ashby, R., & Lee, P. J. (1987) Discussing the evidence. *Teaching History, 48,* 13–17.

Barton, K. C., Levstik L. S. (1996). "Back when God was around and everything": Elementary children's understanding of historical time. *American Educational Research Journal 33,* 419–454.

Bloom, L. R. (1996). Stories of one's own: Nonunitary subjectivity in narrative representation. *Qualitative Inquiry, 2,* 176–197.

Bloom, L. R., & Munro, P. (1995). Conflicts of selves: non-unitary subjectivity in women administrators' life history narratives. In A. Hatch & R. Wisniewski (Eds.), *Life history and narrative* (pp. 99–112). London, Falmer Press.

Bronner, L. L. (1993). From veil to wig: Jewish women's hair covering. *Judaism, 42,* 465–477.

Brophy, J. (1990). Teaching social studies for understanding and higher-order applications. *Elementary School Journal, 90,* 351–417.

Broyde, M. J., Krakowski, L., & Shapiro, M. (1991). Further on women's hair covering: An exchange. *Judaism, 40,* 79–94.

Cooperman, A. (2004, September 16). Openly religious, to a point: Bush leaves the specifics of his faith to speculation. *Washington Post,* p. A01.

Davies, B. (1992). Women's subjectivity and feminist stories. In C. Ellis & M. G. Flaherty (Eds.), *Investigating subjectivity: Research on lived experience* (pp. 53–76). Newbury Park, CA: Sage.

Ellsworth, E. (1997). *Teaching positions: Difference, pedagogy, and the power of address.* New York: Teachers College Press.

Epstein, T. (1998). Deconstructing differences in African-American and European-American adolescents' perspectives on U.S. history. *Curriculum Inquiry, 28,* 397–423.

Fontana, A., & Frey, J.H. (2000) The interview: From structured questions to negotiated text. In N. Denzin & Y. Lincoln (Eds.), *The handbook of qualitative research.* (pp. 645–672). Thousand Oaks: CA, Sage.

Geertz, C. (1973). *The interpretation of culture.* New York: Basic Books.

Goodman, N. (1955). *Fact, fiction and forecast.* Cambridge, MA: Harvard University Press.

Goodman, N. (1978) *Ways of worldmaking.* Indianapolis, IN: Hackett.

Grant, S. G. (2001). It's just the facts, or is it? The relationship between teachers' practices and students' understandings of history. *Theory and Research in Social Education, 99,* 65–108.

Hacking, I. (1986). Making up people. In T. C. Heller, M. Sosna, & D. E. Wellberry (Eds.), *Reconstructing individualism: Autonomy, individuality, and the self in western thought* (pp. 222–236). Stanford, CA: Stanford University Press.

Heilman, S. (1992). *Defenders of the faith.* New York: Schocken Books.

Heshusius, L. (1994). Freeing ourselves from objectivity: managing subjectivity or turning toward a participatory mode of consciousness? *Educational Researcher, 23*(3), 15–22.

Hollway, W. (1989). *Subjectivity and method in psychology: Gender, meaning and science.* Newbury Park, CA: Sage.

Jacobs, M., Munro, P., & Adams, N. (1995) Palimpsest: (Re)reading women's lives. *Qualitative Inquiry, 1,* 327–345.

Kondo, D. K. (1990). *Crafting selves: Power, gender, and discourses of identity in a Japanese workplace.* Chicago: University of Chicago Press.

Lagemann, E. C. (2002). *Useable knowledge in education: A memorandum for the Spencer Board of Directors.* Chicago: Spencer Foundation.

Levstik, L. S., & Barton, K. C. (1996). "They still use some of their past": Historical salience in elementary children's chronological thinking, *Journal of Curriculum Studies, 28*, 531–576.

Levstik, L. S., & Barton, K. C. (2001). *Doing history: Investigating with children in elementary and middle schools.* Mahwah, NJ: Lawrence Erlbaum Associates.

Milgram, S. (1974). *Obedience to authority.* New York: Harper & Row.

Mosborg, S. (2002). Speaking of history: How adolescents use their knowledge of history in reading the daily news. *Cognition and Instruction, 20*, 323–358.

Myerhoff, B. (1978). *Number our days.* New York: Dutton.

Peshkin, A. (1986). *God's choice: The total world of a fundamentalist Christian school.* Chicago: University of Chicago Press.

Peshkin, A. (1988). In search of subjectivity: One's own. *Educational Researcher, 17*(7), 17–21.

Richardson, L. (1994). Writing: A method of inquiry. In N. K. Denzin & Y. S. Lincoln (Eds.), *Handbook of qualitative research* (pp. 516–529). Thousand Oaks, CA: Sage.

Roman, L. G. (1993). Double exposure: the politics of feminist materialist ethnography. *Educational Theory, 43*, 279–308.

Schweber, S. A. (2004). *Making sense of the Holocaust: Lessons from classroom practice.* New York: Teachers College Press.

Schweber, S. A. (under review). "Breaking down barriers" or "building strong Christians": Reflexive affirmation and the abnegation of history. *Theory and Research in Social Education.*

Schweber, S. A. (in press). "Fundamentally 9/11: The mechanics of collective memory in a fundamentalist Christian school." *American Journal of Education.*

Schweber, S. A., & Irwin, R. (2003). "Especially special": Learning about Jews in a fundamentalist Christian school, *Teachers College Record, 105*, 1693–1719.

Shapiro, M. (1990). Another example of "Minhag America." *Judaism, 39*, 148–154.

Seixas, P. (1993) Historical understanding among adolescents in a multicultural setting. *Curriculum Inquiry, 23*, 301–327.

VanSledright, B. A. (1995). The teaching-learning interaction in American history: A study of two teachers and their fifth graders. *Journal of Social Studies Research, 19*, 3–23.

VanSledright, B., & Brophy, J. (1995). "Storytellers," "scientists" and "reformers" in the teaching of U.S. history to fifth graders: Three teachers, three approaches. In J. Brophy (Ed.), *Advances in research on teaching: Vol 5. Learning and teaching elementary subjects.* (pp. 195–243). Greenwich, CT: JAI Press.

Walkerdine, V. (1990) *Schoolgirl fictions.* London: Verso.

Wellen Levine, S. (2003). *Mystics, mavericks and merrymakers: An intimate journey among Hasidic girls.* New York: New York University Press.

Wineburg, S. (2001). *Historical thinking and other unnatural acts: Charting the future of teaching the past.* Philadelphia: Temple University Press.

CHAPTER 7

COMPARATIVE AND INTERNATIONAL SOCIAL STUDIES RESEARCH

Carole L. Hahn

For years, reviews of research in social studies education, and presentations of research on social studies at annual conferences of the American Educational Research Association (AERA) and the National Council for the Social Studies (NCSS), focused on studies conducted in the United States. Recently that situation has begun to change. Today researchers in social studies education recognize that they can gain rich insights from comparative studies conducted in varied national contexts. Such research may be referred to as international (in which phenomena are studied in more than one country or simply outside the researcher's or reader's home country), cross-national (in which the same questions are asked of samples in different countries), or comparative (in which authors deliberately draw conclusions about how phenomena are similar and different across different settings, regions, or national contexts).[1] In the current era of globalization, such comparative international research is growing, as evidenced by recent meetings of NCSS, AERA, and the Comparative and International Education Society (CIES).

Conducting and interpreting comparative international research requires attention to a number of issues that may not arise with research within one's own country or that take on new meaning in a cross-national

Research Methods in Social Studies Education, pages 139–157

arena. In this chapter I address some of those issues in terms of their applicability to research in social studies education. I begin by reflecting on the advantages of doing comparative international research. Then I draw on my own experiences with two cross-national studies, and to a lesser extent research by others, to illustrate issues related to country selection, insider/outsider perspectives, sampling/site selection, and language. It is my hope that consideration of these issues will prove useful to individuals as they plan studies and to readers or consumers of comparative, cross-national, and international research.

RATIONALE

Why do comparative research, and why study social studies from a comparative and international perspective? There are probably as many answers to that question as there are scholars conducting comparative research. Some answers focus on advantages to scholarship, policy, and practice; others focus on advantages to individuals who engage in such work. Arnove and Torres (2003) identify scientific, pragmatic, and international understanding goals of comparative education. The scientific goal is to contribute to theory building and the formulation of generalizable propositions; comparative research enables scholars to look at the world as if it were a natural laboratory to view the multiple ways in which societal factors, educational policies, and classroom practices may vary and interact. From this perspective, both qualitative and quantitative researchers are interested in determining what happens under particular conditions or in differing contexts. For example, comparative international studies have contributed to knowledge about the role of controversial issues discussions in social studies classes in different national contexts and the relationships between such discussions and student knowledge and attitudes (Hahn, 1998; Torney, Oppenheim, & Farnen, 1975; Torney-Purta, Lehmann, Oswald, & Schulz, 2001).

The pragmatic goal of comparative educational research emphasizes finding effective policies and practices in one place that might address problems or contribute to improved solutions at home. The process of such study and transfer has been referred to as "borrowing" and "lending" in comparative education. In the 1970s many elementary social studies educators in the United States "borrowed" ideas about child-centered teaching practices that were used in Britain. At about the same time, the curriculum project *Man: A Course of Study*, which was developed in the United States, was widely adopted in Australia.

The third goal of studying education using a comparative international approach, according to Arnove and Torres (2003), is to contribute to international understanding and peace. Comparative studies enable educators at all levels (primary, secondary, and tertiary or higher education) to educate their students about the causes, dynamics, and outcomes of transnational forces and actors. Arnove and Torres argue that such understanding is a key to reducing international tensions and promoting peace. Comparative studies in social studies education might contribute to this goal by enhancing teacher education, as well as by improving curriculum and instruction in elementary and secondary social studies classrooms.

Kubow and Fossum (2003) argue that a primary benefit of comparative inquiry is that it can lead educators, and their students, to broaden their conceptual lenses as they view similar issues in diverse national settings. In the process, educators are able to see issues anew in their home contexts for the purpose of informing their decision making. For example, as I studied education for citizenship in countries without a tradition of separation of church and state, I observed students learning much about the diverse religious traditions and viewpoints within their societies. I became aware of the missed opportunity when social studies classes in the United States omit or avoid topics and perspectives related to religion. Since then, when addressing the topic of multicultural perspectives on social studies, I give more attention to teaching about a religiously plural society (within the Supreme Court guidelines for such study) than I did previously.

For me, three benefits of doing comparative international research have been personally rewarding. First, I have found that by doing comparative research I have learned much about the cultures in which education is embedded. In a sense, education serves as a window to a society, revealing particular histories and cultural values. From 1986 until 1993 I conducted a five-nation study, titled *Becoming Political: Comparative Perspectives on Citizenship Education* (Hahn, 1998). I combined qualitative and quantitative methodology as I administered questionnaires to students, observed classroom instruction, and interviewed teachers and students. During my years of visiting schools and talking to educators in Denmark, England, Germany, and the Netherlands, as well as in different parts of the United States, I learned a great deal about the cultural and political histories of the countries and how their citizens view contemporary events.

Whether debriefing the nightly news, observing classes like social studies in the United States, or trying to understand the results from student questionnaires, my international colleagues and "informants" in my study were constantly teaching me about their cultures. For example, I remember Ms. De Vries, a teacher in the Netherlands, explaining to me that the Dutch prefer to have court cases decided by judges who are appointed for their knowledge and wisdom rather than rely on ill-informed judgments of a jury of peers. In another instance, a British colleague explained that the British parliamentary system was more efficient and responsive to the public than was the U.S. system of "checks and balances." He reasoned that a parliamentary majority could pass legislation that would be implemented by the government led by the same party, whereas the U.S. system often resulted in "gridlock." German colleagues described their long tradition of defining citizenship by blood (*jus sanguinis*, nationality by descent) rather than by birthplace (*jus soli*, by the soil) and why they were, thus, reluctant to ease the naturalization process. Additionally, German colleagues explained to me that because of their experiences with Nazism, they would not give anti-democratic groups the same rights to free speech, press, and assembly as democratic ones.

In addition to learning about differing cultural values, I also observed culture traits that are prevalent in schools in different countries. In Denmark it is customary for students to call teachers by their first names; in England students write their daily homework and in-class assignments in small exercise books; and in Germany students raise their hands and click their fingers to be recognized. For me, as a social studies educator, each day observing in a classroom and each conversation talking to colleagues is a fascinating opportunity to learn more about the rich diversity of the world's cultures and at the same time I recognize much that is familiar across national contexts.

To me a second advantage of studying social studies—or any other aspect of education—comparatively is to appreciate the extent to which we are part of a global profession. Talking with colleagues who prepare teachers of elementary social studies or high school history, observing teachers as they lead discussions of current world events with their students, and debating how to word items with researchers from other countries, I recognize that we share many common interests. Our vocabulary, priorities, and contexts differ—yet we are all committed to improving the education of citizens-in-the-making.

I became increasingly aware of being part of a global profession when I was carrying out my five-nation study and when I was part of the international research team that worked on the Civic Education Study (CivEd) of the International Association for the Evaluation of Educational Achievement (better known as IEA). In the IEA CivEd study, national research coordinators (NRCs) from approximately 30 countries met annually with an international planning committee to design and execute a two-phase study (Torney-Purta et al., 2001; Torney-Purta, Schwille, & Amadeo, 1999). In discussions about how best to assess students' knowledge and attitudes related to citizenship, it was apparent to me that colleagues from countries as diverse as Australia, Slovenia, Hong Kong, and Israel shared common interests and challenges. It is little wonder that many NRCs from the study remain friends years after its completion. Today, email enables virtual communities of social studies researchers to stay in touch with one another and there are increasingly frequent conferences that enable members of our global profession to meet face-to-face.

The third advantage I have experienced in doing comparative research is benefiting from the new insight one gains by considering alternatives to present practice in one's home country and from seeing previously taken-for-granted practices with fresh eyes. Comparative studies, thus, serve as a mirror reflecting back on one's own cultural context, as well as a window to others' cultures. In my own experience, I learned how Danish students held weekly class meetings to resolve classroom problems, plan class trips, and advise the student council; in the process, I observed children acquiring skills and attitudes of democratic citizenship. In visits to English schools, I saw children learning much about their multifaith society. Recognizing that the practices I observed in Danish and English schools grew out of the history and culture of those countries and would not fit directly into schools in the United States, my observations led me to imagine ways in which our students might benefit from opportunities for decision making and multicultural learning that included school democracy and recognition of religious cultures. My point is that one would not conduct international social studies research to get ideas that could be directly adopted in local schools, because the cultural context in which a practice is embedded is important to its success. However, one can gain insights into potential alternatives to existing practices that would be culturally compatible. As Kubow and Fossum (2003) emphasize, a greater awareness and understanding of the complexities of educational issues and of the processes of educational reform in various nations can foster thoughtful, informed educational practice in each nation. I turn now from reflections on the potential advantages in conducting and using comparative international studies to consideration of four issues that arise in doing and critically reading such research.

ISSUES IN COMPARATIVE
AND INTERNATIONAL RESEARCH

All researchers must address the issues of population and sample selection, but there are particular aspects to be considered in international comparative studies. Additionally, comparative researchers need to consider the role of cultural insiders and outsiders and how to handle issues related to language and translation. As social studies scholars interpret international research and as they plan their own international studies, they will need to attend carefully to these issues.

Country Selection

The first issue to address in undertaking comparative research is selection of countries that are appropriate for studying one's research question. There should be a logical rationale as to why particular countries are the focus of the study. The cases should be comparable in relevant ways while at the same time providing sufficient diversity to enable one to see what differences particular policies or practices make. In reality, most of us conduct research in countries where we are able to gain access. For example, I began my European study with the assistance of colleagues I met at international conferences. Barton (2001a, 2001b) undertook research in Northern Ireland because his wife was interested in conducting research there and his child could attend a local school (K. C. Barton, personal communication, April 10, 2005). Levstik studied children's ideas about history and citizenship in Ghana with the help of a doctoral student who lived in the country (Levstik & Groth, 2005). However, having contacts alone is not sufficient reason to do a comparative study. It is important to be able to give thoughtful justifications to answer the question, "Why these countries?"

In my study of citizenship education, I conducted research in five countries that are generally classified as "Western democracies"—England, Denmark, Germany, the Netherlands, and the United States. They have civic cultures that value individual rights and limited government. They are all economically "developed" and all have had universal suffrage for almost a century. I also selected countries as sites for my study because they had very different traditions with regard to the school's role in preparing citizens. Additionally, educators' approach to a subject like "social studies" (or its equivalent) varied considerably across these countries.

For example, in England there was a tradition of skepticism toward citizenship education. At the time of my research, there was little expectation that schools should prepare young people for citizenship (although that has since changed with legislation requiring all schools to provide education for citizenship from 2002 onward). Students studied subjects including history, geography, personal and social education, and religious studies. It was rare, however, to find a school in England with a subject like social studies or a subject whose purpose was citizenship preparation.

In contrast, Danish *folkskoler*, which students attend until they are 16 years old, are required by law to model democracy. Students were expected to learn democracy by participating in class meetings and student government. In addition, students studied history and geography and a subject like "social science" that included politics, economics, sociology, and international relations. In Germany as well, following World War II schools were expected to prepare youth for their role as democratic citizens, and courses similar to social studies carried a particular responsibility for such preparation. In the Netherlands, on the other hand, policies changed every few years with respect to a low-status subject called "study of society." In the United States, in contrast, there was a long tradition of schools having a civic mission (Carnegie Corporation of New York & The Center for Information and Research on Civic Learning and Engagement, 2003). It was within this mix of similarities and differences in citizenship education that I sought insights into how schools might prepare youth to be politically interested and efficacious. I was particularly interested in looking at the role of controversial issues discussions in school in that process. Subsequent to my study, Lee has been conducting a similar study in four Chinese societies. He deliberately chose four societies with cultural similarities but differing political contexts—Hong Kong, Mainland China, Taiwan, and Singapore.

Country or case selection has been important in other comparative studies in social studies. In their comparative studies of young people's historical thinking, both Barton and Levstik conducted research in countries that not only were accessible to them but also demonstrated approaches to school history that varied from those used in the United States, and in which the perceived importance of historical events were present in contemporary society. In the United States, for example, elementary students are taught a chronological, idealized version of their nation's history, but in Northern Ireland primary-level history is taught as a way of thinking about the way of life of people in societies of the past; no common narrative is conveyed as students study about life in Roman times, Victorian Britain, and other historical periods (Barton, 2001a). In Ghana, meanwhile, history is expected not only to contribute to a sense of national unity but to honor diverse ethnic heritages and identities (Levstik & Groth, 2005).

The IEA Civic Education Study provides another model of country selection. IEA is a consortium of research organizations in approximately 50 countries. All member countries of IEA are invited to participate in studies, but each is expected to pay the costs of conducting the study in their country. This process has resulted in widely different countries participating in studies such as the Third International Mathematics and Science Study (TIMSS). In the case of the IEA CivEd Study, only countries that placed a high priority on education for democracy and that had sufficient funding available were likely to participate. Nevertheless, there is much diversity in the countries from which data were obtained.

As researchers conduct secondary analyses of the IEA data set, it is important that they consider what makes the particular countries similar and different with respect to the questions they are investigating. For example, in one study based on a secondary analysis, Torney-Purta and Amadeo (2004) looked at student and teacher data from countries in the Americas—Chile, Colombia, the United States—and those that shared cultural traditions from the Iberian Peninsula—Chile, Colombia, and Portugal. Other scholars have used the IEA data set to focus on student perceptions in post-Soviet societies, Scandinavian countries, and countries that are members of the European Union (Steiner-Khamsi, Torney-Purta, & Schwille, 1999). Currently, colleagues and I are analyzing IEA CivEd data from three of the former British colonies, with distinctly different postcolonial experiences—Australia, Hong Kong, and the United States.

For researchers doing secondary analyses of the IEA data set, the book of case studies developed in the first phase of the study provides useful information about the context for civic education in 24 countries (Torney-Purta et al., 1999).[2] That can serve as an important starting point in gathering information about similarities and differences across particular countries to be examined in the secondary analysis. Several other books similarly contain useful contextual information for a variety of countries. *Diversity and Citizenship Education* (Banks, 2004), contains chapters on 12 multicultural societies, and *Citizenship Education in Asia and the Pacific* (Lee, Grossman, Kennedy, & Fairbrother, 2004) contains information on nine countries in the Asia-Pacific region.[3] These books are rich resources for helping social studies researchers think through why they might choose to investigate a question in particular countries. Once having selected countries for a particular study, another early consideration relates to the roles of cultural "insiders" and "outsiders."

Collaboration—Insider/Outsider Perspectives

In planning and interpreting comparative research it is important to deliberately consider the role of insiders and outsiders with regard to the culture or nation in which data are collected. Cultural insiders are more likely to share the meanings of participants in a study than are outsiders. However, they are also more likely to overlook much that they have taken for granted in their familiar setting. Cultural outsiders have not been socialized to cultural meanings, but they do have the advantage of coming to a setting with fresh eyes. Ideally, comparative studies will combine the strengths of both roles. That can be done in a variety of ways. In my study of citizenship education, I was an outsider trying to access participant meanings in Denmark, England, Germany, and the Netherlands. Recognizing my limitations, I spent long hours over several years in discussions with colleagues in the four European countries trying to understand what I was observing and hearing from students and teachers. Additionally, I asked my international colleagues to review drafts of chapters when I reached the writing stage.

I recall one instance in which my outsider perspective was problematic as I sought to understand findings from questionnaires I administered. One of the scales I used was the Political Confidence scale; this contained items used by previous researchers to measure students' sense of political efficacy in terms that would be meaningful to young people.[1] When I examined responses from students in the five countries in my study, scores from the Netherlands were significantly lower than scores from students in the other four countries. This puzzled me, as the Dutch students with whom I spoke did not seem any less confident or efficacious than their peers in the other countries. I asked "insiders"—students in several different Dutch schools—if they could explain the responses of their national peers. They said that the questionnaire responses made perfect sense to them. They explained that in the Netherlands, "everyone has the right to his opinion" so you would not try to persuade someone to your view. I later corroborated this explanation with adult colleagues, who agreed with the students' interpretations. They said that although they often had vigorous political discussions with friends at their local pub, the purpose was to express one's own view, not to try to persuade others to adopt the same view. This was logical in a culture that for centuries after the Reformation enabled Protestants and Catholics to live together peacefully; the tradition of "pillarization" accommodated distinct religious and political groups, or pillars of society. Although pillarization has eroded in recent years, the residual effects were apparently internalized by the young people who completed my questionnaires. The meaning of their responses would have eluded an outsider such as myself without the help of insiders' perspectives.

Similarly, Barton (personal communication, April 10, 2005) recalled that as he interviewed children in Northern Ireland regarding their ideas about history, he was puzzled by the fact that they never mentioned national history or heroes, as they inevitably did in the United States, and as he expected them to do in a setting such as Northern Ireland, where national history is so contentious. As an outsider, Barton did not initially recognize the extent to which adult perspectives on history differed from those of children; U.S. children learn national history from an early age, but in Northern Ireland the topic is too controversial for the settings in which children most frequently encounter the past, such as schools and museums. Only after several months of fieldwork did he begin to overcome his outsider's perspective and start to hear the pattern in students' responses—namely, that they thought history was a way of learning about historic societies that were different from their own (Barton, 2001b).

There are advantages as well as disadvantages to an outsider's perspective. An outsider sees phenomena that are taken for granted by participants, in the sense that a fish might not be aware of water or humans of the air they breathe. As I visited schools in different parts of Germany, I was struck by a frequent pedagogical approach that teachers used. I observed many lessons in which teachers asked students to explain advantages and disadvantages of a particular policy, or the arguments for and against a policy. For example, I saw one teacher near Hannover lead a discussion of whether the voting age in local elections should be lowered from age 18 to 16 as students debated the pro and contra positions. In other schools I observed students explaining arguments for and against changing asylum laws and for funding national parks. When I asked teachers about this strategy, they seemed surprised; it was just something they did. When I probed, several teachers said perhaps it was a legacy of the 1970s when many of them went through teacher preparation programs.

In other countries I also observed teachers using instructional methods that were so natural to them they seemed not to be aware that they used them. In Denmark, teachers often assigned students to do research and write essays in which they described alternative policies to some controversial issue. Again, teachers were not consciously aware that they did this. When I probed, the teachers gave various explanations for this taken-for-granted approach: examination questions ask students to exhibit this skill; such an approach is the predominant method used in social science; it is the Danish way to consider alternatives (one referred to Hamlet's ambiguity, "to be or not to be"); and many teachers were products of the 1960s student protests that challenged authority. In England, I consistently noticed that teachers ended a lesson by having students write a paragraph or two in their exercise books. When I asked where they learned to do this, teachers were not aware that they had. However, as an outsider to a pedagogical culture that places such a high value on writing, this technique was quite visible to me.

Finally, doing comparative research helps one "make the familiar strange," as anthropologists seek to do. After having observed classroom instruction in other countries, I saw with fresh eyes how many American social studies teachers worry about motivating students and use a variety of instructional techniques to engage students. A German colleague who brought a group of educators to an NCSS conference told me that the German teachers were troubled by the many sessions in which teachers seemed to be more interested in making social studies fun than in challenging students. Clearly, outsiders and insiders view the same phenomena somewhat differently. For this reason, some researchers deliberately plan to use research teams that can draw on both insider and outsider perspectives.

For the large-scale IEA study, an international steering committee posed common questions to be answered across countries in the first phase of the study. It was left to research teams in each country to gather primarily qualitative data to develop case studies of civic education (Torney-Purta et al., 1999). The case studies were thus written from an insider's perspective, and they were subsequently used as the basis for developing common questionnaires to be administered cross-nationally in the second phase of the study. The international steering committee and the national research coordinators reviewed draft questionnaires before they were administered. A team of international researchers analyzed the quantitative data and wrote the official international reports (Amadeo, Torney-Purta, Lehmann, Husfeldt, & Nikolova, 2002; Torney-Purta et al., 2001). NRCs, as insiders, had the opportunity to review drafts of the final reports written by outsiders. NRCs also conducted national analyses and produced national reports. (See e.g., Baldi, Perie, Skidmore, Greenberg, & Hahn, 2001; Kerr, Lines, Blenkinsop, & Schagen 2002; Mellor, Kennedy, & Greenwood, 2002.)

In two other studies related to social studies, teams of researchers in different countries collected parallel data within their respective countries. Cogan organized a team of educational researchers from nine countries to ascertain opinion leaders' views of future global issues and how schools might prepare youth to address those issues (Cogan & Derricott, 2000).[5] In a series of international meetings, the researchers collaboratively decided on the content and method for their research. Together they met to interpret the results obtained from a Delphi process, in which opinion leaders responded to questionnaires in an iterative process. In another study, Fouts organized a team of researchers from five countries to plan and carry out a study of civic educators in their respective settings (Lee & Fouts, 2005).[6] In both these studies, researchers from different countries came together to decide on items for questionnaires and interviews. They then administered questionnaires and conducted interviews in their first language and shared their results in English with the international research team. Members of the collaborative research team thus served as insiders for interpreting data from their country and outsiders when looking at results from other countries.

Clearly, there are various models for using insiders' and outsiders' perspectives to enhance data collection and interpretation in comparative and international studies. Whether one is planning a study or reading one, the advantages and disadvantages of the approach used should be considered. Equally important are reflections related to site or sample selection, as I discuss in the next section.

Site or Sample Selection and Generalizability of Findings

Decisions about where and from whom to collect data are never easy; they are considerably more complicated when one is conducting international research. Obtaining nationally representative samples is particularly difficult and expensive. That is why the IEA CivEd data set is a valuable resource for social studies researchers to use for secondary analyses. For IEA studies there are rigorous standards that the participating countries must meet in their sample selection. For the U.S. portion of the IEA study, for example, an independent contractor drew a nationally representative sample of schools that contained a ninth grade. Within the 124 selected schools, an intact class of ninth graders was randomly selected. If social studies was a required course for ninth graders, then the class was selected from the available social studies classes. If social studies was an elective or not taught to ninth graders, then another required course (such as English) or a homeroom was used. In addition, up to three ninth-grade social studies teachers in the same schools were asked to complete a questionnaire. (See Baldi et al., 2001, for further details.) Consequently, it is important to realize that in the IEA study, although a nationally representative sample of ninth graders was assessed, the teacher sample was not representative of social studies teachers.

An advantage of using data sets like the IEA CivEd study is that it is appropriate to generalize the findings to the national population of students from which the sample of respondents was drawn. A limitation is that the only information about the contexts in which sample students lived and attended school is that which was obtained in background questionnaires administered to students and school personnel. The case studies from the first phase of the IEA study provide important information about the national context for civic education, but they do not give contextual information about the specific schools in which student and teacher data were collected.

In contrast, most social studies researchers who conduct comparative studies use samples of convenience or purposefully selected sites. In my five-nation study, I tried to select schools in different geographic regions of each country. In addition, I purposefully selected schools to represent different school types in each country—such as state schools and independent schools (called "Public" schools) in England, and *Realshulen, Gymnasium,* and *Gesamtshulen* in Germany. In Germany, however, I was unable to include *Hauptshulen,* which tend to serve the least academically successful secondary school students and those from immigrant and low-income families. The fact that such schools in Germany were not included in my study was a limitation; however, in the other countries, I also tended not to have access to the lowest track of students within comprehensive schools. Because the students I interviewed and who completed questionnaires were not nationally representative, I tried to be very careful in writing my results to emphasize that I could not generalize to all youth in the country; I could only speak about the Danish, Dutch, British and other students *in my study.* Similarly, as people conduct secondary analyses of teacher data in the IEA study, it is important that they speak about teacher respondents in the study, rather than generalize to all civic-related teachers in any given country.

Qualitative researchers are trained to provide rich, thick descriptions of the context for their studies, to make explicit their criteria for purposeful selection of sites, and to be careful about not generalizing beyond their particular cases. However, when one collects qualitative data in international studies it is often tempting to generalize to others in the country— just as it is tempting to generalize from samples of convenience used in quantitative studies. Social studies researchers need to resist these temptations as we plan and use results from comparative studies. It is particularly important for researchers to give as much detail as they can about the specific contexts in which they collected their information. Hopefully, as cases accumulate over time, future researchers will be able to do cross-case analyses from different countries.

Ironically, one of the issues that presents the greatest challenge to comparative researchers is the one that scholars write the least about—language. In the next section I discuss several aspects of that issue that are important to both those who conduct international research and those who are consumers of such research.

Language and Translation

Ideally, comparative researchers would be fluent in the languages of the countries in which they conduct their studies. However, for many monolingual researchers that is not possible. Even multilingual scholars find themselves in the position of conducting research in countries they did not anticipate they would be visiting when they took foreign language classes in school. Furthermore, it would be unfortunate if international studies were limited to including only French-speaking countries, Chinese speaking countries, or some other language group. Consequently, translation is often an important issue.

Translation is not merely a process of substituting words or phrases. Researchers want to capture similar meanings in different contexts. In my five-nation study, I hired professional translators to translate questionnaires that I had developed. Then, I sat down with English-speaking colleagues in each country who were knowledgeable about education for citizenship and subjects similar to social studies. I asked them to hold the Dutch/Danish/German version of the questionnaire in front of them as they back-translated items for me into English. In the process, my colleagues and I caught many points at which another phrase would more appropriately capture the idea I intended. I recall extensive discussions among several political educators in Germany about which words or phrases would be most appropriate.

In the IEA study, draft questionnaires were similarly translated and back-translated. Copies of the English version of the IEA CivEd questionnaire are available on the project website (www.wam.umd.edu/~iea/) and translated versions of the questionnaire can be obtained from some of the national research coordinators. Because the IEA CivEd questionnaires were subjected to a rigorous process of quality control, they are especially useful for researchers planning studies with other populations.

If one is conducting structured or semi-structured interviews, the interview protocol should be similarly translated and back-translated—even if translators are used in the interview itself. This advice also applies to studies in countries such as Australia, Canada, the United Kingdom, and the United States, where people speak different variations of the same language. The British version of my questionnaire, for example, needed to ask if students thought they might "stand" for political office some day, rather than "run" for office as citizens might in the United States—just one of numerous examples of nations being divided by a common language, in George Bernard Shaw's famous characterization. Similarly, I had the pleasure of working with the team planning a study similar to mine in four Chinese societies. It was fascinating to watch researchers from Taiwan, Singapore, Hong Kong, and Mainland China debate about the best translations for concepts in Cantonese and Mandarin/Putonghau.

No matter what we do, we will not be able to capture the exact same meanings across national or other contexts. But there is much that we can do to ensure that we are coming as close as possible, if our intent is to make comparisons about social studies and other aspects of education across national cultures.

CONCLUSION

I believe that scholarship, policy, and practice would benefit if we had more comparative and international studies in social studies education and related fields. I also believe that individual scholars would find such research personally rewarding, as they learn about diverse cultures, feel part of a global profession, and see their own work with fresh insight. As scholars undertake international studies and as teachers and students read the findings from such research, I hope they will give particular attention to the four issues I have discussed here. I hope they will consider the rationale for examining questions in particular countries and reflect on the roles of cultural insiders and outsiders. Additionally, I hope researchers will make explicit their process of site and sample selection and be careful not to generalize beyond their participants unless representative samples are randomly sampled from a wider population. Finally, it is important that social studies researchers give careful attention to issues of language and translation as they undertake cross-national studies. In addition to these issues, which I have discussed in this chapter, other factors may inhibit some scholars from exploring their research interests internationally.

The first of these is expense. Certainly studies such as those conducted by IEA are expensive, and national governments have been less willing to spend scarce resources on civic or social studies education research than they have been in the areas of science and mathematics. However, in recent years there has been a growing interest in education for democracy in many nations. I am hopeful this will lead to more large-scale studies that can be used in social studies education.

For single scholars seeking to investigate research questions in more than one country, there are barriers of time, cost, and language to overcome. With determination and persistence, however, these can be addressed. Barton, Levstik, and I used sabbatical leaves from our universities to enable us to spend extended time in other national contexts. I continue to use my summer "vacation" to visit schools in countries that are in session during North American summer months. The Fullbright programs for teachers and professors have enabled other social studies scholars to conduct research cross-nationally during the summer, as well as during the academic year. Studies that use teams of researchers to collect data in their own countries enable researchers to work within their academic calendars.

International studies incur greater expenses—associated with questionnaire development, administration or transcription of interviews, and observations—than those set within a single nation or culture. In addition, they may require added expenses for translation assistance, airfare, and living abroad. Increasingly, in their efforts to become global centers of scholarship, many universities have competitive programs to support international scholarship. In addition, a number of granting agencies have been willing to support research done internationally. In my own case, I have used grants from my university's research and international programs, as well as small grants from the Spencer Foundation. Barton used grants from his university and from the German Marshall Fund of the United States to support his work. Torney-Purta and her colleagues have used grants from diverse organizations to enable them to conduct secondary analyses of the IEA data set. One advantage of doing secondary analyses is that they are far less costly than conducting the initial study. In recent years I have been doing such secondary analyses with international colleagues and graduate students without the benefit or necessity of external funding. I encourage others to use this valuable—and free—resource for further analyses (see www.iea.nl/iea/hq; CDs are also available from the international data center).

I suspect that another hurdle that may inhibit potential comparative social studies education researchers is language. I encourage individuals with dual language facility to consider doing comparative research. Gloria Contreras, a bilingual social studies scholar, has been conducting important research on citizenship education in Texas, Mexico, and Chile. Greg Fairbrother's facility with Putonghua has enabled him to do research on patriotic and civic education in China and Hong Kong. Other scholars take refresher language courses in adult education programs in their community or enroll in language courses at their university. I joined Emory University freshmen and sophomores to take introductory courses in German, and I joined undergraduates in our summer abroad program in Vienna (although I must confess I was a slower learner than the 20-year-olds). Earlier in this chapter I discussed several examples of research teams in which researchers collected data in their first languages. That may be the most widely used approach to dealing with multilingual studies in the future, as social studies educators meet colleagues at conferences and through email communication.

I am optimistic that researchers will find ways to overcome challenges in doing international comparative research if they are inspired to engage in such work. It is my hope that social studies education professors will make an effort to include more comparative and international studies in methods courses for beginning teachers and in seminars for graduate students. As they encourage their students to discuss the strengths and weaknesses of such studies, I hope they will draw attention to issues of country selection, insider/outsider perspectives, sampling/site selection, and language, as I have discussed here. As the next generation of social studies education professors and teachers encounters comparative international studies, I hope that they will begin to imagine themselves engaging in comparative work.

Despite the challenges to conducting and wisely consuming research cross-nationally, the rewards to the individual and the profession are immense. But a warning is in order: Doing international research is addictive. After finishing my five-nation study, I wanted to continue doing research in the same countries, and my interest was piqued in doing similar research in other countries. My experience is not unusual—doing comparative international research is so intellectually stimulating and fun that one cannot stop. It becomes a way of life.

I hope this chapter will inspire others to start down that path. As our research "goes global," I look forward to reading about many comparative studies in future issues of social studies journals and hearing about such research at meetings of NCSS and AERA, as well as at sessions of the new special interest group on civic education of the CIES and international conferences on social studies–related themes.

NOTES

1. As Bray (1999) and others have noted, although it is possible to compare classrooms, schools, and other units both within and between countries, most of the writing in the field of comparative education has focused on cross-national comparisons of school systems. In this chapter I focus on comparisons across countries, nations, and macrocultures. Some of the recent work on citizenship education in Hong Kong, Macau, Taiwan, and Mainland China is noteworthy in making comparisons across societies that have different educational, economic, and political "systems"; these are more accurately classified as intracultural or intranational, rather than international, comparative studies, yet the principles I discuss here would apply.

2. The countries that are included are Australia, Belgium (French), Bulgaria, Canada, Colombia, Cyprus, the Czech Republic, England, Finland, Germany, Greece, Hong Kong SAR, Hungary, Israel, Italy, Lithuania, Netherlands, Poland, Portugal, Romania, Russia, Slovenia, Switzerland, and the United States. However, Canada, Israel, and the Netherlands did not participate in Phase 2 of the IEA CivEd study; consequently, there are no quantitative data from their students. Chile, Denmark, Latvia, Finland, Norway, the Slovak Republic, and Sweden were added in Phase 2.

3. The countries included in the Banks (2004) collection, organized regionally, are Canada, the United States, South Africa, Brazil, England, Germany, Russia, Israel, Palestine, Japan, China, and India; chapters in Lee et al. (2004) deal with various aspects of education in Indonesia, Hong Kong, Taiwan, mainland China, Singapore, Malaysia, South Korea, the Solomon Islands, and Vanatu.

4. Items on the Political Confidence scale were: "I am able to influence decisions in groups"; "Although it is not the most popular thing to do, I can often get my way in groups"; "I am the kind of person who is able to influence others in decision-making situations"; "I am the kind of person who can influence how other people decide to vote in elections"; "I can convince others to support candidates I am supporting for in elections"; "If I joined a political (party) organization, I would be the kind of member who is able to change people's minds on important issues"; "I can usually persuade others to agree with my opinions about political matters"; and "I can be effective in political situations."

5. The research team collected data from opinion leaders in England and Wales, Germany, Greece, Hungary, the Netherlands, Canada, the United States, Japan, and Thailand.

6. Teachers in Australia, China, England, Russia, and the United States were assessed for their perceptions of education for citizenship.

REFERENCES

Amadeo, J. A., Torney-Purta, J., Lehmann, R., Husfeldt, V., & Nikolova, R. (2002). *Civic knowledge and engagement: An IEA study of upper secondary students in sixteen countries.* Amsterdam: International Association for the Evaluation of Educational Achievement.

Arnove, R. F., & Torres, C. A. (2003). *Comparative education: The dialectic of the global and the local.* Lanham, MD: Rowman & Littlefield.

Baldi, S., Perie, M., Skidmore, D., Greenberg, E., & Hahn, C. (2001). *What democracy means to ninth-graders: U.S. results from the international IEA civic education study.* Washington, DC: U.S. Department of Education. Retrieved July 8, 2005, from http://nces.ed.gov/surveys/cived

Banks, J. A. (2004). *Diversity and citizenship education: Global perspectives.* San Francisco: Jossey-Bass.

Barton, K. C. (2001a). A sociocultural perspective on children's understanding of historical change: Comparative findings from Northern Ireland and the United States. *American Educational Research Journal, 38,* 881–913.

Barton, K. C. (2001b). "You'd be wanting to know about the past": Social contexts of children's historical understanding in Northern Ireland and the United States. *Comparative Education, 37,* 89–106.

Bray, M. (1999). Methodology and focus in comparative education. In M. Bray & R. Koo (Eds.), *Education and society in Hong Kong and Macau: Comparative perspectives on continuity and change* (pp. 209–223). Hong Kong: Comparative Education Research Centre, University of Hong Kong.

Carnegie Corporation of New York, & The Center for Information and Research on Civic Learning and Engagement. (2003). *The civic mission of the schools.* New York: Carnegie Corporation of New York.

Cogan, J., & Derricott, R. (Eds.) (2000). *Citizenship for the 21st century: An international perspective on education.* London: Kogan-Page.

Hahn, C. L. (1998). *Becoming political: Comparative perspectives on citizenship education.* Albany: State University of New York Press.

Kerr, D., Lines, A., Blenkinsop, S., & Schagen, I. (2002). *England's results from the IEA international citizenship study: What citizenship and education mean to 14 year olds.* Nottingham, UK: Department for Education and Skills.

Kubow, P. K., & Fossum, P. R. (2003). *Comparative education: Exploring issues in international context.* Upper Saddle River, NJ: Merrill Prentice Hall.

Lee, W. O., & Fouts, J. T. (Eds.). (2005). *Education for social citizenship: Perceptions of teachers in the USA, Australia, England, Russia, and China.* Hong Kong: Hong Kong University Press.

Lee, W. O., Grossman, D. L., Kennedy, K. K., & Fairbrother, G. P. (2004). *Citizenship education in Asia and the Pacific: Concepts and issues.* Hong Kong: Kluwer Academic.

Levstik, L. S., & Groth, J. (2005). "Ruled by our own people": Ghanaian adolescents' conceptions of citizenship. *Teachers College Record, 107,* 563–586.

Mellor, S., Kennedy, K., & Greenwood, L. (2001). *Citizenship and democracy: Australian students' knowledge and beliefs.* Camberwell, Australia: Australian Council for Educational Research.

Steiner-Khamsi, G., Torney-Purta, J., & Schwille, J. (1999). *New paradigms and recurring paradoxes in education for citizenship.* Amsterdam: Elsevier Press.

Torney, J., Oppenheim, A., & Farnen, R. (1975). *Civic education in ten countries.* New York: Wiley. (ERIC Document Reproduction Service No. ED132059)

Torney-Purta, J., & Amadeo, J.-A. (2004). *Strengthening democracy in the Americas through civic education.* Washington, DC: Organization of American States.

Torney-Purta, J., Lehmann, R., Oswald, H., & Schulz, W. (2001). *Citizenship and education in twenty eight countries: Civic knowledge and engagement at age fourteen.* Amsterdam: International Association for the Evaluation of Educational Achievement. Retrieved July 8, 2005, from http://www.wam.umd.edu/~iea/.

Torney-Purta, J., Schwille, J., & Amadeo, J.A. (1999). *Civic education across countries: Twenty four national case studies from the IEA civic education project.* Amsterdam: International Association for the Evaluation of Educational Achievement. (ERIC Document Reproduction Service No. ED431705

CHAPTER 8

COMBINING COGNITIVE INTERVIEWS AND SOCIAL SCIENCE SURVEYS

Strengthening Interpretation and Design

Wendy K. Richardson

Much of what we know about students' knowledge and attitudes in social studies is based on responses to survey questions. Since we can not directly observe students' thinking, this is one important way to begin to understand the process by which students acquire knowledge and develop attitudes. Researchers can make more informed interpretations of survey results if they understand how students' interpretation of survey items (or their beliefs about a particular topic) influence the ways in which they respond. Social studies educators may find that they gravitate toward qualitative research because such methods provide a descriptive glimpse of classroom practices about which educators have personal experience and might offer more direct advice about how to improve instruction. However, survey methodology is likely to remain valuable because it is an efficient way of collecting information (in cost and other respects) from representative samples, and these offer greater generalizability to larger populations than non-representative samples. Furthermore, surveys maintain the privacy of respondents.

Research Methods in Social Studies Education, pages 159–181
Copyright © 2006 by Information Age Publishing
All rights of reproduction in any form reserved.

This chapter examines what research in cognition has to offer to our understanding of students' thinking when responding to surveys, ways in which surveys help/don't help us uncover this thinking, and how other methodologies can help improve researchers' use and interpretation of surveys. The development of survey items is a time-consuming and often expensive endeavor. Therefore many researchers are likely to use or adapt items developed for studies with other purposes. In this case, use of cognitive interviews can enrich interpretations that researchers make about quantitative results of their own studies using preexisting survey items, and such interviews can improve revisions to the items researchers select to use. Although particularly useful for interpreting survey results, cognitive interviews can also contribute to the body of knowledge about students' understanding of social studies concepts.

To illustrate the contributions possible from combining cognitive interviews and survey results, this chapter presents findings from a study I conducted using retrospective cognitive interviews as a tool for improving my understanding of results from a statistical analysis using a previously developed survey. A brief overview of the original design of the International Association for the Evaluation of Educational Achievement (IEA) survey is presented, followed by details about my follow-up study and relevant items from the IEA instrument, as well as a discussion of potential issues complicating interpretation that remained as a result of the survey design. My use of the cognitive interview as a post-hoc interpretative tool was exploratory. My study differed from the typical application of cognitive psychology to surveys in that mine was not intended to be a study of cognitive processes used by students but rather aimed to gather additional information about the student experiences measured by the survey items, and to improve my understanding of what the statistical results represented in order to better relate them to the needs of social studies educators and researchers.

THE INFLUENCE OF COGNITIVE PSYCHOLOGY ON SURVEY METHODLOGY IN SOCIAL SCIENCE RESEARCH

There are a number of ways in which cognitive psychology has influenced survey research methods in social studies, such as having students think aloud as they respond to survey items to identify potential problems with question wording. The theories and research behind methodologies such as these are probably less familiar than their application to research. This section provides a brief overview of the interaction of cognitive psychology and survey methodology and examines the use of one method (cognitive interviews) as a way to enhance what we can learn from surveys.

Since the 1950s, most attempts to improve survey research have focused on sampling errors—that is, problems resulting from making generalizations about a population from a sample. The application of cognitive psychology to survey design represents a departure from this approach and focuses instead on response effects, or problems resulting from the ways in which a respondent interprets and responds to survey questions (Tourganeau, Rips, & Rasinski, 2000). Certain aspects of cognitive psychology, such as memory structures, access to prior knowledge, and language, are especially relevant to this focus on response effects.

Information processing theories in cognitive psychology represent efforts to understand how humans obtain, retain, and use information (Bjorklund, 2000). Attention is paid in these theories to sensory input, short- and long-term memory, representation of knowledge in memory, and access to memories. Because a major purpose of surveys is to obtain information that is unattainable by direct observation, these theories provide a useful tool for considering how best to design surveys to obtain the desired information. For example, providing respondents with rating scales with all the categories labeled can improve the accuracy and consistency of their answers. When asked to recall the frequency of a particular behavior, respondents may use various methods, such as counting or estimation, and this may lead to different response patterns.

Theories in cognitive psychology have primarily been used in pretesting survey items to identify and uncover potential problems with question wording. But they also have been used to develop theories about the process respondents use to answer questions. Although there is no clear consensus about any one model of the processes used in survey response, Tourangeau and colleagues (2000) offer a conceptual framework that contains elements common in many other theories. Their model of the response process contains four major components: *comprehension* of the item, *retrieval* of relevant information, use of the information to make the required *judgment*, and the *response* (selection and reporting of an answer). Unlike information processing theories, the four parts of this model are not intended to be serial in nature. For example, respondents may believe they comprehend an item and therefore go on to retrieve appropriate information from memory, but when faced with the survey response choices, they may need to reconsider their comprehension if none of the choices fit the memory they have selected.

Cognitive interviews have been the main technique used to evaluate the response process. Ericsson and Simon (1993) first used the technique as a way to uncover the thinking of experts during problem-solving tasks. As originally conceived, a cognitive interview (also referred to as a think-aloud protocol or verbal protocol) asks a respondent to think aloud while performing a certain task. The objective is to capture the thinking process of the respondent *as it happens.*

In the area of social studies, various forms of cognitive interviews have been applied to research on historical thinking and problem solving. The tasks included as part of these protocols have most often asked respondents to think aloud as they read historical texts (VanSledright & Afflerbach, 2000; Wineburg, 1991), compare evidence or clues about different historical situations (Lee, Ashby, & Dickinson, 1996), or solve social science problems (Torney-Purta, 1992; Voss, Tyler, & Yengo, 1983). Even though cognitive interviews are probably used informally in the design of surveys in social studies, such efforts have not been the focus of significant research.

Criticisms regarding the use of cognitive interviews, and think alouds in particular, include the degree to which verbalizing is an accurate representation of respondents' thoughts, whether the process of verbalization influences thinking, and whether interpretation of the data can be considered an objective method (Crutcher, 1994; Lee et al., 1996). Studies addressing these criticisms conclude that these factors are influenced both by the type of task involved and the method of administration of concurrent protocols (Ericsson & Simon, 1993). Similar studies addressing potential problems with nonconcurrent cognitive interviews, however, have not been conducted in social science research.

Despite increased use of cognitive interviewing strategies for the development of surveys across all fields, empirical evidence about improvements to the validity and effectiveness of survey design resulting from cognitive interviews are not well documented. The relative effects of survey design processes remain inconclusive in the few empirical comparisons of survey pretest methods that have included cognitive interviews (Lessler, Tourangeau, & Salter, 1989; Presser & Blair, 1994).

There are several challenges to studying the effectiveness of these techniques. Most prominent is that problems with a survey are not necessarily known in advance of conducting the cognitive interviews. In order to assess empirically whether the cognitive technique identified problems with items, problems would have to be purposefully incorporated into the survey. Most often, cognitive interviews generate a list of issues by item, which the designers then address based on project goals and expert review. In some cases, problems represent the verification of a suspected problem; however, in other cases the problem represents the discovery of something unanticipated, such as respondents' interpretation of a word or phrase in a manner not intended by the researchers (Willis, DeMaio, & Harris-Kojetin, 1999). For example, cognitive interviews were used to investigate suspected problems with items from the National Assessment of Educational Progress (NAEP) fourth- and eighth-grade math and science background questionnaires (Levine, Huberman, & Buckner, 2002). In that study, potential problem items were initially identified using statistical analyses of variations within a class. Items asking students about their use of calculators for homework and class work, and items about how often they discussed mathematics problems in class and with other students, were found to have the most variation within a class and were subsequently included in the cognitive interviews.

Part of the problem with evaluating the effectiveness of cognitive interviews in survey design is that the results of cognitive interviews used for pretesting of survey items are often available only to the original researchers. And even in that case, the documentation of such findings may frequently remain at the level of field notes. An exception is an early political socialization study in which the interview excerpts used in the formulation of items were extensively quoted in the book in which the statistical results of the survey appeared (Hess & Torney, 1967). It is more frequently the case that the original researchers carry some of the knowledge about problems (or respondents' interpretations) forward with them to the interpretation of findings, but the underlying assumption is that items work in a similar way for respondents in the final study as they did for those in the pilot. This may or may not be a sound assumption, and it may depend in part on the degree to which the pilot sample is similar to that of the final study.

Concurrent protocols are often considered more reliable and valid than retrospective ones, because asking respondents to recall their thinking after the task has been completed is likely to introduce changes in their reporting. However, variations on the concurrent technique provide useful information difficult to obtain by other methods. Some of the most commonly used methods are the retrospective think aloud, probes, and paraphrasing of the items (Tourangeau et al., 2000). These protocols are often referred to in the research literature using the term "think-aloud protocol," thereby blurring important distinctions between concurrent and non-concurrent methods.

Concurrent cognitive interviews are best applied to research where the main objective is to learn about the thinking process that takes place *during* task completion. In the case of social science surveys, it is probably a research method most useful to survey methodologists—those interested in understanding how participants respond to survey questions. However, many social scientists could benefit from using this technique to improve the development or revision of survey items.

Retrospective cognitive interviews could also be a useful method for survey design, because they can provide an efficient means for reviewing items. In many cases, conducting concurrent interviews can be both time- and cost-prohibitive. Furthermore, using the technique retrospectively allows researchers to use initial statistical analyses to identify items with a high level of within-class variation (see Levine et al., 2002, for an example of this approach). Conducting retrospective cognitive interviews can be a useful first step for researchers who plan to revise items originally developed for another study. A new sample of students can take the battery of items and later be interviewed about the thinking they did while completing each item.

In addition, retrospective cognitive interviews can enhance interpretations of survey findings. Because the retrospective technique already introduces a degree of distance from task completion and therefore potentially leads to reliability errors, including probing questions or paraphrasing survey items might help fulfill study objectives not possible with concurrent methods. For example, exploring participants' interpretation of concepts that are part of survey items is especially important in social studies research because such concepts might have contested meanings or multiple legitimate perspectives. In general, survey methodology has found the interpretation of attitudinal concepts to be part of the purpose for posing such questions in the first place (Tourangeau et al., 2000). While not all social science surveys contain attitudinal questions, many items asking respondents about factual information or experiences represent an intersection between recall of experiences and attitudinal concepts. For example, in asking respondents to report the frequency of their political discussion with others, respondents' attitudes about politics can influence the number of experiences they elect to include in their estimates. Interviews, although not retrospective cognitive interviews per se, have already been used successfully to learn more about students' understanding of social studies concepts (Berti & Andriolo, 2001; Brophy & Alleman, 2002).

A STUDY OF IEA CIVIC EDUCATION SURVEY RESULTS USING COGNITIVE INTERVIEWS

The use of cognitive interviews as a way of uncovering adolescents' understanding of items from the IEA instrument was part of a larger study designed to examine the relationship between political discussion and civic engagement (Richardson, 2003). Statistical analyses were conducted on the 1999 IEA sample of students from the United States to examine the degree to which the IEA items measured students' experiences with political discussion and open classroom climate for discussion, as well as the relationship of these discussion experiences to civic engagement.

The survey used was an instrument developed and administered by countries participating in the IEA Civic Education Study (Torney-Purta, Lehmann, Oswald, & Schultz, 2001). Development of the instrument included findings from case studies in more than 24 countries about core concepts of citizenship education, input from experts in participating countries, and extensive pilot testing. However, no official or explicit widespread use of cognitive interviews with 14-year-olds was a part of the pilot process (Torney-Purta, personal communication, November 4, 2004).

The instrument was administered to more than 90,000 14-year-olds in 1999–2000 in 28 countries, including the United States. The full survey instrument assessing students' understanding of democratic concepts, attitudes, and actions and 16 publicly released items from the 38-item test of knowledge of civic concepts are available at www.wam.umd.edu/~iea. Additional details about the IEA survey development are provided both in the international report (Torney-Purta et al., 2001) and a chapter of the technical report (Husfeldt & Torney-Purta, 2004).

Findings on Discussion from the 1999 IEA Study

Statistical analyses conducted using the 1999 IEA Civic Education Study data indicated associations between political discussion and civic engagement. This section provides data about student experiences with discussion from the 1999 IEA Civic Education Study across all 28 countries and for students in the U.S. sample, followed by a summary of the analysis of the relationship between discussion and civic engagement for the U.S. sample.

There are two sections of the IEA instrument that include items asking students about their experiences with political discussion. One section asked students their perception of how open their classroom is for discussion (Appendix A). Six items from this section were combined to form a scale called Open Classroom Climate. A second section asked students about their discussion of national and international politics with peers, parents, and teachers (Appendix A). Response options for both sections were 4-point scales ranging from 1 = never to 4 = often.

Although a majority of students responded on the positive side of the 4-point scales for all six items in the Open Classroom Climate scale, fewer than 40% of students across all 28 countries and fewer than 50% in the United States believed these activities happened "often" in their classroom. A simple regression model analyzing the relationship of several variables with civic knowledge and voting found that when students report a more open classroom climate they are also more likely to have higher scores on the test of civic knowledge and are more likely to believe that they will vote in the future.

Across all 28 countries fewer than 40% of students reported that they discussed what was happening in their national government or international politics "often" or "sometimes" with peers or teachers. Just over 50% of the students reported discussion with parents about these topics. In the

United States fewer than 30% report such discussion with peers, whereas close to 55% report political discussion with parents and teachers. The items about engaging in political discussion with others were not analyzed as part of the regression model for the international report (Torney-Purta et al., 2001). However, in subsequent statistical analyses, with a subset of participating countries, discussion with parents was found to have a positive association with civic engagement (Richardson & Amadeo, 2002; Torney-Purta & Richardson, 2002, 2004).

Relating Discussion to Engagement Using 1999 U.S. IEA Data

Although 28 countries participated in Phase 2 (the instrument administration and data collection) of the IEA Civic Education Study, the statistical analysis in my 2003 study was limited to the U.S. data (Richardson, 2003). A confirmatory factor analysis was modeled to evaluate the possibility of four distinct types of political discussion: discussion with peers, discussion with parents, discussion with teachers, and a classroom climate open to the discussion of different issues. With two minor changes to the model, the fit between the proposed model and the data indicated a good fit. The six items about discussion with others regarding national and international issues were combined to form three composite variables.

The relationship between these four types of political discussion and three forms of civic engagement in the 1999 U.S. IEA data were then examined using a series of hierarchical regressions, controlling for the effects of home literacy resources and gender. The statistical results found that all four types of political discussion did relate to students' reports that they were likely to engage in future conventional political activities (such as being a candidate for a local office or joining a political party). Political discussion also related to expected future social movement–related participation (e.g., volunteering to solve problems in the community). Discussion with peers, parents, and teachers also predicted higher levels of students' current participation in civic-related organizations (e.g., student council). Open classroom climate did not significantly predict students' current participation in organizations.

Drawing conclusions about the experiences with discussion represented by these analyses remained difficult. Therefore, one of the reasons it was important to learn more about how students responded to the items regarding political discussion with others and open classroom climate was to provide descriptive data about the possible meanings of the association between discussion and engagement.

Cognitive Interviews

In an effort to deepen my understanding of the statistical findings, in 2003 I administered an abbreviated version of the IEA instrument containing the discussion and engagement items to a new sample of 14-year-olds that then allowed me to interview them about thoughts they had when responding to the items (see Appendix A for the discussion items). I conducted cognitive interviews with a sample of 32 ninth-grade students (19 females, 13 males) from a high school in the Northeast in late spring 2003. Students volunteering for participation were part of a larger sample (N=80) that completed the abbreviated version of the IEA instrument, including items about political discussion with others and open classroom climate. Nearly all of the students were white (95.6%), and only a small portion qualified for free or reduced-price lunch (<5%). While the findings from these interviews should therefore not be generalized to adolescents in the United States more broadly, their responses do offer insight about how 14-year-olds think about political discussion and civic engagement and suggest potential explanations for the statistical findings from the nationally representative sample of students from the United States in the 1999 IEA data.

I developed a cognitive interview protocol that included both retrospective questions about thoughts on specific survey items and more general probes about understanding of terms and concepts that appeared in the items. (Items relevant to findings presented in this chapter can be found in Appendix B.) One or two days following the students' completion of survey items, they were asked a series of questions designed to help them elaborate on their thinking about political discussion and civic engagement germane to this study (see Appendix B). Despite the possible changes that might have occurred in students' thinking between their completion of the survey and the interview, I opted to use a retrospective cognitive interview because it allowed me to interview a larger number of students in a shorter period of time and to gain specific information about their understanding that might not have occurred if I had followed a concurrent think-aloud process.

Specifically, I intended to learn more about how adolescents interpreted the survey items about political discussion and open classroom climate and the meaning they attached to terms such as "discussion" and "politics." In order to get a broader understanding of how students experience political discussion, a few open-ended questions asked them to describe the connections they saw between political discussion and civic engagement both inside and outside the school context.

My intention here is to argue that using cognitive interviews after the administration of the final instrument, even with a different sample, can provide researchers with an understanding of response effects that may have influenced accuracy, as well as the intentions with which the students responded to the items, and can therefore lead to insights into the items' validity. Understanding response effects can aid researchers by offering possible interpretations for survey findings and could be used to improve future versions of items.

Analysis of Interview Data

Analyses of interviews began with an initial review of each transcript. Themes and categories were developed based on patterns across students' responses. In some cases these categories were limited to short, specific answers provided by students, especially for interview questions pertaining directly to students' interpretation of the survey questions (i.e., categories for frequency included "once a month" and "almost daily"). In other cases, categories were developed to capture my interpretation of the students' explanations for their responses. For example, the question that asked about whether participation in school leads to action as adults produced categories such as "model of larger community" or "experience increases probability of participation." Transcripts were reviewed a second time using these categories. Simple frequency tallies were made using the categories, and examples were selected to illustrate both student interpretations and characterizations of discussion. Some revisions were made to the categories during this second review and responses were reconsidered wherever necessary. The purpose of the interviews was to enrich the interpretation of the statistical analyses. Therefore, more rigorous evaluation of the reliability of these categories was left for future analyses.

Findings from Cognitive Interviews Related to Response Effects

Discussing Politics

An analysis of the means for the composite variables of political discussion with others about U.S. and international politics from the 1999 U.S. IEA sample found that in general most 14-year-olds "rarely" discuss politics with peers (M = 1.90, s.d. = 0.79) and "rarely" or "sometimes" with parents (M = 2.45, s.d. = 0.89) and teachers (M = 2.56, s.d. = 0.89). Furthermore, these youth perceive that their classroom is open for discussion only "sometimes" (M = 3.02, s.d. = 0.63) (Richardson, 2003). However, the average response choice of "rarely" or "sometimes" might not provide an adequate description of adolescents' participation in discussions about politics. There are a number of ways in which this question format could have led respondents to understand the item and response choices differently. One limitation of survey research is that response choices can be interpreted in multiple ways. Respondents were offered four choices (never, rarely, sometimes, often) that did not have exact numerical equivalents. Studies of surveys using similarly vague choices have found extensive overlap between adjacent categories and differences in individuals' responses based on level of education (Tourangeau et al., 2000). Overlap between adjacent categories of response choices, for these IEA items, was evident from my interviews. Based on data from my 2003 interviews, "rarely" was generally interpreted to be either once a month or several times a month. However, nearly as many students also reported that "sometimes" meant several times a month.

In the 1971 version of the IEA instrument, response options for the discussion with others items were "several times a week," "about once a week, or less often," and "almost never" (Oppenheim & Torney-Purta, 1974). Changing the response options to be consistent with the open classroom climate measures probably facilitated improved student consistency in using the options, but eliminating the weekly timeframe approach to the discussion with other items may have introduced response effects in the type of information students retrieved from their memory and the way they reached a judgment about their frequency of participation in political discussions.

Not only did students perceive the response choices differently, but they may have differed in their ability to recall relevant discussions. Errors in estimating the number of experiences with discussion are therefore another example of a possible response effect. Some respondents might use counting to derive a total number, whereas others might employ various methods of estimation. As noted by Sudman, Bradburn, and Schwarz (1996), both methods of retrieving memories present possible sources for error, such as the omission of relevant events or adjusting an estimate to fit the available response choices. One of the probing questions from my cognitive interviews examined the frequency with which students engage in political discussions and thus offered a comparison to survey items. This question asked students to quantify the percent of all of their conversations that contain political topics. In response to the question, "What percentage of your discussions with others is about political topics?" nearly half of the students estimated that they spent 10–20% of their conversations with others discussing politics. This finding was consistent with a study conducted by Keeter, Zukin, Andolina, and Jenkins (2002), in which slightly older youth (ages 15–25) estimated that they spend 22% of their conversations discussing politics. However, about a quarter of the students I interviewed estimated their conversations are about politics 30–40% of the time, and another quarter estimated that less than 10% are about politics. A number of students appeared to have difficulties with estimating percentages. For example, one student noted that "sometimes I'll bring it [politics] up.... It's not a huge hobby of mine" but then also reported that 15–20% of all the discussions he or she has with other people are about politics. If the student is really spending one-fifth of his or her discussions on the topic of politics, it might be argued that politics is something that he or she demonstrates a large interest in. Finally, not all students interpreted the response categories in a calendar timeframe, but instead described categories relative to one another. These two possible response effects, interpretation of response choices and different estimation processes, may have attenuated relationships of discussion to engagement. While there were some differences between the relationship of discussion and engagement depending on the partner, more accurate, consistent estimate procedures used by respondents might also have yielded stronger variation across experiences.

Contexts

The results from my statistical analyses suggested that discussions of what is happening in the United States and international politics have distinct qualities for adolescents when they occur with people their own age, with parents, or with teachers. Furthermore, these one-on-one or small group discussions are distinct from students' perception that their classrooms provide environments where respectful discussion of political and social issues is encouraged. However, response effects might have decreased variation across contexts identified from the statistical analyses. The cognitive interviews strengthen these conclusions.

The 1999 IEA Civic Education Study made several changes from the 1971 instrument in the terms used to refer to different discussion contexts in the series of questions asking, "How often do you have discussions of what is happening in the U.S. government (or international politics) with people your own age, parents or other adult family members, and teachers?" Some of these changes probably improved response validity and reliability, while others introduced potential response effects. The phrase "other family members" was added to "parents," demonstrating sensitivity to the social prevalence of non-nuclear families and the importance of nonparental adult role models. It is likely that this made the selection of a response more accurate for students from non-nuclear families. The response "friends" was changed to "people of the same age." Developmental research suggests that these terms may have different meanings. Therefore, use of the phrase "people of the same age" might have been understood by some students as "friends," whereas other students might have recalled discussions with both friends and same-age peers. Dropping the phrase "in class" for the teacher questions may have captured different meanings depending on school climate. In some school settings, students may have substantial opportunities to talk with teachers outside of the class setting or may discuss political topics in classes other than civic-related ones.

Students interviewed in my study were asked how they interpreted these different contexts. About half the students interviewed interpreted "people your own age" to mean other students in ninth grade, but nearly as many considered it to mean all students in high school. While some students said they had their friends in mind, some other students considered both friends and classmates. Distinctions between friends and classmates, often prominent in other studies of adolescent development, were not apparent in this study. Nearly all the students mentioned that they discussed politics with their mother or father, but grandparents, siblings, aunts, and uncles were also mentioned. When asked about discussion with teachers, the majority of students mentioned that they mainly considered this to mean conversations with their social studies (history) teacher in class. More than one quarter of the students appeared also to have considered discussions in other classes and with teachers outside class. The different ways in which students interpreted the contexts in which discussion occurs is a potential response effect impacting the relationship between discussion and engagement. These findings offer one explanation for the finding that open classroom climate and current participation in civic organizations has a nonsignificant relationship, whereas discussion with teachers is positively associated with current participation. The interviews indicate that some students perceive discussion with teachers as an experience that extends beyond the classroom. This type of discussion with teachers could be more influential on current participation than classroom climate.

What is Politics?

Different interpretations about which topics are considered "political" is another source of a possible comprehension response effect that might have reduced the amount of time students reported discussing politics. A typical approach to items about political discussion used frequently in political science surveys asks respondents how often they discuss "politics." However, following the approach used in the 1971 items, the items about national issues in the 1999 IEA study used language that avoided this vague term. Instead the item asks respondents how often they discuss what is happening their country's national government. However, the next three items used the phrase "international politics."

In order to draw practical inferences from the statistical analyses assessing the relationship between political discussion and civic engagement, it is important to understand the boundaries of what 14-year-olds consider political. The interviews helped provide detail about these boundaries in three ways. First, students were asked to describe or give detail to the topics they thought of when answering how often they talked about politics. Then they were asked how they interpreted the phrase "political and social issues," and finally, whether or not this was the same as current events.

The question designed to assess what sort of topics students considered when responding to the survey question about how often they discussed politics was significantly influenced by prominent current events and their curriculum unit on the United Nations. All but two students mentioned the war with Iraq for both the discussions about the United States and internationally, and nearly one-half mentioned the United Nations as an international topic. Clearly students responding to the IEA instrument in the fall of 1999 would not have mentioned the war with Iraq. It is impossible to determine from this study whether the magnitude of the war influenced its dominance in students' minds for the interviews. However, a majority of students noted later in the interviews that the media was the main way conversations about politics typically got started. Slightly more than half the students mentioned watching something on television, but nearly that many mentioned reading something in a newspaper. Therefore, it is also possible that prominent coverage of topics in the media serve as the main topic of discussion for adolescents regardless of whether events are of significant magnitude. Findings from my 2003 cognitive interviews suggested that "international politics" was not well understood by students in the United States. Some students seemed to be less confident about international topics, with one-quarter noting that they weren't sure what was considered an international topic or indicating that they responded to the question without distinguishing it from the previous one about topics in the U.S. government.

The section with the Open Classroom Climate scale was changed between 1971 and 1999, and these changes may have guided students' thinking in a number of ways that were not part of the first study. This was likely intended to achieve more accuracy in students' responses about civic-related social studies classes. In the directions for this section in 1999, students were asked to think about "history, civics/citizenship, or social studies." Some of the items also added phrases about "political and social issues in class," perhaps to avoid having students respond about all discussions in class or related discussions outside the classroom.

The Open Classroom Climate scale used for the statistical analyses in this study contained two questions that asked students to consider their opportunities for discussion in the classroom on political and social issues. Since this was different than the other discussion questions of what is happening in the U.S. government or international politics, asking students to describe how they interpreted "political and social" issues provided more insight about what sort of issues adolescents consider relevant to discussions of politics. Students demonstrated varying abilities to respond to this question. A few defined "social" only in terms of relationships between people. However, when they were probed to distinguish between political and social, most students gave responses that demonstrated a relatively complex understanding of the relationship between political and social issues. Most often students associated "political" with the government or elected representatives and "social" with community. Their comments implied that the size of the issue and the distance from the people affected were also part of the difference between political and social. Political issues were those that were bigger and more abstract, whereas social issues were more local and were therefore perceived as directly affecting more people. They either did not see or failed to mention issues, such as racism or health care, that affect large numbers of people and may cut across communities. A few students attempted to describe the distinction between the two, as in the following two examples:

Student 1: I think that more social issues are political issues, but you know, not really the other way around. Cause something that's political isn't necessarily social, but all social issues really are, you know, political problems also.

Student 2: Well, like terrorism is both political and social, usually.

Interviewer: And can you tell me how you think it would be political and social?

Student 2: Cause a lot of the times, terrorists are motivated for political reasons, like that's why they're doing what they're doing. But they're also using the social aspects of things to prove their point, sort of.

Interviewer: What kind of social aspects are they using?

Student 2: Like, using the population to do what they want to do. Like, if they had the population, if they threaten the population.

These two students demonstrated an understanding of the distinctions between political and social issues that many students struggled to articulate. However, despite uncertainty with their responses, many students provided distinctions similar to the examples above.

Research in social studies education has often asked students about how frequently they discuss "current events," but it is unclear whether students interpret this in the same way as questions about discussing political and social issues. Therefore, these interviews were used to explore the degree to which students distinguish between classroom discussions on "political and social issues" and discussions of current events. The majority of students considered discussing current events to be the same thing as discussing political and social issues. However, explaining their reasoning proved to be challenging for these students. Several students tried to explain that a political or social issue was a current event if it had taken place recently; however, this did not lead them to conclude that there could be political and social issues that were not recent—and therefore not the same as current events. Some students did have a more sophisticated approach for making this distinction and tried to explain how the implications of the current event could make it political or social, as illustrated by the comments of one student:

> Um, yeah, I think that's [political/social issues and current events] pretty similar. I mean, sometimes, current events are…like there was a flood…but it kind of wraps around to political, because there's money that has to go into it, and how it'll affect the economy.

Students are not necessarily grasping the political and social implications of current events. Placing current events in a political or social (and often historical) context is a primary purpose for social studies education, but few of the students interviewed here appear to be able to make these distinctions or links. This may be another possible reason why the association between students' reports of participating in political discussion and civic engagement found in the statistical analyses of this study was not larger. If students are not able to grasp the implications of current events for politics, they may also be unable to grasp the future implications for political issues, including civic engagement related to that issue.

In sum, details about potential limits of the items and variations between students became more apparent by asking students to reflect on their thinking about selected IEA survey items on political discussion. The different ways in which students interpreted terms in the items and the various response choices might have influenced the validity of their responses. These findings suggest that the validity of items might be limited in scope. The topics considered relevant to "politics" were likely narrow, and the level of participation in discussions likely contained some errors in estimation (with both over- and underestimation possible). More accurate and valid information about adolescent experiences with political discussions could provide more insight into why discussion is related to civic engagement.

Contributions of the Cognitive Interviews to Interpreting Results from the IEA Survey

Although the magnitude of the association between political discussion and civic engagement is only moderate in the data from the 1999 IEA study, there are several response effects that may have attenuated the relationship. Survey items about the frequency of participation in political discussion offered response choices "never," "rarely," "sometimes," and "often," and as noted, interviews indicated that these categories could be estimated in different ways. For example, both "rarely" or "sometimes" were considered by some students to mean several times a month. Furthermore, these categories did not ask adolescents to consider the quality or length of these discussions. By comparison, Conover and Searing (2000) asked respondents to consider only "serious" discussions lasting more than 5 minutes. Moreover, interviews with adolescents revealed that they held a rather limited interpretation of "what is happening in the U.S. government" or "international politics." The limited number of topics they provided, considered in conjunction with the topics they provided for explaining how they interpreted "political and social issues," make it seem likely that students reported participation in political discussions only for instances that had direct connections to issues they perceived as related to government (mostly national government) or elected representatives. If they had specifically been asked to include topics such as poverty or pollution, the strength of the relationship between their participation in political discussions and civic engagement might have been stronger. A broader conceptualization of politics is an issue that is especially important for this generation, when conventional politics is relatively unpopular among adults, and community volunteering in poor neighborhoods or participation in environmental cleanup is likely to be part of adolescents' experiences but unlikely to be labeled "political." Although the distinctions between discussion contexts also received confirmation from the interviews conducted for this study, the nature of political discussions with peers, parents, teachers, and in class was not described in the same way by all students. It was clear that most students perceived each of these contexts to have distinct qualities. These various response effects likely influenced both the way students understood the survey questions and the process they used to select and estimate discussion experiences from their memory.

IMPLICATIONS FOR USING COGNITIVE INTERVIEWS IN CONJUCTION WITH SOCIAL SCIENCE SURVEYS

For the cognitive interviews described in this chapter, asking students to provide examples of their thinking certainly fulfilled the goal of gaining an understanding of how they experienced discussion, as well as the meaning they attached to terms such as "political" or "social." Using cognitive interviews after the students completed the survey suggested conclusions about students' experiences with discussion that would not have been possible with statistical analysis alone. The descriptive statistics from the 1999 IEA U.S. sample demonstrated that political discussions were not an activity that adolescents engaged in often. However, the cognitive interviews suggest that students responded to this item in a very narrow fashion and included mostly issues pertaining to government.

Cognitive interviews offer promise beyond their role as a research method to examine subjects' thinking as they complete tasks. They also offer the opportunity to improve interpretation of results from surveys and the design of survey items. Such interviews can also add to a growing body of research aimed at learning more about students' understanding of social studies concepts. One way to make these research methods stronger is for social studies researchers to collaborate with cognitive psychologists and survey methodologists to conduct studies comparing the reliability and validity of concurrent and retrospective protocols in social studies surveys. In addition, studies measuring the error of estimation or counting strategies used by participants when responding to social studies surveys would be helpful. This could be accomplished, for example, by comparing student responses to items about frequency of participation in political discussions with student journals and reports by their teachers, peers, or parents. Finally, at a more basic level, requiring researchers to make the pilot study process more transparent—or a study of publishable quality in and of itself—would help improve the quality and usefulness of cognitive interview techniques.

ACKNOWLEDGMENT

I would like to thank Judith Torney-Purta for feedback provided on an earlier draft of this chapter.

REFERENCES

Bjorklund, D. F. (2000). *Children's thinking: Developmental function and individual differences.* Belmont, CA: Wadsworth.

Berti, A., & Andriolo, A. (2001). Third graders' understanding of core political concepts (law, nation-state, government) before and after teaching. *Genetic, Social and General Psychology Monographs, 127,* 346–377.

Brophy, J., & Alleman, J. (2002). Primary-grade students' knowledge and thinking about the economics of meeting families' shelter needs. *American Educational Research Journal, 39,* 423–468.

Conover, P., & Searing, D. (2000). The democratic purposes of education: A political socialization perspective. In L.M. McDonnell, P.M. Timpane, & R. Benjamin (Eds.), *Rediscovering the democratic purposes of education.* (pp. 99–124). Lawrence: University Press of Kansas.

Crutcher, R. J. (1994). Telling what we know: The use of verbal report methodologies in psychological research. *Psychological Science, 5,* 241–248.

Ericsson, K. A., & Simon, H. A. (1993). *Protocol analysis: Verbal reports as data* (Rev. ed.) Cambridge, MA: MIT Press.

Hess, R., & Torney, J. (1967). *The development of political attitudes in children.* Garden City, NJ: Anchor Books.

Husfeldt, V., & Torney-Purta, J. (2004). Development of the cived instruments. In W. Schulz & H. Sibberns (Eds.), *IEA Civic Education Study Technical Report* (pp.17–26). Amsterdam: International Education Association.

Keeter, S., Zukin, C., Andolina, M., & Jenkins, K. (2002). *The civic and political health of the nation: A generational portrait.* College Park, MD: Center for Information & Research on Civic Learning & Engagement, School of Public Affairs, University of Maryland.

Lee, P., Ashby, R., & Dickinson, A. (1996). Progression in children's ideas about history. In Martin Hughes (Ed.) *Progression in Learning* (pp. 50–81). Bristol, PA: Multilingual Matters.

Lessler, J.T., Tourangeau, P., & Salter, W. (1989). *Questionnaire design in the cognitive research laboratory: Results of an experimental prototype.* Vital and Health Statistics, Series 6, No. 1 (DHHS Pub. No. PHS 89-1076). Washington, DC: U.S. Government Printing Office.

Levine, R., Huberman, M., & Buckner, K. (2002). *The measurement of instructional background indicators: Cognitive laboratory investigations of the responses of fourth and eighth grade students and teachers to questionnaire items* (Working Paper Series, Report No. NCES-WP-2002-06). Washington, DC: National Center for Educational Statistics.

Oppenheim, A. N., & Torney, J. (1974). *The measurement of children's civic attitudes in different nations* (IEA Monograph Studies No. 2). New York: Wiley.

Presser, S., & Blair, J. (1994). Survey pretesting: Do different methods produce different results? In P. V. Marsden (Ed.), *Sociological methodology* (Vol. 24, pp. 73–104). Beverly Hills, CA: Sage.

Richardson, W. K. (2003). *Connecting political discussion to civic engagement: The role of civic knowledge, efficacy and context for adolescence.* Unpublished doctoral dissertation, University of Maryland, College Park.

Richardson, W. K., & Amadeo, J. (2002, April). *Civic discussion with peers, parents, and teachers: Outcomes and contexts for adolescents.* Paper presented at the annual meeting for the American Educational Research Association, New Orleans, LA.

Sudman, S., Bradburn, N., & Schwarz, N. (1996). *Thinking about answers: The application of cognitive psychology to survey methodology.* San Francisco: Jossey-Bass.

Torney-Purta, J. (1992). Cognitive representations of the political system in adolescents: The continuum from pre-novice to expert. In W. Damon (Series Ed.) & H. Haste and J. Torney-Purta (Vol. Eds.), *The development of political understanding: A new perspective* (New Directions for Child Development, pp.11–25). San Francisco: Jossey-Bass.

Torney-Purta, J., Lehmann, R., Oswald, H., & Schulz, W. (2001). *Citizenship and education in twenty-eight countries: Civic knowledge and engagement at age fourteen.* Amsterdam: International Association for the Evaluation of Educational Achievement.

Torney-Purta, J., & Richardson, W.K. (2002, August). *Trust in government and civic engagement among adolescents in Australia, England, Greece, Norway and the United States.* Paper presented at the annual meeting of the American Political Science Association, Boston.

Torney-Purta, J., & Richardson, W.K. (2004). Anticipated political engagement among adolescents in Australia, England, Norway and the United States. In J. Demaine (Ed.), *Citizenship and political education today* (pp. 41–58). London: Palgrave.

Tourangeau, R., Rips, L. J., & Rasinski, K. (2000). *The psychology of survey response.* Cambridge, UK: Cambridge University Press.

VanSledright, B., & Afflerbach, P. (2000). Reconstructing Andrew Jackson: Elementary teachers' readings of revisionist history texts. *Theory and Research in Social Education, 28,* 411–444.

Voss, J. F., Tyler, S., & Yengo, L. (1983). Individual differences in the solving of social science problems. In R. Dillon & R. Schmeck (Eds.) *Individual differences in cognition* (pp. 205–232). New York: Academic Press.

Willis, G. B., DeMaio, T., & Harris-Kojetin, B. (1999). Is the bandwagon headed to the methodological promised land? Evaluating the validity of cognitive interviewing techniques. In M. G. Sirken, D. J. Herrmann, S. Schechter, N. Schwarz, J. M.Tanur, & R. Tourangeau (Eds.), *Cognition and survey research* (pp. 133–153). New York: Wiley.

Wineburg, S. S. (1991). On the reading of historical texts: Notes on the breach between school and academy. *American Educational Research Journal, 28,* 495–519.

APPENDIX A:
Selected IEA Instrument Items Related to Political Discussion

A1:Open Classroom Climate Items

> N1: Students feel free to disagree openly with their teachers about political and social issues during class.
>
> N2: Students are encouraged to make up their own minds about issues.
>
> N3: Teachers respect our opinions and encourage us to express them during class.
>
> N5: Students feel free to express opinions in class even when their opinions are different from most of the other students.
>
> N7: Teachers encourage us to discuss political or social issues about which people have different opinions.
>
> N8: Teachers present several sides of an issue when explaining it in class.

Response: 1 = never, 2 = rarely, 3 = sometimes, 4 = often, 0 = don't know

A2: Political Discussion Items

    Stem: How often do you have discussions of what is happening in U.S. government?

           L1: with people of your own age.

           L2: with parents or other adult family members.

           L3: with teachers.

    Stem: How often do you have discussions of what is happening in international politics?

           L4: with people of your own age.

           L5: with parents or other adult family members.

           L6: with teachers.

Response: 1 = never, 2 = rarely, 3 = sometimes, 4 = often, 0 = don't know

APPENDIX B:
Interview Directions and Selection Questions

Interview Session Directions

Purpose: There are two main purposes for this interview. First, I'd like to learn more about how you interpret certain survey questions. Second, I'm trying to develop a description of how young people experience political discussion and civic engagement and would like you to describe your own perspective on these topics.

Directions: First, I'm interested in learning more about the interpretation you have of specific survey questions. I'm going to ask you to respond to some questions about the survey. Providing more detail is more useful than one-word answers. Remember there is no right or wrong answer to these questions and the answers you provide will be kept confidential. So you don't have to worry about carefully planning out each of your answers. Just respond with the ideas that come to your mind. At any time you may decide not to answer any question or stop the interview altogether. Do you have any questions before we begin? (Note: Follow-up probes appear in italics.)

Part 1: Political Action 1 Questions (IEA Survey Section L)

    4. What kinds of topics or issues did you consider part of a discussion about "what is happening in the U.S. government?"

       Is there anything else that comes to mind?

    5. What kinds of topics or issues did you consider part of a discussion about "international politics?"

       Is there anything else that comes to mind?

These questions were repeated for several different kinds of people. I'd like to know how you interpreted each phrase.

6. What does "people of your own age" mean to you?

   When you answered the questions were you thinking about discussions with friends, classmates, anyone in your age group, or some other group?

7. Who did you have in mind when you responded about discussion with "parents or other adult family members"?

8. When you responded about discussion with teachers, what did you interpret that to mean?

   Did you consider classroom discussions or just discussions you have with teachers outside of class?

   Did you consider only conversations you have with teachers of politically related subjects or all of your teachers?

   Did you have one particular teacher (a few) in mind or an average of your discussion with all your teachers?

9. You were offered several choices about the frequency with which you engage in political discussion—Can you tell me what you interpreted "rarely," "sometimes," and "often" to mean?

   Would "often" be every day, several times a day, or something else?

Open Classroom Climate Questions (IEA Survey Section N)

This section asked questions about what happens in your social studies classes. Several questions ask you about discussion of "issues."

10. What did you interpret "political and social" issues to mean?

    Do you distinguish between political and social issues? If so, what's the difference?

    Can you give me an example of each one (a political issue, a social issue)?

    Do you consider discussion of current events to be the same as discussing political and social issues?

Part 2: Student Descriptions of Political Discussion and Civic Engagement

Directions: Next I'm going to ask you a series of questions that will help me develop a description of your own perspective on political discussion and civic engagement. Remember, providing more detail is more useful than one-word answers and there is no right or wrong answer to these questions.

12. Could you please describe your participation in political discussions that occur outside of the classroom?

13. What percentage of discussions that you have with other people are about political topics?

14. Where do you talk most often about politics *(home, work, school, car)?*
15. How many people do you usually have political discussions with at one time?
16. How do the political discussions typically get started *(media, school, observation)?*
17. Do you make connections between political topics discussed at home and discussions at school? What kind of connections do you make?
18. How frequently do you talk with your parents about school topics?
19. What is your role during political discussions *(initiate, listen, give and take)?*
20. Is national politics something you like to talk about, or is it something other people bring up?
21. How might the political discussions you have differ depending on who you are talking with?
22. How often do you talk with people whose ideas are different than yours? Are these discussions different from discussions with people who have similar ideas?

    When you talk with (parents, friends, teachers), how often do you disagree with their point of view?
23. What do you think is the purpose of political discussion?

    Can you tell me more?

CHAPTER 9

CAPTURING CANDOR

Accessing Teachers' Thinking About the Cultivation of Historical Empathy

Deborah L. Cunningham

The first time I interviewed Ms. Hayes, a teacher participating in my doctoral study, I was struck by her articulateness, her ease in mapping out teaching dilemmas, and her willingness to level with me about the realities (even inconsistencies) of her practice. Discussing the tensions between present and contemporary understandings of past situations, she noted,

> We have to realize that there is a real problem here. It's like the saying "to take the historian out of the history." We've almost got to take ourselves out and our own experiences out before we can empathize and have a real understanding [of people in the past].... It's not a case of how you would feel if you were in a trench. Yes, that is largely the way we approach it, to be honest: "How would you feel in this situation?" In a way your feeling...is going to be so different to how it was.

Educational and psychological literature regarding teacher knowledge and its elicitation had not led me to expect such candor, or the accompanying flow of nuanced insights about her efforts to foster historical empathy. I had read that teachers often struggled to express their implicit knowledge and assumptions, lacked awareness of differences between

Research Methods in Social Studies Education, pages 183–206
Copyright © 2006 by Information Age Publishing

their ideas and practice, and tailored comments to the researcher, fore-grounding the favorable. So her open expressiveness caused me to ask, were the theories off, or inapplicable? Had I managed to make her feel comfortable? When the other three teachers in my study proved equally capable of rigorous self-scrutiny and lucid sharing of their views, I began to think: probably both.

This chapter explores a cluster of methodological issues centering upon how to evoke the knowledge that experienced teachers possess about cultivating historical empathy in their students. After introducing the study design, I briefly trace the literature on accessing thinking and illustrate four teachers' typically fluent accounts, then examine the signifi-cance and methodological implications of occasional gaps between their ideas and practice. Next I outline the principles guiding my interactions with participants, which mattered for the type and quality of data they helped to engender. Key themes and dilemmas in teachers' thinking that were revealed by the use of multiple data sources follow, and then I explain how triangulation added depth of insight to my emerging analysis even as it highlighted some methodological complications. Finally, I chart my basic rules for developing analytical categories and interpretive propo-sitions, and assess which methods seem to have contributed most to the validity of the study.

THE RESEARCH DESIGN

Embarking upon my doctoral research in England, I wanted to understand and codify teachers' knowledge in one area much debated in British schools during the 1980s and 1990s: the cultivation of historical empathy. I hoped to discover how experienced teachers conceptualized empathy—generally conceived as entertaining the perspectives and values of people in the past through consideration of the circumstances they faced—and what they thought and knew about effective means of teaching it. I also wondered, what did they do in practice to bring it about? How had they learned what they knew? What factors facilitated or constrained their work in helping students to develop empathetic understanding? Because most studies of history education had focused on mapping students' thinking or the philosophy of the discipline, little was empirically known about history teachers' own ideas and practice. Describing and explaining their present work thus seemed the logical starting point for my study, and the success of such a project would rest upon my ability to gain access to teachers' authentic thoughts and aspirations. I attempted to ensure validity through the study design, planned adherence to certain principles, and had momentary responses and adaptations as I interacted with teachers—all of which will be addressed in this chapter.

Because I wanted to portray the contours of teachers' work in their natural settings, I elected to do a collective case study (Stake, 1995) exploring the phenomenon of empathy-teaching across the work of four teachers. I opted to work with four because this number offered the possibility of comparison and allowed for the development of propositions (as opposed to idiosyncratic observations). The teachers were typical of the area in their professionalism, and each had an undergraduate history degree and the equivalent of an M.Ed. The sample included two teachers who had 10 or more years of experience (Ms. Joslin and Mr. Dow) and two with 3–5 years (Ms. Hayes and Mr. Ingram).

THE CENTRAL METHODOLOGICAL CONCERN: ACCESSING TEACHERS' TACIT KNOWLEDGE

For several decades, educational and psychological researchers have questioned whether professionals, including teachers, can explicate their implicit thinking, particularly regarding their decisions during active classroom teaching. While I felt confident on the basis of trial interviews that teachers *could* articulate much of their thinking, I had no illusions that I could capture its totality. Any interview methods I devised would necessarily miss some sorts of data—perceptions, distinctions, and feelings "too fine-grain to be caught accurately in a web of words" (Claxton, 2000, p. 36). Along this line of logic, Schön (1983) characterized professional cognition as "knowing-in-action," meaning tacit knowing generated through "reflection-in-action." However, Eraut (1995) convincingly responded that teachers' thinking and knowledge creation resulted mainly from "reflection *on* action," which happened during slower, "cooler" moments in the classroom or from more deliberative reflection out of the action—thus in circumstances where it might be collected or shared. Though surely teachers possess tacit knowledge that may be difficult to bring to the surface, it seems likely that its extensiveness and especially its ineffability has been overestimated. Indeed, when reminded—through quotations or paraphrases from my field notes, student coursework, or occasionally transcripts—of specific moments of classroom life, the teachers in my study usually could recall some of their interactive thinking and aptly articulate their reasoning. What accounted for their fluency? Research indicates that training or mentoring relationships as well as continuing education (such as serious reading) endow people with greater ability to think and talk about their work (Eraut, 2000), and all of my teachers mentored student teachers and kept abreast of their own professional development.

Ultimately, too, it was not only interactive cognitions that interested me in this study, but teachers' conclusions and how they viewed their own work during less harried reflection—what has been called the substance and logic, not psychology, of their thinking (Brown & McIntyre, 1993). The teachers generally proved adept at explaining their logic; because I interviewed them about classes I had just observed (guaranteeing a strong degree of shared experience), they spent little time recounting what happened and focused instead on my questions about why they had chosen certain approaches. Various interview methods elicited particular features of teachers' thinking and beliefs, as explained below in the section on data sources.

In many cases, my "why" questions resulted in their articulating teaching *principles*. For instance, Dow explicitly introduced empathy as a concept, explaining,

> I think if you want someone to achieve a particular skill then you have to show them what they are trying to achieve. No one can hit a dartboard blind, so to speak...I think it's vital to be open about the actual skill as well as the content.

However, teachers did not always have reasons for certain approaches they used. Observing classes and analyzing transcripts, I could sometimes detect uses of language or patterns of discourse of which they were not conscious. Hesitations and qualifications tended to mark times when they were uncertain or formulating a new principle. For example, when I asked Dow how he differentiated between framing questions as "How would *you* feel about the situation?" and "How would *they* understand the situation?," he seemed to be working through his ideas afresh:

> I think I'm not quite clear in my mind. I think there is a bit of confusion there and...a hell of a lot of overlap. I think, going from the top of my head, that the second of what you said ["they" version] is a more developed sort of style, where you're trying to achieve a higher level that requires a deeper understanding of the context or the historical situation...I think I'm just being a bit contradictory in the words I use [in class], so I don't want to read too much into it.

From these and many other examples, it seemed to me that experienced teachers could voice their rationales, or communicate (directly or through their affect) when they didn't have one—a finding supported by other studies (Cooper & McIntyre, 1996; Husbands, Kitson, & Pendry, 2003; Mitchell & Marland, 1989; Pendry, 1994). However, I still wondered whether teachers' comments after one lesson would match their practice thereafter, a question arising from warnings in the research literature.

Argyris and Schön's work (1974) highlighted possible incompatibilities between *espoused* theories of action and *actual* theories-in-use, but I found that reflecting after our shared experience of the lesson minimized the risk of gaps between what teachers said and did. The concern turned out to be minor, casting doubt on the applicability of the thesis to their case (and teachers notably were not part of the researchers' sample). It was *exceptional* when their reflections and classroom practices were not in accord. How might I account for this?

I believe the main reason for the congruity was that the content of teachers' theorizing grew organically from and in turn shaped their actual practice; the two were tightly bound up with each other. Where discrepancies existed—and they only diverged significantly with issues of whether to promote moral or historical judgment, how to harness students' powers of imagination, and stated desires for *historical* empathy but actual questions about students' *own* feelings—they pointed not so much to befuddled or wishful thinking as to a desire to reconcile conflicting obligations in a fair and sufficiently flexible way. Sometimes the two less experienced teachers had not yet worked out systems of resolution, or decided to "enforce" them, in ways that were as consistent or faithfully principled as the others. But they generally recognized the fissure between espoused and enacted ideas; the real issue was how to *manage* persistent dilemmas. Analytically, I had to distinguish between lack of awareness and lack of a clear solution. Methodologically, this would require drawing out what they believed to be true, not what they perceived I wanted to hear.

RESEARCHER–PARTICIPANT ISSUES

Because much of the validity of the interview data in this study relied on teachers' speaking their thoughts candidly, I attempted to build rapport and to create motivation. Two of the principles guiding my work were respect and clarity about the process and my role. Respect for teachers and their knowledge was fundamental to my approach, and indeed to my reasons for undertaking the study. Following the methodology of Brown and McIntyre (1993), I tried to show positive regard for them and their work (hardly a matter of effort); I refrained from negative judgments, and took an interest in all that they said, for instance, "I'm interested that you were worried about your questioning. Were you picking up signals that they *weren't* understanding the questions?" When a teacher appeared disappointed with a lesson, I encouraged a balanced approach by asking about what had gone well: "Let's talk just for a minute about *strengths*.... What did you think were the strengths of the video in helping them understand how women were viewed?" Maintaining a stance of openness about their rationales was also my aim; I tried not to impose my assumptions onto their work or to lead them in questioning, and I made it clear that I was not there to evaluate them but to learn from them. This generally approving, indeed *empathetic*, orientation seemed to have the effect of allowing them to speak honestly, and they were not hesitant to critique their own lessons when displeased.

A second principle I followed was to be clear with teachers about the research process and what it entailed. I explained the obligations and time commitment involved at the outset, and I let them know when I was gathering data as opposed to just chatting. I also drew up a Research Ethics statement involving issues of data collection, confidentiality, and mutual rights, and I made sure at the beginning of the research that they had no concerns about it. (Such procedures are still less standard in the United Kingdom than in the United States.)

I also tried to be clear about my own role and identity. While I tried to gather data in ways that promoted authenticity, I knew that my presence would definitely alter the teaching scene as well as influence my own interpretations and reactions. Ultimately I could not control how teachers perceived my role, but I took steps to make it clear and unthreatening (noting research effects all the while so I could later document them). I emphasized that I did not want them to "perform"—not that this would have been sustainable over so many lessons. I also mentioned that I was a history teacher myself, which seemed helpful for breaking down feelings of distance or formality. Yet I was clearly visiting their schools as a researcher, on top of which I was American, which made me a kind of "outsider" but aided me in seeing things with unhabituated eyes (see Hahn, Chapter 7, this volume). While I doubt the teachers were bothered by my nationality—all were cosmopolitan in outlook; three had lived in America, and Joslin was American though a long-term resident of England—I myself experienced the transnational differences in schooling as profound, and through reading and discussion tried to familiarize myself with the British school context. Especially at the beginning, I frequently found myself comparing British and American modes of teaching and learning, marveling at British teachers' conversance about historical skills, musing over images I had held about orderly British classrooms, and asking many questions about the (to me, puzzling) content of the curriculum and relatively low weighting of coursework, issues they took for granted. These tendencies are important insofar as they reveal that I had my own empathetic work to do to enter into the worlds of British teachers, in schooling contexts quite unlike those I had known.

My principles for interacting with teachers helped evoke many remarks notable for their candor and self-awareness. After teaching a disengaged group of ninth graders, Joslin noted, "As soon as I find them being distant and quiet, I don't relax with them…," and Ingram acknowledged, "I'm hopeless at remembering how I learned things, or what processes I've gone through." Multiple remarks of this nature from each teacher in the study led me to feel that they were seriously scrutinizing both their lessons and their role in them.

TYPES AND TRIANGULATION OF DATA SOURCES

Once I had chosen the sample of four teachers, other aspects of the research design required attention. I knew that a valid study required more than simply sitting down with a few teachers for a wide-ranging interview; such an approach would provide data largely limited to general beliefs and principles abstracted from the specifics of actual lessons. This would make a useful starting point, but I wanted to explore particular moments in their teaching, delving into their logic and beliefs at a fine-grained level. To maximize the validity of the study through the data collection processes, I utilized triangulation of data sources, cross-checking classroom observations with three different kinds of interviews (some of which used stimulated recall methodology) as well as curricular documents, a card-sorting exercise, and examples of students' work. I also employed triangulation of question types—open-ended, probes, multiple choice, responses to theoretical statements from educational literature, and member-checking of past statements—to build an understanding of the teachers' thinking and practice. Finally, I observed whichever two grade 6–8 classes the teachers happened to be teaching in 2001–2002, as well as one of their grade 9 or 10 classes. These lessons spanned historical time periods and degrees of examination pressure—both potential influences on empathy.

The individual methods used in the study offered different sorts of data, which (except for written documents) I converted from tape-recordings into transcripts so I could cross-check them for similarities and differences and see how each contributed to answering particular questions. These methods are outlined below.

Initial Interview

In September of the data collection school year (2001–2002), I conducted an initial interview with each teacher. Lasting from 1–2 hours, this session gave me an opportunity to learn about the teachers' educational backgrounds and philosophies. I arranged the questions with a gradually narrowing focus, from broad-based queries about the teachers, to their beliefs and values about history, to their ideas about empathy and the strategies it involved. The interview was semi-structured and the stem questions, though not associated probes, were sent to teachers a few days in advance so that they had a chance to reflect; I felt some of the questions were demanding and unfair to confront them with on the spot. I wanted to support teachers in answering questions like "How do you think your own experiences of empathy have shaped your thoughts about how to help students develop it?" This advance notice was offered from an awareness that fleeting classroom events could be difficult to recollect and that teachers might not even be conscious of aspects of their performance, especially those that had become automatized with experience (Berliner, 1986).

Within the initial interview, I utilized triangulation of question types and a stand-alone card-sort exercise. Elements to which I wanted them to react without prior reflection were not included in the protocol sent ahead of time but were written into my copy, since the ordering of questions mattered. For example, to avoid prejudicing their responses through the questions, I first inquired what they felt the purposes of school history were, *then* asked them to complete a standardized card-sort exercise, grouping or ranking different purposes that I had culled from the history teaching literature. I likewise asked them for their own definition of empathy before checking that they agreed with a rudimentary one I had drawn up from the literature, meant to establish that we were talking about the same basic idea.[1] The interview concluded with a multiple-choice question asking them which of three statements about the role of empathy in producing historical understanding was closest to their own view, and why. Triangulating questions and methods produced an important source of corroboration or modification of claims about each teacher's beliefs, exemplified at the end of this section.

Classroom Observations

In order to gather data that was as ecologically valid as possible, I observed teachers on multiple occasions, teaching different topics to several grades and attainment levels, at a variety of times of day and of the school year. This gave me the opportunity to see a broad range of ways that teachers both used and nurtured empathy. I asked them to identify lessons in which promoting empathetic understanding was one of the goals or a main goal, without altering their usual modes of teaching or contriving lessons for my benefit. However, because innovation is actually a normal part of a teacher's work, some was captured in the study.

Ultimately I joined each teacher for between 9 and 15 lessons, recording them with a sensitive but unobtrusive radio-microphone device that usually picked up students' comments as well as teachers' words except in louder group work situations. I supplemented this with my own field notes to highlight nonverbal communications, special circumstances, and students' comments too soft in volume to decipher on tape.

The role I adopted during these lessons was "observer as participant" (Robson, 1993, p. 198), meaning that I presented myself as a researcher, not a teacher, but sought to help out in small ways as requested, passing out materials, helping with equipment, or running a quick errand on rare occasions. I attempted not to interfere, and positioned myself on the margins of the action when possible—though all parties were aware of my presence and occasional roving around the classroom during group work.

Post-Lesson Interviews

As soon as possible after a lesson, I sat down with the teacher and conducted a follow-up interview ranging from 10–30 minutes (usually 15–20 minutes) that focused on their thinking about events in the lesson. While I crafted questions during the lessons—or on the spot—three core questions were the staple: "Why did you choose these particular strategies?", "How did they contribute to empathetic understanding?", and "Did they work as you had hoped, in terms of pupils' responses?" Often I reported teachers' words to them and asked them to elaborate on what they were doing.

For the first few months I kept the questions very grounded in the specifics of events, not building in any ideas for them to respond to. In February, I reviewed all questions posed to each teacher to check for biases and gaps in my own interviewing, and to note important issues mentioned by a certain teacher so I could be alert for chances to raise them with the others. Thus while these follow-up sessions remained focused on lesson events, they also became testing grounds for emerging ideas and theories.

This review also enabled me, as a starting point in analysis, to evaluate whether trends were emerging in teachers' responses. I was concerned, for instance, about Bromme's (1987) assertion that teachers remembered "peak phases" of introducing new material better than other parts of a lesson, and Berliner's (1988) claim that experienced teachers tended to focus their attention on what was *atypical*—problems or outstanding events. Perhaps because I was fairly systematic in asking teachers about the various parts of a lesson, including "nonpeak" elements like review of former learning, and often cited or paraphrased their own or students' statements back to them, these distortions were not arising except for a particular attentiveness to matters they wanted to change in the future. For instance, Joslin commented after a lesson on witchcraft,

[T]he effect that religious changes of this degree could have on people whose lives were dominated by religion is completely lost on them…. I would revise [review] the Reformation course in 20 minutes with them. Just to bring it familiar in their minds. Because I was taking that for granted and I obviously shouldn't have.

Although I tried to conduct interviews directly upon the conclusion of a lesson, when teachers' memories were freshest, or at the next available hour, in three cases no time of the day was available. For these, I used stimulated recall methods, giving teachers a full transcript of the lesson to prompt their recollections. The status of this interview data is different: It doesn't capture immediate post-lesson thoughts, and it shows reflection at greater leisure. Perusing the transcripts drew forth metacognitive interpretations from the teachers and allowed them to notice more detailed aspects of their own speech than they normally picked up. Joslin realized how much talking and explaining she was doing, and she worried that this "could be detrimental and frustrating for pupils if I am filling in too much without letting them figure it out for themselves." Stimulated recall proved to be a promising learning mechanism; since the teachers did not usually have access to "frozen" portraits of their work, they seemed to enjoy and value the opportunity (though some might not react this way!).

Coursework Interview

In September 2001, I asked teachers to identify a piece of coursework assigned during the year that focused on historical empathy, and around which we could discuss how they assessed students' empathetic performance. I specifically requested that they select two examples each of work they considered excellent, middle-range, and poor. After they had marked these and added such comments as they chose, I sat down with teachers for about 45 minutes and asked them to talk me through students' writing, explaining what they looked for and how they knew a student had or had not empathized, why they had made particular comments, and how they had graded the work. I gathered background information on the assignment, such as how it was worded, what resources were available to students in completing it, why it was valuable, and how the assignment had developed over time, if it had. I also asked whether there were empathetic matters teachers had considered addressing, but had not, to get at their broader pedagogical or specific empathetic philosophies.

This method, a form of stimulated recall, had the advantage of allowing teachers to comment in greater depth on students' performances and on their uses of language. It also elicited more of teachers' implicit cognitions than most methods, as teachers "relived" their marking process as they walked me through page after page. The stimuli of written documents, in the exact form in which they originally had been encountered, served as helpful memory prompts. Eraut (2000) has linked such "mediating objects" (p. 120) as student work or transcripts to an increased capability for practitioners to talk explicitly about their knowledge—another contributor to teachers' fluent articulation of their thoughts in my study.

Curricular Documents

Throughout the year I collected documents relating to lessons taught and to teachers' ways of thinking about the curriculum. These included "schemes of work" (written curricula), lesson handouts, syllabi, examination questions, National Curriculum guidelines, and photocopies of textbook pages. These helped me understand transcribed lessons, and I sometimes analyzed the empathetic content of handouts in their own right. Curricular artifacts also assisted in understanding the wider teaching context.

Final Interview

The questions for this semi-structured interview, which lasted from 1–2 hours, were to a considerable extent tailored to the individual teachers, though there were also common questions. I used the interview partly for respondent validation: It began with my presenting the cluster of statements about empathy I had gathered over the year from each teacher to check that I had them all correct, to clarify where necessary, and to serve as a prelude to asking whether their ideas had changed at all. I then inquired about the lesson identification process, about effects of the research itself, about strategies they used that I had not seen, about constraints, influences on pupils, and a handful of other issues about which I felt some gaps still existed. I also used this opportunity to request that they respond to brief statements about empathy teaching made in the research literature. Formerly I had resisted presenting them with any empirically based *or* theoretical ideas, and now I wanted to see what they thought. To a person, they appeared intrigued by what the literature had to say, but they did not allow themselves to be led by it; they challenged claims that failed to square with their experience.

Bringing together various forms of data offered by triangulating methods allowed me to note when teachers' ideas and practices aligned closely (which was most of the time). A matching of insights across data types provided powerful indicators of a teacher's values. For instance, observing Hayes's lessons showed a teacher extraordinarily tuned in to her students' lives and needs as individuals, a fact that harmonized with her interview comment that "people fascinate me," her classroom tendency to spin out the full human significance of events, and the fact that four of six "purpose of history" goals she ranked most highly in her card-sort exercise concerned effects on pupils and their growth.

The topics on which triangulating sources might cast light did not necessarily line up on their own; insights from an observation, for instance, might not be accompanied by an unprompted comment explaining their rationale. I needed to use one method to build questions for another method. Significantly, when teachers were asked what they did to encourage understanding, they usually spoke at the level of activities that organized the lesson. However, they also guided pupils toward empathy by what they said: their language in the classroom and how they used it. Though often arising spontaneously and organically from interactions, and less often recognized or discussed as strategies by the teachers, their discourse contained a mix of verbal devices that assisted the empathetic cause. Joslin, for instance, would suddenly speak in a historical role to personalize a viewpoint and show the feeling behind it. This strategy was frequently used by all the teachers, but I had to first identify it as a strategy in order to ask about it. Joslin then explained,

> I do that quite often...I just do a bit of a role play from time to time. I'm sure that's because I feel it helps them to understand a particular point of view, but I don't necessarily plan it. In fact, I never plan it into my lesson as such.

Likewise, as a listener and researcher, I could hear that on some subjects teachers added fewer fresh details or illustrations to students' statements or questions, and used more tentative language like "might," "could," "possibly," and "probably" to a greater extent. This cued me to ask in interviews about their level of content knowledge—and usually to find out that such hedges marked topics where they felt they knew less.

By making possible the comparison of interview statements and lesson actions, triangulation also showed where ideas and practices diverged. For instance, when asked his feelings about making moral judgments about history, Ingram expressed that he was "a wee bit concerned" about making value judgments, and in class would "always try and emphasize the fact that you can't judge these people, because at the time they probably thought the same as we would." In reality, he never once emphasized restraint in the lessons I saw—sometimes just the reverse—and overall he rarely invited students to discuss values inherent in his own approach to topics. Without observations, I would not have known that Ingram held discrepant positions, or followed through with enough questions to learn that he was still working out his own beliefs and the contexts in which they applied. Similarly, the teachers often claimed in interviews to be cultivating *historical* empathy while actually asking questions that evoked students' *current* thoughts and feelings. Subsequent interviewing uncovered different levels of awareness and thoughtfulness about the issue, varying conceptions of what qualified as empathy, and ideas about steps in its cultivation based on assessments of students' capacities. Triangulation, then, mainly indicated where I needed to "dig" further for a richer story.

Exploring these disjunctions, I realized that they usually emerged when teachers faced conflicts and dilemmas arising from the multiple goals they held, both moral/civic and historical. Which came uppermost had to be negotiated because they could not be permanently or formulaically resolved. Once sensitized to areas of inconsistency, I could identify new instances while active teaching was happening, and I could ask in follow-up interviews why they had pursued a certain course on one occasion and a different approach in a seemingly similar situation. (I ultimately learned that teachers were taking 13 different types of factors into account in making decisions about empathy teaching.) I could ask directly about theory–practice alignment using evidence from the lesson and then, in the final interview, from across the year. The value of beginning analysis early with Glaser and Strauss's (1967) constant comparative method became apparent here; I could see discrepancies when there was still time to explore them.

Apart from triangulation and the corroborating or jarring fit between data sources, respondent validation—having the teachers in the study verify the findings—posed another means of clarifying or checking my grasp of their views. I opted to only pursue it in the most limited of ways: I solicited feedback from teachers during the follow-up interviews about various hunches, and I tested my characterization of their ideas about empathy on them in the final interview. I did not present them with the full claims of the study because of evidence that teachers tended to focus on different aspects of the contents than the researcher (especially their own words) and not to offer much response or further insight to analytical or theoretical claims (Jaworski, 1994; Norman, 2000).

METHODOLOGICAL COMPLICATIONS: MOVING TARGETS AND RESEARCH EFFECTS

Lesson observations and follow-up interviews generated the bulk of data gathered in this study, so identifying which lessons would be the best to observe for empathy was a central concern. This proved complicated at times; teachers occasionally felt in retrospect that lessons had turned out either more or less pertinent than anticipated, often due to time constraints. With empathy involved to some degree in many lessons, picking the most fruitful could be hit or miss.

Teachers' selection of lessons was particularly important because it was one way they revealed what they believed empathy to be; I asked them to choose which sessions I should observe. This was informative in its own right, and useful because they knew their plans best. Initially, the challenge was to have them identify lessons based on *their* definitions of empathy, not (as happened during my trialing of methods) their perceptions of *my* ideas. Part of the rationale for having them define empathy at the initial interview was to focus the discussion of identifying lessons upon their views. I also explicitly stated at the start of the research, and dropped reminders during the year, that I wanted to see lessons *they* considered relevant to empathy, taught in their normal fashion—that this would be of most value for the study. This worked in a straightforward manner with teachers whose conceptions of empathy held stable during the data collection year.

However, teacher identification of lessons introduced tricky methodological issues and tradeoffs when teachers' concepts shifted, subtly or fundamentally. For most of the year, Ingram identified empathy lessons as those with specific exercises involving a written or acted empathetic performance. The methods were the empathetic part, and could be applied to different topics as befitted them. Equally, empathy was not to be mixed with other goals: Lessons on primary evidence needed to be separated from empathy lessons so as not to overwhelm students. This view gradually changed over the year as Ingram spent time debriefing about lessons with me (unusual for him, coming from a small and scattered department) and participated in a Diploma course at a local university, where he began conducting his own research on historical interpretations and reading the literature on history teaching. He came to feel that empathy was "not a standalone thing, but…something that underpins all of the study that we do." While his basic means of identification continued to focus on methods, his conception of empathy-related methods broadened. For Ingram's final three lessons, all in May, he chose lessons where his standard strategies, such as role-play, formed a significantly smaller component of the total lesson, and knowledge accretion, sourcework, and discussion played a more prominent role. That these shifts in action were beginning to form a trend indicative of new underlying thinking became fully visible to me only during subsequent analysis, through the subtle comparisons afforded by slower examination of tapes and transcripts. Ingram only expressed most of his new thinking during the final interview, and in the form of plans; even examining his last few lessons in light of his shifting thinking, I could not detect changes already enacted beyond the lesson identification differences noted above.

If when Ingram first broached new ideas I had more aggressively pursued the question of how they might be specifically affecting his lesson identifications, I may have gained a clearer picture of the scope of his thoughts a few weeks earlier. However, even in retrospect such a methodological principle is not simple: For one, pinpointing the earliest stages of change would have required extraordinary sensitivity to—perhaps overinterpretation of—the few comments he made prior to the final interview. In the end, I focused on what I could control, which was ensuring that Ingram's various definitions were all captured in the study as ways of conceptualizing empathy, and a whole chapter of the dissertation dealt with teachers' conceptions and how they related to specific teaching strategies.

The tradeoffs of observing teacher-identified lessons were more costly in data collection terms with Dow. After an initial flurry of lessons in which empathy was either the focus or one of several goals, there was a lull in invitations for a couple of months. Ultimately, it emerged that he had defaulted to a more traditional notion of almost "pure empathy" lessons involving empathy exercises, a notion he thought interested me and for which he could not find time in the exam-driven upper grades. Concerned, I inquired into observation possibilities beyond the originally chosen grades, and we established that an upcoming 11th-grade lesson had potential in terms of its subject matter. Through reflection and conversation about empathy, Dow came to be "more aware of how much you use it without necessarily realizing that you're using it, that it's quite an important component"—crucial, in fact.

Something of an epiphany seemed to occur in a discussion of the lesson noted above—a class on Henry VIII, Anne Boleyn, and the Church. Dow began by saying, "The empathy comes through developing an understanding of what was going through Henry's mind. I'm not going to make a claim that that was pure empathy as such...most history teachers probably wouldn't describe it as empathy."

As Dow pondered it further, he began to shift his view:

And so if you are trying to understand someone's conscience then you've got to start trying to get on the *line* in which he was thinking. When you start doing that you are effectively putting yourself in someone's shoes, which is, effectively, empathy...yes, I would say that at heart there is an empathetic exercise there. So yeah, I'll come off the fence!

By the end of the year Dow had expanded his definition from the "traditional, pure kind" of empathy (where it is the sole focus) to a "gray area" where it is not just an exercise, but also a *route* or *vehicle* involved in many things—"as much a route to a goal as a goal in itself." And through this altered awareness he realized that it was not just for younger students, but for grades 9–12, too.

As a researcher, these incidents taught me the importance of ongoing vigilance about how teachers conceived of the concept I was studying; I could not assume that their definitions were static. I had to keep asking how they were thinking about empathy, noting how this looked in practice (and whether the two matched), and reminding them to follow the line of their thinking to its natural if "untraditional" end-point in new lessons for me to see. While I regretted the loss of data caused by my slow response in Dow's case, I was heartened that the very process of talking about empathy in a contextualized way actually served as a catalyst for fresh ideas and interest into the phenomenon of empathy teaching—to the point that one teacher undertook a separate research project looking at aspects of her work the following year.

DEVELOPING PRINCIPLES FOR DATA ANALYSIS AND INTERPRETATION

Faced with an alpine heap of transcript data and other documents, I decided to use Glaser and Strauss's (1967) constant comparative method for analysis and the highly compatible computer software program *ATLAS*. As an inductive and pattern-seeking approach, it suited my study of historical empathy, a topic where few analytical concepts were available for borrowing from the literature. It also offered sufficient flexibility to be tailored to my research, allowing me to check that the categories I was capturing made sense to teachers and reflected classroom realities.

As I approached the task of formulating and assigning codes, I found it necessary to compile a set of principles to guide my work, ensuring consistency, validity, and rigor. I adopted the following rules: Codes had to be *clear* and *applied coherently* and *systematically* to the data. Data would be *grounded* in evidence, not forced to fit preconceived constructs. In some cases, concepts were brought in from the literature, but only if they were also substantiated by the data itself, as in the case of "analogies." Adequate account would be taken of all data of relevance, and the *comprehensive* system arrived at would suffice to represent the thinking of those studied. Although teachers were not asked to validate the coding system as respondents, constructs needed to be *recognizable* in their connection to their practices and thinking (as in "exploring paradox"). Coding categories had to be *relevant* to the research questions, and *named precisely* to capture the essence of their content, as in "knowledge of the world today—how things work." The codes should *identify initiative*, reflecting who (teacher or student) started a new direction or theme of empathetic significance ("student judgment"), and thus accurately reflect the conditions of dialogue and interaction in the classroom.

Furthermore, each code would be assigned to an *independent* unit of meaning (Lincoln & Guba, 1985). This unit might range in length from a word to an exchange of several paragraphs, depending on the content; typically in this study, it involved a phrase to a few sentences. Finally, codes must be applied with *economy*, meaning in mutually exclusive fashion, although overlaps would be permitted in two quite prevalent cases: when a statement by a teacher represented use of several types of knowledge at once (a major purpose of analysis being to understand how teachers brought to bear a variety of forms of knowledge—separated only for heuristic purposes—to advance empathetic understanding), and when a statement represented different levels of analysis, or performed multiple simultaneous (and theoretically interesting) functions at the same level of analysis. So, for example, the teacher question about proper burials by soldiers of corpses in World War I, "[Would] you [have] got the *energy* to do it? Is it likely you're going to have *time* to do it?" was coded both as "encouraging humility/respect" and "logical reasoning—teacher initiates," because it performed both these functions. Likewise, a statement could be coded at the descriptive level as "role-taking: teacher" if that was the strategy she was employing, and at the inferential level as "what it means to empathize" if that was what she was seeking to illustrate.

Where, though, did the categories come from? Glaser and Strauss skip this question in their first book, but Strauss and Corbin (1990) later take it up, as do other writers. There are three main sources: from the data, from one's impressions, or from other studies or writings. For my research, a primary analytical challenge followed from the fact that no *a priori* set of concepts or categories particularly related to teachers' work on historical empathy existed. While the teacher knowledge literature offered a few helpful ideas, and the empathy-teaching accounts sensitized me to some strategies I might expect to see used (such as "anachronism highlighted"), the bulk of the categories had to be generated from the "ground up," reading the transcripts and identifying codes that captured what was happening in them. Observing how my advisor coded part of a transcript helped me learn to create relevant categories. Attending to the language of the teachers allowed me to generate some codes borrowing their words, such as "knowledge of feelings" or "encouraging differentiation"; it was obvious they viewed these as important. Other codes were suggested by the research questions: "what it means to empathize," for example, derived from the question "How do teachers conceptualize empathy and its role in historical understanding?" So while I had a small "start list," as Miles and Huberman (1994, p. 58) call it, I mostly held an awareness of possibly valuable ideas in my head. This was particularly true of my approach to categorizing teachers' knowledge; an almost overwhelming number of frameworks for parsing it existed, and I decided that as I trial-coded the first 16 transcripts (four per teacher), I would first see which categories made sense empirically, then refer to the literature for substantiation and clarification.

Toward the end of this stage of analysis, I decided to write holistic portraits of two of the teachers in action, in order to assess whether my fledgling coding system was sufficiently picking up on elements of their work that seemed important for empathy. I wanted these portraits to be grounded in detail, so I did close readings of three transcripts for both of them. The combined effect of profiling the teachers and reading scholarship that affirmed the importance of classroom dynamics for empathy (Blake, 1998) caused me to add new codes to capture these aspects, such as "teacher interactional style" and "teacher's empathy/wonder."

Finally, my attempt to code the data comprehensively converged with insights from my reading in another way: I realized I could not make sense of what was happening in the classroom without attending to both how students were contributing and how structural factors (those outside of teachers' direct control) were impinging on events. I came to share the perspective of Clandinin and Connelly (1996) that curriculum is not so much a document, or even set of potentialities, as what actually happens in a classroom. Cooper and McIntyre (1995) had noted the recursive patterns of teacher–student influence in the classroom, and called for work combining the two. While a thorough examination of students' perspectives was outside the scope of my study, my own attempts at coding convinced me that teachers' and students' comments and behaviors simply were not comprehensible in isolation from one another and that they employed many of the same strategies for grasping past actions. As a result, I created a set of codes specific to students and began to systematically examine their input.

Finally, my own observations of lessons, in addition to teachers' interview statements, substantiated the attention given in the teacher knowledge literature to the importance of multiple external factors in the construction of the curriculum (Doyle, 1986; Nott & Wellington, 1994; Parker, 1991; Romanowski, 1996), as well as the "major role of sociocultural context in shaping teachers' practice" (Ben-Peretz, 1995, p. 105; see also Yinger & Hendricks-Lee, 1993). In response, I made an effort to take account of the wider factors influencing the empathy curriculum, for instance by coding the "constraints" and "facilitating factors" on their work, or by looking at "sources of teacher ideas/knowledge development." Much of what I learned about structural factors (such as time or resource availability) or student factors arrived through the lens of teachers' thinking, but the analytical system also contained many independent examples of how context shaped events.

Ultimately I reduced my system to 71 codes derived from various sources and tested from transcript to transcript. What I possessed at the end of the grounded theory process was a finding in its own right, a map of the constituent elements in four individuals' teaching of empathy—a kind of definition of empathy teaching as reflected upon and operationalized. It offered a starting point for new, more far-reaching studies that might be conducted in the future. I had also gained a picture of what sorts of remaining analyses would be profitable—namely, fine-grained analysis and quantification of teachers' strategy use.

Fine-grained analysis proved necessary because the *ATLAS* coding system could not shed sufficient light on significant aspects of teaching for empathy, including the sequencing of classroom events, the ways students shifted the direction of the curriculum, and many finer points of teachers' language use, such as how they framed questions or injected new historical content as queries arose. Some were too diffuse and omnipresent to work well as separate units of meaning; others were too micro-level to bear in mind with 71 other codes. Through a close and systematic reading of 12 transcripts—two for each teacher of largely successful lessons, and one each in which the teacher's expectations were not met—I honed in on 16 characteristics of talk that seemed to affect empathetic outcomes and developed note-taking methods for examining them.

I also occasionally employed simple counting or calculated the mean number of instances of a phenomenon per lesson to compare certain aspects of a teachers' work. Units of meaning had to be discrete instances of a concept, not dialogic exchanges, and of roughly the same length; only codes applying to lesson data could be used; teacher and student statements could not be mixed; and examples of the content had to be meaningful in comparative terms. The quantitative approach offered insight into which aspects of historical knowledge certain teachers emphasized as foundational for empathy, into historical subjects with whom they encouraged empathy, and into their preferred activities and discourse strategies. It yielded further evidence and added clarity for qualitative claims.

Adhering to certain principles in interpreting my data also helped ensure that the end products would have validity. All propositions had to be supported by evidence from the original data and qualified in accordance with how strong or weak that evidence was; all relevant data had to be collated for consideration; inferences had to be logical; propositions could not exceed the limits of what the data allowed; teachers' actual language had to be preserved as far into the process of abstraction as possible and where possible into the findings; and a check for disconfirming evidence had to be conducted.

As a procedure for interpretation, I first extracted all data that I deemed pertinent to a particular research question (poring through the instances of all associated codes), then performed a within-case interpretation of a single teacher. Only when I had a clear picture at this level did I take the step of comparing the results across teachers. As I went through, I began to identify trends and categorize what I was seeing, and to reflect about how the teacher's thinking or actions fit together. I wrote all the details into a new document—a findings summary, with illustrative quotations and typologies—then reviewed it *alongside* my fine-grained analysis summary. Finally, I distilled propositions, often referencing claims in the literature. In grouping these into emergent themes, I found I needed to report them in a way true to their highly interlinked nature, rather than prying them apart to conform to a research-question-and-answer format. So I first penned portraits of each teacher at work, to give a holistic flavor of his or her style, then divided my findings from the cross-case analysis and interpretation (or the single case of empathy teaching), into chapters in ways that felt most natural for the data.

CONCLUSIONS: WHICH METHODOLOGICAL FACTORS MATTERED MOST?

While case study research involving only four teachers limits the sorts of claims that can be made, collecting data over the course of the year showed me that building multiplicity into the study was a useful principle for ensuring the quality and depth of the data and ultimately the validity of the study. Multiplicity of teachers, of methods, of ages of students, of question types, of observation and interview sessions all played a complementary role. In terms of the teachers, their sex did not seem to affect their teaching for empathy, but experience—particularly in terms of their awareness of politicized debates in the press during the 1980s and early 1990s—mattered for how they assessed empathy, and how they structured work in the classroom. Their mentoring of student teachers and their involvement in continuing education, as well as this study, appeared to contribute to their ready explanations of their beliefs and knowledge. Rapport with me as a researcher, while surely not the only factor in their frankness, nonetheless appeared to assist in their willingness to critique (as well as affirm) their own approaches.

Similarly, the study of teachers interacting with multiple grades and ages—as well as capacities—of students proved vital in understanding how they tailored strategies according to these variables. Older students took exams; this significantly influenced how much time for "processing" information teachers would allot. Younger students tended to be more fanciful in their interpretations, and they generally had a weaker sense of societal institutions. While the time period of the historical subjects studied seemed relatively unimportant—chiefly because whether the history was 20th century or more ancient, the thinking was far removed from their own—there was some evidence that whether students identified with the empathetic subjects mattered. Sixth-grade boys were sometimes unwilling to role-play girls; girls showed much more interest in their own views than in Victorian attitudes toward women; and patriotic feelings affected students' preconceptions and motivation to empathize when discussing war or national conflicts.

In terms of what I as a researcher could control, factors that influenced the quality of data included triangulation of methods—for the important reasons of illuminating new issues and sensing dilemmas they faced that were hard to resolve—and facilitating recall through the timing of interviews (right after the lessons usually) or through the provision of "mediating objects" such as transcripts or quotations. Attentiveness to the ways teachers defined the focus of my study, empathy, was also vital, because this could change and affect how they invited me to their classrooms.

Finally, reactivity to me as a researcher mattered, despite my efforts to minimize teachers' self-consciousness and inclinations to change their practice. All of the teachers said that my presence in the classroom did not worry them, and two remarked that they were accustomed to having visitors around, but naturally the research process had affected them in ways large and small. How it influenced their lesson identification (particularly Dow's) has been addressed above. I also asked teachers to review its impact in the final interview. For Ingram and Dow, being involved simply meant that they were thinking more about empathy; their awareness of how they used it and presented it was deeper. They felt they had intentionally not innovated or changed their practices, except for Ingram's switching the sequence of a couple of lessons to accommodate conflicts in my schedule. Hayes too felt that she had tried hard not to tailor curriculum, but thought that possibly a new lesson on poverty had more of a feelings focus because she knew I would be watching—though she later backtracked on this idea. Overall she felt there had probably been more "How would you feel?" questions due to thinking about the research.

Joslin also said she had thought more about some of her methods; because I was asking her to evaluate outcomes, she had considered reasons why some strategies were not working well. Reactivity emerged across several lessons in various ways. Joslin claimed to have prepared for her existing lesson on the medieval church more precisely, with improved sources, knowing I would be present, and she was influenced by having thought about empathy all year when she came to design her new World War I unit. She also felt she had been a bit more ambitious in a couple of lessons, knowing another history teacher was in the room in case pupils needed help (though I did not actually offer much help, since I was focused on listening to her). Joslin also drew attention to the taping of lessons in some classes, notably when students were presenting or when she wanted the noise level to be low; despite my questioning this practice, she claimed she was pleased to be able to use recording as a motivator, a sign that pupils' ideas were valued, and a way to discourage "shouting out." How much these adaptations affected the outcomes is difficult to say. Though her own consciousness of the research probably led to slightly enhanced empathetic performances, especially since for other reasons she was creating several new lessons that year, her knowledge of how to carry out her vision was clearly embedded already, a product of years of experimenting and honing. This was true for all the teachers; having practiced their craft thoughtfully for several years, they had accrued knowledge that was ready for articulation if I evoked it with similar thoughtfulness and care.

NOTE

1. To achieve empathy is to enter into some informed appreciation of the circumstances of people in the past, and to entertain their perspectives on issues and events (Department of Education and Science, 1985a, 1985b; HMI, 1985; Lee, 1983).

REFERENCES

Argyris, C., & Schön, D. A. (1974). *Theory in practice: Increasing professional effectiveness.* San Francisco: Jossey-Bass.

Ben-Peretz, M. (1995). An essay-review of *Making sense of teaching. Teaching and Teacher Education, 11,* 103–106.

Berliner, D. C. (1986). In pursuit of the expert pedagogue. *Educational Researcher, 15*(7), 5–13.

Berliner, D. C. (1988, February). *The development of expertise in pedagogy.* Paper presented at the annual meeting of the American Association of Colleges for Teacher Education, New Orleans, LA. (Eric Document Reproduction Service No. ED298122)

Blake, C. (1998). Historical empathy: A response to Foster and Yeager. *International Journal of Social Education, 13,* 25–31.

Bromme, R. (1987). Teachers' assessments of students' difficulties and progress in understanding in the classroom. In J. Calderhead (Ed.), *Exploring teachers' thinking* (pp. 125–146). London: Cassell.

Brown, S., & McIntyre, D. (1993). *Making sense of teaching.* Buckingham, UK: Open University Press.

Clandinin, D. J., & Connelly, F. M. (1996). Teacher as curriculum maker. In P. W. Jackson (Ed.), *Handbook of research on curriculum* (pp. 363–401). New York: Macmillan.

Claxton, G. (2000). The anatomy of intuition. In T. Atkinson & G. Claxton (Eds.), *The intuitive practitioner* (pp. 32–52). Buckingham, UK: Open University Press.

Cooper, P., & McIntyre, D. (1996). *Effective teaching and learning: Teachers' and students' perspectives.* Buckingham, UK: Open University Press.

Department of Education and Science. (1985a). *GCSE: The national curriculum for history.* London: Her Majesty's Stationery Office.

Department of Education and Science. (1985b). *General Certificate of Secondary Education—The national criteria: History.* Southampton, UK: HP Ltd.

Doyle, W. (1986). Classroom organization and management. In M. C. Wittrock (Ed.), *Handbook of research on teaching* (3rd ed., pp. 392–431). New York: Macmillan.

Eraut, M. (1995). Schön shock: A case for reframing reflection-in-action? *Teachers and Teaching: Theory and Practice, 1,* 9–22.

Eraut, M. (2000). Non-formal learning and tacit knowledge in professional work. *British Journal of Educational Psychology, 70,* 113–136.

Glaser, B. G., & Strauss, A. L. (1967). *The discovery of grounded theory: Strategies for qualitative research.* New York: Aldine DeGruyter.

Her Majesty's Inspectorate. (1985). *History in the primary and secondary years: An HMI view.* London: Her Majesty's Stationery Office.

Husbands, C., Kitson, A., & Pendry, A. (2003). *Understanding history teaching.* Buckingham, UK: Open University Press.

Jaworski, B. (1994). *Investigating mathematics teaching: A constructivist enquiry.* London: Falmer Press.

Lee, P. J. (1983). History teaching and the philosophy of history. *History and Theory, 22*(4), 19–49.

Lincoln, Y. S., & Guba, E. G. (1985). *Naturalistic inquiry.* London: Sage.

Miles, M. B., & Huberman, A. M. (1994). *Qualitative data analysis.* London: Sage.

Mitchell, J., & Marland, P. (1989). Research on teacher thinking: The next phase. *Teaching and Teacher Education, 5,* 115–128.

Norman, N. (2000). *The use of television for the teaching and learning of mathematics in secondary school.* Unpublished DPhil, Oxford University.

Nott, M., & Wellington, J. (1994). Science teachers, the nature of science and the National Science Curriculum. In J. Wellington (Ed.), *Secondary science: Contemporary issues and practical approaches* (pp. 32–43). London: Routledge.

Parker, W. C. (1991). Achieving thinking and decision-making objectives in social studies. In J. Shaver (Ed.), *Handbook of research on social studies teaching and learning* (pp. 345–356). New York: Macmillan.

Pendry, A. (1994). *The pre-lesson pedagogical decision-making of history student teachers during the internship year.* Unpublished DPhil, Oxford University.

Robson, C. (1993). *Real world research.* Oxford, UK: Blackwell.

Romanowski, M. H. (1996). Issues and influences that shape the teaching of U.S. history. In J. Brophy (Ed.), *Advances in research on teaching. Vol. 6: Teaching and Learning History* (pp. 291–312). Greenwich, CT: JAI Press.

Schön, D. A. (1983). *The reflective practitioner: How professionals think in action.* Aldershot, UK: Ashgate.

Stake, R. E. (1995). *The art of case study research.* London: Sage.

Strauss, A. L., & Corbin, J. M. (1990). *Basics of qualitative research: Grounded theory procedures and techniques.* London: Sage.

Yinger, R., & Hendricks-Lee, M. (1993). Working knowledge in teaching. In C. Day, J. Calderhead, & P. Denicolo (Eds.), *Research on teacher thinking: Understanding professional development* (pp. 100–123). London: Falmer Press.

CHAPTER 10

OH, THE TROUBLE WE'VE SEEN

Researching Historical Thinking and Understanding

Bruce VanSledright, Timothy Kelly, and Kevin Meuwissen

What an ominous sounding title for this chapter. We hope that it inspires intrigue rather than apprehension, for we believe that what we discuss here will allow readers to benefit by learning from others' difficulties, namely ours. Research, we suggest, needs to be as much about learning from the troubles of our own research designs and practices as it is about adding to what we know of the social and educational worlds we study. To serve this pithy aphorism, we take up an array of research-related troubles, from technical glitches and problems associated with studying the historical thinking of young learners, to attempts at understanding the historical epistemologies of teachers and their practices, to theoretical-construct concerns that arise in conceptualizing and carrying out studies of historical thinking and understanding. We begin with a vignette that illustrates how a small technical glitch can otherwise foil a good beginning and create theoretical troubles that take creative energy to work around.

Imagine for a moment that you are sitting with a fifth grader. Her name is Julie. She's 10 and very excited that you wish to interview her and hear her ideas. She's also a bit nervous because she has never recorded her

Research Methods in Social Studies Education, pages 207–233
Copyright © 2006 by Information Age Publishing

voice for such an "important research project," as she puts it. You and Julie are in a small, quiet room adjacent to her classroom. You have obtained your permissions to conduct research and Julie's parents have signed off on the interviews you wish to conduct with her and several of her classmates. The tape recorder sits on the desk in front of you both. You are preparing her for her first "formal interview" by trying to get her comfortable with you and the prospect of her speaking clearly into the microphone.

Things begin inauspiciously. Julie settles down to the task at hand after you've explained the details and given her some practice. The activity involves having Julie read aloud three documents concerning the early Jamestown colony and what has been referred to as the "starving time" in the winter of 1609 to 1610. Julie is to read the documents out loud, projecting her voice clearly into the tape recorder. Her goal is to use the content of the documents to build an interpretation about what caused the starving time. On each of the documents, at the end of every two to three lines, is a large red dot. The dots signal that Julie is to pause when she reaches them and explain out loud what she is thinking about, what ideas her reading of the document is bringing to mind. She has never done this before aloud, but the practice you have given her on unrelated texts before presenting with the Jamestown documents suggests that she can manage the task. You begin by clicking on the recorder and off she goes, handling the exercise with considerable aplomb.

You see, she has been doing a version of this sort of activity in class. The curriculum in fifth grade is embedded with what the curriculum writers call "exercises in historical investigation." Julie's teacher, who is learning to conduct these investigations herself, has been diligently working with this curriculum to teach her fifth graders some of the rudiments of the practice; that is, the use of multiple original and secondary sources to construct interpretations around questions such as, What caused the starving time in Jamestown in 1609–1610? As a researcher, you are interested in how kids like Julie take to this process, how they handle the documents, how they read and make sense of the texts, whether the texts enable (or not) the building of robust, evidence-based historical interpretations, among other things. In short, you are interested in Julie's source work. The data collection strategy you are employing here is the verbal report protocol, otherwise known simply as the "think aloud." Julie is the third student you have worked with today. And things have gone quite well. The equipment is capturing the voices of the children effectively, even with soft-spoken Kent, the first child you interviewed.

The protocols have been taking about 20 to 25 minutes per child. The tape you are using contains 60 minutes of recording time. You realize that, within a few minutes after Julie begins, you will need to switch tapes. You are counting on your tape recorder to snap off as it ends the tape, signaling you to tell Julie to hold her idea while you insert a clean tape from the stack you brought for the purpose. Julie embarks on the task in a cheerful, animated way. She turns out to be an excellent reader of these rather difficult documents, two with archaic, original language and spelling intact (you want to see what she does with these "authentic" documents). You become fascinated with her text work and with her comments following the red dots. For a 10-year-old, what you are getting here is really quite amazing. Apparently Julie's teacher is enjoying considerable success with students like Julie as she teaches them to conduct these types of historical investigations. Well into the third document and after about 20 minutes during which you found yourself completely immersed in what Julie was producing, you abruptly come to your senses, realizing that you have not heard the tape shut off. Oh, the trouble that now ensues.

Attempting unsuccessfully to disguise your alarm, you immediately tell Julie to stop. You grab the tape recorder off the table, hitting the rewind button to see where Julie was in the process before the tape ended. To your profound dismay, you discover that it has only recorded about four minutes of Julie's stellar reading. The last 15 to 17 minutes are, well, simply missing. You shudder quietly and try to summon up a smile for Julie. But you know this activity is likely a bust; most of this excellent data is gone for good. Why? You could simply apologize and ask Julie to start over. It turns out to be anything but that simple.

In trying to understand how young learners come to make sense of historical documents, how they read and analyze them on their way to building historical interpretations and understandings, we have few more powerful tools than the verbal report protocol. However, verbal reports are tricky to elicit and they have their limitations. In giving verbal reports, children like Julie are providing their thought processes at a particular moment, in a particular context. Verbal report specialists (Ericsson & Simon, 1993) caution that prior ideas play an important role in how verbal reports are generated. They need to be taken into account as data that influence what cognitive processes occur on line as the report is given. In the case of Julie and the 17 missing minutes, we could say that the content of this initial verbal report is indeed that sort of data and, therefore, could seriously influence any subsequent reports she was invited to provide. In effect, we would argue that, if a second report was immediately requested to "recover" the missing minutes, that second report would contain cognitive-processing residue for the first report. The residue would impact the sort of subsequent report Julie would offer, changing the nature of her cognitive processing, and, we would contend, potentially enhancing the quality of the second report because she had already "practiced" on the texts and her interpretations of them. As a result, it would be difficult to say that the second report was cognitively clean, seeing as how it would suffer from a practice effect. In this sense the verbal report data collection moment was lost when the tape shut off and recording ceased for 17 minutes.

What could be done? You might be thinking that it would be wise to wait a week and return to elicit a second report from Julie. Indeed, this is possible. But again, verbal report specialists would indicate that there is no clear way of determining how the second report a week later would be influenced by the first report. Even if you asked Julie to talk beforehand about what she recalled from the first report as a means of understanding residual impact, her articulations at that point would serve to influence the ensuing report you elicited from her. There seems to be no way to win here. Unfortunately, all manner of similar research and data collection problems crop up from time to time. Such are the occupational hazards.

In what follows, we lay out an additional array of these sorts of research difficulties, discuss them, and offer a few tentative ideas about how they might be resolved. We say tentative because, to date in our work, these difficulties continue to trouble the types of research work we do as we attempt to come to grips with making sense of historical thinking and understanding among learners of all types.

RESEARCHING HISTORICAL THINKING AMONG YOUNG LEARNERS

When asking young children to recount what they have learned, say, about the American Revolution, they often tell you less than they actually know. This does not typically occur because they do not like researchers or answering their questions (although that surely could be the case with a few children). In fact our experience is that youngsters enjoy the attention such exercises afford them. This telling-less-than-you-know has more to do with how children hear a question, and what sort of cues it provides. To paraphrase Jerome Bruner, when children give wrong answers to our adult questions about what they remember of the Boston Tea Party, they actually are giving a correct answer to a different question, perhaps what they remember about another disruptive act in the colonies around the same period. It does not necessarily mean that they have no knowledge of the Boston Tea Party; it's that they heard a different question than the one the researcher asked. Sometimes children might hear the word Boston and focus on it, thinking that the researcher wants to hear about all manner of things dealing with historical (or even occasionally contemporary) Boston. If the child skips over a discussion of the Boston Tea Party, it could simply be an oversight. When this occurs, it frequently pays to ask the question again, in a different way. It may take several attempts before it becomes completely clear that the child was simply dead asleep or absent the day the Boston Tea Party was discussed in class.

Telling less than one knows also has to do with the process of turning stored ideas into verbal articulations, the latter being a bit cumbersome for young and cognitively maturing learners. Adults typically are much more facile with language than are, say, 10-year-olds (as always, there are exceptions to this rule, and we have heard from some). On more than a few occasions, we have become impatient with children as they struggle to articulate an idea that they genuinely know about but lack many of the better words that could form a coherent articulation. As adults, we tend to impose our articulation capacities on children, forgetting that they still are learning to master language. For second-language students, this can be even more the case. It is tempting to draw the all-too-quick conclusion that such semi-articulate children really do not know the answers to your questions. Patience here can offer important dividends.

Sociocultural differences between children and the researchers asking them questions can also play a defining role in what informants have to say. During the Great Depression, efforts were made to collect oral histories from the few surviving former slaves and other African Americans who experienced the effects of slavery in the South firsthand. White interviewers were not as likely as African American interviewers to obtain detailed accounts, a result some former slaves explained had to do with their (understandable) suspicions of white interviewers and their motives.

In Epstein's (1998) work with African American and white students in the Detroit area on questions of historical significance, she asked her African American research assistant to interview the African American students in the study while she worked with the white students. To an important degree, the wisdom of following this practice depends on the kinds of questions a researcher is asking. In Epstein's case, she effectively wanted students to tell her about people and ideas and historical events they valued and held significant. She hunched that, not unlike former slaves talking to white interviewers about their lives, the black students in her study might not tell her, as a white interviewer, what they truly valued and believed significant historically. School-age students become quickly adept at telling adults what they think adults want to hear. And when racial or ethnic differences also intervene, it can intensify this response. The result can be less about students not knowing something and more about them trying to figure out what you, the researcher, are really trying to discover. In efforts to "read through" the questions, ones that can be shot through racial and ethnic implications, they miss what you might be after, or they intentionally avoid revealing too much about themselves as an exercise in self-protection. Again, knowing how to listen carefully to a child, how to rephrase a question, or how to pair interviewer with interviewee—

and gender can matter here as well—can go some distance in attenuating the problems that can arise.

When it comes to historical thinking, a subject of considerable interest among history education researchers, most elementary-age children are very much novices. They have had few opportunities to learn to think historically in any deep way. That does not mean they cannot think historically at all. It is just that their ideas are often nascent and only partially formed compared to what we know about how history experts reason. History education researchers, who arguably are much more expert in how they engage in historical thinking, bring that capacity with them to the research setting. Caution here is important. We, as researchers, have caught ourselves projecting our own historical thinking capacities onto novices in research contexts, either misunderstanding what the learners are actually doing cognitively, or unintentionally assisting the novices in learning new ways of thinking while assuming that these new cognitions were that of the learner in the first place. As a consequence, we have attributed to novices greater expertise in historical thinking than they have possessed.

The reverse of this situation is perhaps even more problematic. By this we mean thinking of such novices as bereft of the capacity to think historically because they show no signs that they can in an interview or a verbal report protocol, for example. We have come to realize how important it is to carefully listen to what these children are doing when they try to engage in acts of historical thinking. If they are not acts we recognize as such, the question then must turn on what the children *are doing*.

Understanding what novices are doing when researchers give them opportunities to think historically is crucially important to the process of being able to map starting points of academic development in the history domain. Where is it that young learners begin? How is it that they think about history at these starting points? Answering these questions—even if they appear dismaying because the kids do not appear to be engaged in acts of historical thinking at all—is vital to making sense of how historical cognition develops and blossoms over time. Researchers in history education need starting points from which to measure change. If researchers are to plot a learning path toward greater competence in thinking and understanding in the domain, then we need markers of progress along the way. Gathering data all along this path will provide many such markers. Researchers need to resist the temptation to foreclose on novices' ideas and thinking processes, especially if they appear understated and/or somewhat inarticulate and unsophisticated by the lights of what we know of expertise.

What can make studying historical thinking among school-age children frustrating and problematic is that kids often do not receive many opportunities to learn what it means and to engage in it in any deep way. This is particularly the case in the United States, where the history curriculum consists of survey-coverage courses, typically at fifth and eighth grades, and at some point in high school. Such coverage models span vast, complex, and meaty periods of American history. Time is short and teachers are pressed to push through the periods they need to cover in rapid succession. The efficiencies of lecturing, textbook reading, historical film viewing, and testing become deeply attractive. This is the terrain of what we would call school history. Under the circumstances and understandably, little time is left for students to engage in in-depth analyses of particular historical events, to pursue understanding by examining the *residua* of the past (documents, images, artifacts) on the way to learning how to wrestle with the it and construct interpretations of their own. Models of historical thinking practice that lead to deeper historical understandings so described are obviously limited in such classrooms because they consume too much precious classroom time. Students learn early that in school history the task is to identify and describe the correct historical idea or detail, the one contained in the book or the lecture or the film, and reproduce it on the test. Such is the grammar of schooling (Tyack & Tobin, 1994).

Recently, however, one could argue that a quiet revolution (some might prefer the term quiet evolution) has taken place in school history. Judging by the interest in firsthand accounts and original testimonials and their appearance in the sidebars of textbooks and in compendia of such sources on book shelves and at teacher-conference exhibits, the proliferation and use of these types of documents and sources portends to reshape history teaching practice.

However, two contemporary studies indicate that these documents and sources are used primarily—in keeping with traditional school history grammar—to augment the search for the correct names, term, and storylines that will later appear on the test (Hicks, Doolittle, & Lee, 2003), and to provide, as some teachers believed, motivational enhancements, prompting reluctant students to read (Grant, 2003). Consequently, although materials that might promote extended preparation in historical thinking grow ever more present in classrooms, opportunities for that preparation do not necessarily follow. Therefore, it becomes difficult to find students at almost any grade level in the United States who have learned the rudiments of historical reasoning and working with source material, and who have had much prolonged practice. This may suggest that students—even those at the high school and college levels (see, e.g., Stahl, Hynd, Britton, McNish, & Bosquet, 1996; Wineburg, 1991; Yeager & Davis, 1996)—are simply dull and are incapable of engaging in complex acts of historical thinking. Researchers need to resist the temptation to draw such conclusions.

One way around this issue is to give students opportunities to put on display what they can do. Using verbal-report protocols with students of various ages in the context of exercises in using multiple documents that encompass a specific historical incident that has wide historical significance do provide some idea of what they can accomplish. However, picking the right incident and combination of documents (e.g., whether differing perspectives exist, how perspectives are juxtaposed), attending to the texts' reading complexities and how they are arranged sequentially (e.g., so as to anticipate a storyline), and providing adequate verbal reporting practice beforehand can significantly influence how well students perform and therefore what sort of progressional markers they display. Nonetheless, the results of such work can begin to provide teachers with important feedback on what kids are doing with these texts and documents, and point in the direction of where they still might go if taught how.

You may now be asking, but what if teachers do not know much about source work themselves? Will knowing what the markers are in their students' intellectual progression be enough? If not, where will teachers learn how to interpret those markers and what to do about them in the classroom? We do not have ready answers to these questions; but next we consider them indirectly by way of a discussion of the epistemic nature of historical thinking and understanding and the complexities of studying it among teachers (and, by implication, students).

STUDYING TEACHERS' (AND STUDENTS') HISTORICAL EPISTEMOLOGIES

By now it should be obvious that studying historical thinking is no simple matter. Much of this complexity has to do with the epistemological nature of the practice. Acts of historical thinking and reasoning are historicized cultural practices that, at present anyway, are designed principally to lead to deeper, richer ways of understanding the past. Such understandings are often (but not exclusively) displayed in books and narrative accounts that we call histories. These histories might be described colloquially as bricks in the wall of historical knowledge. (That we remake this wall repeatedly only shows us how tentative and unstable the nature of our knowledge is.) But what counts as understanding, and, more importantly, what counts as understanding that is vetted in book form and becomes what we call historical knowledge? These questions effectively ask about the warrants for constituting such knowledge. And asking about warrants implicates the cultural practice of how participants in communities that wish to investigate the past make decisions concerning what gets to count. Rules and criteria typically guide participants' decisions. Knowing rules and criteria that circumscribe warrants for knowledge defines the practices by which participants in communities that investigate and study the past get to say what counts and what does not.

What makes all this tricky is that communities can vary in the types of rules and criteria they choose to employ. For instance, professional historians have theirs, informal clubs or societies that study, say, genealogical paths have theirs, and teachers and students engaged in studying the past in the classroom using various texts and documents and artifacts can have theirs. None of these groups must necessarily agree with the others about what counts as the best warrants for knowledge. Communities can agree to disagree and justify their rules and criteria based on their differing goals and teleological frameworks. To make things more complex, rules and criteria change over time as communities evolve. Disputes over rule applications even within the same community are not uncommon—see, for example, the debate between professional historians Robert Finley (1988) and Natalie Zemon Davis (1988) on the pages of the *American Historical Review.*

Two key issues concern us here as researchers interested in studying the substance of history teachers' (and students') epistemological standpoints. First, it is important to be as clear as possible about which community's rules, criteria, and goal frameworks will serve as the focus of comparison. That is, in eliciting epistemological standpoints (the question of how we will get to in a moment) from teachers, a robust scheme for interpreting what they might say is crucial. This means knowing something about how different communities engaged in attempting to make sense of the past construe the rules and criteria about what understanding should entail and which ones get to count. At the risk of oversimplification, some examples here may suffice.

In school history, in the United States at least, it is not uncommon for the goal of history education to be about a cultural practice in which teachers teach students to acquire and then display historical knowledge produced by others, not the teachers or students themselves. The rules and criteria for this practice hinge on the capacity of the students to read a textbook and accompanying study sheets and guides, the teachers' lectures, and an occasional videotape, and to reproduce the key ideas on an assessment designed to measure them. Success is calibrated by how well the students engage the rules and, by some lights, enjoy themselves along the way. The criteria for what it means to come to understand the past are defined by how students score on the assessments.[1] Claims for saying that a student now possesses understanding and knowledge about the past is arbitrated by what these assessments measure. Warrants for these claims, epistemologically speaking, are tied up in an enterprise that is less about knowledge *production* and more about knowledge *reproduction.*

Among professional historians, warrants for claims are the reverse; they are less interested in reproducing historical understandings generated by others and more compelled by producing new understandings (notwithstanding the observation that there is nothing new under the sun). Rules and criteria therefore look different. Claims to understanding must be vetted in the tribunal of peer review. Peers pay particular attention to how new arguments about what the past means are supported and defended by documentary evidence. Being able to read and assess source material critically, synthesize deftly, and argue interpretations cogently are central practices. Reproducing and displaying understandings on assessments are rare. The epistemological landscape is markedly different than that of school history's (for more on this, see, e.g., VanSledright, 1996).

For several years now, we have been exploring this double-sided terrain. We have attempted to hold fourth- and fifth-grade teachers up to the prism cast by the epistemological standpoints assumed within the community of professional historians in order to understand how the two groups compared. The effort has been both deeply problematic and subtly promising. Before we had theorized much about the distinctions between cultural practices within these two communities, the elementary teachers in our sample, as you might imagine, appeared epistemologically shortsighted when compared to the positions staked out by professional historians. However, when it occurred to us that if we made the comparison in the other direction, historians seemed similarly myopic. The point here is that we needed a theory of cultural practices guiding these two groups. We needed to understand their epistemological standpoints within the context of each group's teleological or goal-oriented position.

Epistemological standpoints must be studied with respect to the community contexts in which they are employed. To hold teachers to the rules and criteria for knowledge warrants shaping the practices of historians is a normative move that in itself must be justified by researchers. This necessitates building such a justification. It must turn on making a case that the knowledge warrants held by historians are somehow more powerful than those deployed by history teachers, or vice versa. In turn, it means theorizing about and explaining, as only one possibility here, why the rules and criteria used to make knowledge claims within the community of historians could serve to develop deeper, richer, more finely nuanced historical understandings than rules and criteria employed in school history classrooms. Accomplishing this task is no mean feat. But, if such a case can be made, then it may make sense to say that *this* is where teachers *are* epistemologically, and *this* is where they *might go* along a progression to a more powerful and sophisticated (in the sense of warrants for making knowledge claims) epistemological standpoint. Such assertions may hold the subtle promise suggested a moment ago. Making a case is the responsibility of history education researchers (for more on specific arguments that can be made about goals and epistemological standpoints, see Barton & Levstik, 2004; Lee, 2004; VanSledright, 2002b; VanSledright, Alexander, Maggioni, Kelly, & Meuwissen, 2004).

A second key issue that faces us, and one we have sidestepped so far, is designing research tools that help us measure epistemological standpoints of history teachers. If we agree that a history teacher's epistemological position, in part, defines the nature of her teaching practice and in turn shapes what rules and criteria her students have opportunities to learn as they develop understandings of the past and warrants for claims that they understand, it makes sense that the task could be valuable in figuring out what it means to learn to teach the subject. But we need sensitive tools to do the work. We have been testing out various approaches in the context of large groups of fourth- and fifth-grade teachers who teach (among other subjects) American history to their students (VanSledright et al., 2004).

Following our foregoing argument on being clear about the community culture of history teachers and goal frameworks influencing it, we (with considerable help from our research associate Liliana Maggioni) created a series of 21 statements that put epistemological standpoints in the context of teaching history. We ask the teachers to rate their agreement with the statements (e.g., knowledge of historical research methods are fundamental for historians and school students alike; students need to be aware that history is basically a matter of interpretation) on a 6-point scale (since the teachers take this measure on three occasions, the scale allows us to track changes in positions over time). The statements are about evenly divided between a rules-criteria-warrants structure of the disciplinary community and a knowledge-acquisition criteria of the school history community. The statements are designed to see if the teachers' positions cohere best with which community practices. We have been using this measure experimentally, as we test its validity. And this is precisely where the trouble begins.

To begin, we theorized each statement as a factor. We performed factor analyses on the 21 statements to see how they would load. Ten of the 21 statements loaded with some statistical power on two factors. We presumed we were witnessing the two communities' normative practices nicely divided before us, with some teachers selecting for one community's norms and the rest opting for the other. In other words, initially we believed we were seeing a measuring tool that validly sampled teachers' positions on the two communities' criteria. Teachers high on one factor (say, the school history community practice) would therefore sample low on the other (the criteria of guild historians). A closer analysis of which statements (as factors) loaded together revealed that there was no such neat bimodal division. In fact, several statements loading together on one factor appeared to us to contain opposing epistemological standpoints.

For example, historical knowledge is both a fixed and chronically stable entity *and* largely the result of historians' shifting interpretations and revisions. How could this be?

We are still unclear on a good answer. On the one hand, we could conclude that the teachers in our sample are simply confused epistemologically, that they wish to hold both positions, and have not thought much about reconciling their incompatibilities, a clear possibility. Another interpretation might be that such statements sound good to the teachers and that social desirability suggests that they opt for agreement on both. A third possibility is that teachers' knowledge of history and history teaching is so tacit that corresponding epistemological standpoints are weak and prone to various and sometimes conflicting conceptualizations. Conversely, a fourth possibility is that the teachers agree with both statements and know something about the difference between the communities to which they apply, but because the measure has no avenue for allowing them to elaborate on the nature of their compartmentalized agreements, they have no means of recording them.

As this last possibility implies, it could be the instrument itself: it simply is not up to the challenge of sensitively sampling for epistemological standpoints. Because the statements describe tenable and attractive positions, but ones held by two different communities, it confuses the teachers' responses. Or, as we suggested, a powerful social desirability effect is a work that the Likert-scale response format only exacerbates. Finally, it may have something to do with the fact that we have structured the instrument theoretically, drawing from the domain of history but also from epistemological work undertaken that is not domain specific (e.g., King & Kitchener, 1994; Kuhn & Weinstock, 2002). Mixing these theoretical assumptions may have confused us and we in turn only confused the teachers, semantically more than anything. In other words, it could be troublingly problematic to assume that the teachers intersubjectively subscribe to an epistemological vocabulary we appropriated from the research literature.

Our work on this approach continues because we believe understanding teachers' epistemologies is valuable and important to sample in a broad way. One strategy we intend to pursue is to check in with our teachers on how they do make sense of the vocabulary of the statements. We would like to study a subsample of the teachers and conduct verbal report protocols with them as they respond to each statement and select responses on the Likert scale (for parallel suggestions, see Richardson, Chapter 8, this volume). We are hoping that this process will teach us about how our vocabulary choices shape responses, to what degree social desirability plays a role, and to what extent the measure samples only epistemological standpoints on history *teaching*. It may turn out that there is no reasonably valid, constructive way to sample epistemological standpoints in history using such measures. What other tools might we use?

Our sample includes approximately 220 teachers. We could interview them each to develop portraits (as King & Kitchener, 1994, have done). However, the cost of doing so has proven to be prohibitive with a sample this large. We have experimented with attempting to infer epistemological standpoints from the ways in which these teachers have responded to interpretive essay prompts based on reading and analyzing sets of documentary accounts. This has been intriguing and useful, but it remains relatively high-inference work that clearly needs triangulatory support from other measures. The effort begs for clarity and a degree of precision that eludes our grasp. We think this is the case with many efforts at researching how teachers think about their teaching practices, the history subject matter they teach, and the community practices and goals that influence both. One approach that we think is promising but also has troubling features is the study of teachers' knowledge and ideas about teaching via detailed case studies.

STUDYING TEACHERS' KNOWLEDGE GROWTH AND CHANGE IN PRACTICE

As the foregoing makes obvious, a good deal of our research in history education has examined beginning and practicing teachers' engagement with learning experiences designed to enhance their domain knowledge and to influence their pedagogical decision making in relation to the use of potentially powerful knowledge-domain tools. This line of research has forced us to wrestle with a number of methodological concerns that appear to be intimately connected to the kinds of questions we are asking. These questions turn on the extent to which teachers' changes in historical thinking and their purposes for teaching history manifest themselves in classroom practice. Do transformations in teachers' knowledge and beliefs about a domain necessarily translate into pedagogical change? Conversely, do new instructional approaches show that more fundamental epistemological shifts are taking place?

These substantive questions, among others, have led us to consider how we document such changes, and in particular, how we account for the relationship between knowledge growth and pedagogical change. We are also interested in how our use of particular research methodologies influences understandings we develop around teacher education and professional development in the social studies and the meanings we construct with our research participants.

The troubles we have encountered in trying to make sense of these cases of teacher change are not novel. More than a decade ago, Cohen (1990) offered the case of Mrs. Oublier. Charged to teach a reformed elementary mathematics curriculum, Oublier employed a number of innovative activities designed to engage students in the exploration of mathematical concepts. These efforts were triggered by her involvement in a professional development experience, one closely aligned with the new curriculum. In her mind, she was teaching for the kind of deep understanding that characterizes thinking in the domain and championed within the development experience.

While her embrace of the curriculum appeared to signal a shift in her thinking and practice, Cohen (1990) argues that Oublier actually adopted new strategies and materials without altering her more fundamental ideas about mathematical knowledge and pedagogy. So, even when new ideas, curricular materials, and activities are presented to teachers, evidence indicates that they may interpret these in the context of their prior conceptions, reconfigure them to fit within existing conceptual frameworks, or simply ignore or reject what does not fit (Cohen, 1990; see also McDiarmid, 1990, 1994). For Mrs. Oublier, the "new math" seemed to offer a new method of solving an old problem: finding the right answer. And yet, it is Cohen's research methods that are of particular interest to us here, for they are the tools used to construct the case of Mrs. Oublier and the nature of the revolution in her classroom.

Such case study research appears to share a common methodological thread with many studies that reveal discrepancies between articulated knowledge and pedagogical practice. They usually involve observations of classroom instruction and interviews or questionnaires through which teachers report on their conceptual understanding of a particular discipline and their beliefs about teaching and learning within that domain. Through our use of similar methods, we have become familiar with cases where teachers espouse a set of beliefs that seem to contradict other data emerging from the study. Specifically, we have asked teachers where history comes from, what they perceive the purpose of teaching history to be, and how they handle conflicting accounts of the past. We then crystallize their responses with what we observe in their classrooms and the circumstances we find within the local school context. Teachers, it turns out, tend to talk to researchers in interview settings about idealized versions of practice, images of what they might be, all other things being equal. Once 25 students walk through the door, things change, often dramatically.

Take the case of Alison Stanton, an elementary teacher of 5 years who participated in a professional development experience designed to support her efforts to teach a new district social studies curriculum. That curriculum draws in part on an investigative approach to learning history. At a number of points, students are invited to investigate the past and develop evidence-based interpretations. In order to make sense of the potential changes experienced by Stanton as a result of the professional development project linked to changes promoted by the new curriculum, we began by spending time in her classroom. These observations provided evidence that she was using the primary sources and deploying protocols provided in the curriculum to engage her students in historical investigations. Using district curricular guidelines, Stanton also taught a number of lessons that appeared to be aimed at developing students' understanding of the nature of historical knowledge. She encouraged her fifth graders to make connections between the sources they were examining and the types of residual evidence historians use when reconstructing the past.

Initial readings of our field notes and assessments of analytic memos suggested that Stanton was in fact moving toward more complex and nuanced domain understandings. Interview data reinforced what we thought we were seeing in the classroom. But Stanton's interaction with the curriculum materials and her dialogue with students in the course of the investigations described above suggested a deeper epistemological resilience. Even though Stanton touched on issues of source perspective and reliability, as outlined in the curriculum, much of the language she used with her students suggested that history amounted to an accumulation of information and facts found in sources, rather than a deeply interpretive act. Stanton appeared to have adapted the investigative tools and methodologies of the domain while retaining a conceptual framework that hinged on reproducing "correct answers." All that was needed, Stanton emphasized to her students on more than one occasion, was more historical research, the accumulation of more information.

How did we, as researchers, move beyond our preliminary reading of the data? In other words, how did we come to know what we know now? And how does the story we tell about Stanton reflect the methodologies we employed, *our* purposes, and *our* perspectives? Observations of classroom practice, especially the combination of teaching strategies and classroom dialogue, suggested inconsistencies between espoused and enacted beliefs. Comparing thematically coded field notes and analytic memos across case studies—Stanton's was one of three cases conducted simultaneously—also proved to be an effective means of making sense of change. When examined in relation to each other, we were able to see degrees of change, with the different teachers showing evidence of more or less marked epistemological shifts. Situating cases in relation to progression scales (Lee, 2004; VanSledright et al., 2004) proved to be another powerful analytic tool. One drawback of these kinds of comparisons, though, is the potential to ignore the intrinsic value of the individual case.

This raises an issue of data interpretation and reporting. For how we choose to represent participants involves not simply a rigorous application of case study methodology but a moral choice. Lest the case of Stanton be tossed onto an already accumulating heap of teacher deficit literature, it needs to be placed in the context of contemporary research in history education and professional development, which points to knowledge of subject matter, both substantive and strategic, as one of the most important factors contributing to teaching practice and powerful professional judgment. In fact, we see it contributing to this body of research. However, how it contributes is a matter of careful analysis and clear representations that do justice to teachers' knowledge growth and change in practice. And it must be situated in the contexts of the communities in which they work, as we stressed earlier.

Both Oublier and Stanton were the focus of studies aimed at understanding epistemological and pedagogical changes experienced by practicing teachers as a result of their involvement in professional development experiences. Alternately, some researchers have focused their attention on the experiences of prospective history teachers in teacher education programs or novices during the induction phase (e.g., McDiarmid, 1994; Slekar, 1998). While studies that follow students through their teacher education experiences, into their early years of teaching and professional development, and through their careers are rare, researchers are beginning to acknowledge the importance (if not the feasibility) of such comprehensive explorations (e.g., Hartzler-Miller, 2001; van Hover & Yeager, 2003).

We turn now to some of our work with preservice teachers. Popular wisdom would have us believe that most teachers, like Oublier and Stanton, advance similarly through teacher education programs, into the classroom, and toward expert practice via experience and professional development opportunities aimed at the knowledge growth and refinement of teaching practice. Along the way, they build upon their existing knowledge, occasionally accounting for the cognitive dissonance caused by practical dilemmas. The research literature on teacher education and professional development contradicts this "received wisdom" model of learning to teach (e.g., Ball & Cohen, 1999; McDiarmid, 1990). Ball and Cohen (1999), among others, point to the powerful socializing factors that effectively reinforce "the conservatism of practice, with its didactic approaches to teaching and facts-and-skills conceptions of knowledge" (p. 5).

Familiar with the apprenticeship of observation and the deeply embedded and interconnected web of beliefs novices wear like protective armor, many teacher educators consider their work a quixotic undertaking (McDiarmid, 1990). Considering the goals we have framed for the prospective teachers in our methods classes and teacher education programs—demonstrate a clear instructional purpose rooted in critical, evidence-based thinking and a knowledge of how and why history is constructed, a firm grasp of teachers' roles as curricular arbiters, a realistic conception of school and classroom contexts and the means to foster democratic discourse within them, and mastery of the subject matter— one gets the sense that we are tilting at windmills (see Barton & Levstik, 2004; Grant, 2003; Thornton, 2005).

Conceivably, these orientations toward theoretical and practical knowledge ought to play largely into how teachers teach. But whether or not they do depends on some very complex factors. Studies suggest that deep disciplinary knowledge or an articulated penchant for historical inquiry do not, by their very nature, safeguard against didactic, unidirectional instruction (see, e.g., the cases in Hartzler-Miller, 2001; van Hover & Yeager, 2003; VanSledright, 1996; Wilson & Wineburg, 1993). Thus, as we have been saying, it is reasonable to ask how we can better understand the relationship between developing knowledge and changing practice, as well as the personal and contextual factors that impact teachers' work.

We see the research methodologies discussed above as moving us toward these understandings, but it is difficult to say with authority that any specific factor is a primary reason why teachers' knowledge and pedagogy do not always connect. Grant (2003) describes a number of dynamics that influence teachers' practices, from personal beliefs, knowledge, and learning experiences to organizational culture, curriculum mandates, and instructional resources. The trouble is how, then, can we better examine teachers' knowledge in the context of such influences and make sense of the ways in which these factors variously influence teachers' thinking and practice?

Journaling is one means by which we can gather more in-depth data on teachers' knowledge and pedagogical beliefs and practices. Depending on our research question, we might ask history teachers to work through a historical analysis and write about it, to discuss their own experiences and interests as history students, or to offer an image of an ideal history classroom and indicate what factors stand between their current practices and that image. Furthermore, we reap similar benefits in drawing upon think-aloud exercises with teachers as we do when using them with students. Certainly it makes sense to have teachers grapple with historical accounts as a means of documenting their thinking strategies and epistemological positions.

Also we could use what Ball and Cohen (1999) call portraits or materials of practice in researching both what teachers know and how that knowledge plays into their teaching. This might involve having teachers talk their way through an analysis of student work, examine a challenging classroom scenario, or evaluate curricular materials (see Cunningham, Chapter 9, this volume, for similar suggestions). By employing these portraits, we are able to better make sense of teachers' theories about historical thinking, teaching, and learning and the influences on their work within the context of practical school-based dilemmas. However, even these creative efforts will not fully be up to the task of getting us the sorts of understandings of teachers' knowledge and practice, and the complex contexts in which they interact. Yet, we need to attend to all these dimensions and being clear about how we conceptualize them cannot be underestimated.

GETTING CLEARER ALSO ABOUT THE THEORETICAL CONSTRUCTS WE USE?

Perhaps at the risk of a redundancy, we want to elaborate on some of these conceptual issues that arise in studying historical thinking and understanding. They emanate from the types of work we have been describing. Here again, research efforts and how studies get conceptualized and carried out benefit considerably from possessing a degree of clarity about these constructs (noting, though, that stabilizing them will always escape us). We have had to learn such lessons the hard way—failed studies, uninterpretable results, misleading questions, misguided claims, contradictory assertions, and the like—and we are still learning, as the foregoing testifies. The following ideas have proven useful to us in our work. The suggestions the ideas entail, however, permanently fix and anchor nothing. They need to be considered as position points on a perpetual journey toward generating questions that can serve to sharpen theoretical touchstones guiding research work in this domain.[2]

Is There a Difference between History and the Past? Between Historical Recall and Historical Thinking?

We have already discussed the importance of theorizing about the distinctions (and occasional overlaps) between the goal and teleological frameworks guiding school and disciplinary history communities. In a related vein, in studying knowledge growth and change among teachers and students, another important distinction to make is between history and the past. To say in describing a study that a student's understanding of the past has changed is different from saying that her understanding of history has changed (although saying both could be true). For us, saying the former requires that the learner has encountered points of access to this bulky, massively complex admixture of events and actors we call the past, understands the nature of those points of access, and can identify and attribute them and make sense of the perspective they contain (an original source testimony, a historian's secondary source narration, a photographer's visual statement, an artist's depiction). In effect, the student knows that the purpose of coming to understand the past is chiefly associated with investigating it in the raw, so to speak, with a goal of reinscribing it in accessible ways.

Because a history is an interpretive reduction, it is necessarily tentative, unstable, and less than the past. Therefore, in our minds, to say that a student's understanding of history has changed is a reference to the role school learners typically play as consumers of others' tentative (his)stories. It suggests to us a change in the child's capacity to traffic in the sorts of details contained in textbook-like compendia, details already selected out from a much larger past. Making this distinction goes to the differences in goal frameworks between acts of reproducing other people's knowledge and producing one's own.[3] Putting a point we made earlier another way, communities of historical investigators occupy themselves with the slow, arduous task of wrestling with the temporally vast and complex past (as exemplified by its *residua*) on their way to producing new ideas. (That they occasionally reproduce old ideas while thinking of them as new certainly occurs, but it is not the purported goal.) These investigators try to bring some order to the complexities and unruliness of the past. They do so by producing histories. Students in school are more apt to be placed in acquisition roles in which they are those histories' consumers.[4] Making such theoretical notations are useful, for example, in being able to hear what children are saying in interview settings, to gather in something about the reference system that describes the culture of their classroom and school learning experience (e.g., knowledge acquisition and reproduction) and its possible connections (or not) to other community systems and vocabularies (e.g., production of knowledge, historical thinking and reasoning).

Following this same line, we have tried to interpret talk of historical thinking and understanding in school history contexts—among teachers and students—as fundamentally rooted first in language about reproducing the details and minutiae of others' ideas, a vocabulary consistent with the knowledge acquisition and socialization missions of schools (as appears to have been the case with Alison Stanton). The practice of reproducing these details appears to require less cognitive effort (memorization, recall) than understanding them as they appear in the raw and then assembling them coherently (interpretation, analysis, synthesis). So, to say that reproducing details of others' historical ideas qualifies as historical thinking can be a stretch, especially if we mean by such thinking those cognitive activities that help bring the unruly past under the control of the stories investigators want to tell. Theorizing historical thinking and understanding, as well as historical detail-reproduction practices, in these ways has helped us to make sense of differences between the linguistic systems of school history and history-as-investigation, where they overlap, and in which places they diverge among the teachers and students we study.

What's Significant in Studying Historical Significance?

History education researchers in the United States have been much attracted to studies of what Seixas (1996) referred to as historical significance. The construct, as with the others just noted, is complex and can quickly get researchers into trouble if it is undertheorized. And if this were not enough, historical significance in itself is also a complex construct about which to theorize (see Seixas, 1997). What appears to attract researchers to the study of historical significance is an interest in how minority racial and ethnic individuals come to make sense of the history told in schools and epitomized by the contents of the 7-pound U.S. history textbook. This history is frequently referred to as the "official history," and is just as frequently contrasted with the "vernacular histories" (after Bodnar, 1992) making up the understandings of minority groups. Researchers collect data that comprises this contrast (or the lack thereof) as a means of describing how the two—official and vernacular—reside (sometimes in striking opposition) in the historical consciousnesses of those studied (e.g., Barton, 2001; Epstein, 1998; Seixas, 1994). In our studies in the diverse classrooms that characterize the types of urban schools in which we often work, questions of what counts as historically significant have surfaced repeatedly.

Again, the benefits of being theoretically clear regarding this construct are immediately apparent. From our perspective, being able to specify the actual contents and properties of official and vernacular histories provides the framework in which comparisons can be made between, say, a group of Latino/a children's conceptualizations of significance in United States history and what the textbook accounts "officialize." Without this level of specification, comparisons can become fuzzy and interpretations of data can be misleading because how the children express their understandings only rarely reveals the two types of histories in sharp relief. Second, it can be valuable to construct a theoretical understanding of how the official history becomes officialized. In other words, what are the sociological underpinnings and structural components that permit one history to become more official than others? Wertsch's (2000) discussions of mastery and appropriation of narratives (official and otherwise) as cultural tools can be useful here.

Third, it may also help to develop a theoretical understanding of the criteria used by scholars in the field about what counts as historically significant (e.g., Phillips, 2002). These criteria could be contrasted with what can be inferred to be the criteria at work in the selection of contents for a U.S. history textbook. Or researchers could begin with the history textbook criteria and work toward applying them to efforts within the community of Americanist historians. Either way, such applications of criteria would go some length in sharpening up what we mean when we discuss official and vernacular histories and how they function in the lives of teachers and students.

Studying ideas about historical significance among learners remains only a partially successful endeavor without collecting sufficient data on their biographies. In an effort to describe the contents of the children's vernacular histories, and if and how they then reside alongside the official history, biographical data is crucial. But how is it to be collected? There are a variety of strategies possible from obtaining interview and written accounts, to inviting respondents to provide drawings or photographs of family about which they tell stories, to generating genealogical trees. However, none of these methods is foolproof, and the chance that critical details will be left out is reasonably high enough to render the contents of any vernacular history troublesome to produce. Nevertheless the effort must be made, as a means of providing some sociocultural context within which to situate the children being studied and the vernacular, "unofficial" nature of their histories.

Who's an Ambitious History Teacher?

Of concluding concern is the construct of "ambitious history teaching." This term has found some favor among history education researchers of late, in part as a way of talking about changes in teaching practice that have followed reform movements that have traversed education in waves since the early 1990s. What do researchers mean by the terms "ambitious history teaching" or "ambitious history teachers"? By what criteria does a teacher become ambitious? Ambitious compared to what? In our work, we often have used the term rather absentmindedly, without much concerted effort to theorize what we meant by it beforehand. As we have been noting all along, for us, trouble has not been far off in the absence of this theoretical work.

Part of the problem with the construct of ambitious teaching is that it is a relative term, often applied in a particular educational context. For instance, it may be applied to teaching practice in California, or Virginia, or New York, certainly places in which state standards and testing practices have some influence on what those teachers do and have done. What might be "ambitious" in one state's educational context could be construed as pedestrian in another. When used as a descriptor, the term contrasts itself at least implicitly to teaching practices that are unambitious. Without clear and reasonably precise definitions of what constitute the relationships between ambitious and unambitious practices, it is difficult to know whether a teacher being described is truly what researchers claim him or her to be. Some comparative/contrastive lexicon must be employed so that readers of the research studies can make sense of the indexes to which the construct refers. This necessitates the development of clear criteria for what counts as ambitious teaching practice. It also necessitates a description of a teaching–learning context that has a historical dimension, one that allows for cataloging pedagogical changes over time. Historical and local/state contexts (among other matters such as teacher subject-matter knowledge) become pivotal in considering how ambitious practice is understood and used. Again, at the risk of oversimplifying, an example might help. What follows is based loosely on other case study work that we have done.

In a state that we shall call Pandora, an effort was undertaken in the early 1990s to rewrite history standards for learning and the target outcomes expected for students. In Pandora before 1992, the guiding curricular expectations for schools had been that they would cover American history in three course sequences. Students were expected to learn the story of national development, once in elementary school, once in middle school, and again in high school. During the rewriting of the standards and learning outcomes, Pandora's State Department of Education officials decided that the children were not learning enough about the nation-building effort, that they lacked sufficient knowledge of those famous Americans who brought the country into being and helped propel it toward becoming the most powerful nation on the planet. As a result, their standards and outcomes reform demanded that teachers teach more about this history. In effect, they asked for a doubling of intensity of effort from history teachers and held them accountable by assessing students more rigorously on their recall of the ideas, terms, dates, and actors contained in the story of national development. Higher detail recall capacity would serve, the officials reasoned, as a proxy for understanding nation building in the United States.

In a neighboring state—we will call it Cassandra—state education leaders followed a different tack at about the same point. Instead of asking for greater intensity of survey coverage effort from teachers and increased recall by students, they pursued an approach that asked teachers to teach about how knowledge of American history has been produced. To that end, they asked teachers to spend more time engaging students in working with historical documents and writing interpretive essays following their study of a variety of source materials on identified curricular topics. (Stanton taught in a school district influenced by this shift.) They also reduced the spread of the suggested scope and sequence, limiting elementary school American history to the period from 1600 to about 1800, middle school American history to the 19th century, and high school to 20th-century America. They added a number of document-based questions to the state assessment, effectively requiring that teachers teach students to read, interpret, and draw inferences from a set of source materials on topics specified in the standards, as a means of deepening students' understanding of the past.

Faye, a teacher in a school district in Pandora, took the charge of the new state reform efforts to heart. She pushed her middle school history students to work harder and more efficiently at committing key names, dates, and events to memory. She was rewarded when 90% of her students passed Pandora's standardized assessment. Sarah, a middle school teacher in a district in Cassandra, also took her state's new standards and learning outcomes to heart. She gave her students much practice working with documents and spent many hours teaching them how to write clear, thoughtful interpretive essays that reflected close attention to the evidence presented in the sources. Sarah too was rewarded when 88% of her students passed Cassandra's standardized exams.

If we use the contexts (historical and current) of each state's standards and learning outcomes as the point of reference for assessing the history teaching practices of these two teachers, we would have to conclude that each teacher was ambitious. However, one need not look very close to surmise that Faye and Sarah were ambitious in very different ways. Is Faye's practice more ambitious than Sarah's? Or is it the other way around? The answer we give depends. It depends on a serious normative move we might make, a move that reflects what we value about what it means to teach history and to what end. If we hold Faye and Sarah up, say, to the light cast by the kinds of history teaching exemplified by much of the research literature on historical thinking pedagogies, then Sarah becomes the more ambitious of the two. In fact, by these lights, Faye only does more of what we know has been common—and often maligned—practice for at least a hundred years (see Cuban, 1991). Calling what she does ambitious seems misleading and perhaps even disingenuous. On the other hand, it may well be that Faye's students know and can recall more American history than Sarah's students. By this criterion, Sarah appears to be the much more unambitious history teacher.

Our point is that a normative move here is virtually unavoidable if the construct "ambitious history teaching" is applied. We are arguing that researchers like us need to be clear about our own theories of what counts as ambitious history teaching and the criteria we employ in arriving at a normative position. This means that we must theorize about what types of history teaching approaches teachers might utilize, the goals they pursue, and with what consequences—from an array of various possibilities (on this point see, e.g., Barton & Levstik, 2004; Seixas, 2000; VanSledright, 2002a). If we use the construct in our studies, we need to place it up against or next to a description of the context in which the teachers work. Finally, we must explain to readers the nature of our normative position and offer a rationale for why we value it over others. This means we have to discuss the consequences of choosing to endorse one approach in relationship to others. Otherwise, our use of the term rings hollow.

There are a number of other constructs in this work of research on history teaching and learning that can get us into trouble quickly. The ones we describe in the foregoing are only some of the more pressing of the lot. These constructs are important because they form the vocabulary of our research work. It is difficult for researchers in history education to speak without them. Theoretical clarity makes the work, its applications, and its results more powerful.

TROUBLE, TROUBLE, GO AWAY?
SOME CONCLUDING THOUGHTS

History education research can be an exciting undertaking. No doubt the upsurge in interest in doing this work by teacher educators, cognitive psychologists, and curriculum theorists reflects the excitement and the possibilities it portends for influencing educational practice in constructive ways. However, the work as we have testified can also be filled with pitfalls and difficulties that shadow researchers ceaselessly. Technical troubles can often be overcome. Theoretical problems, on the other hand, are more like dilemmas: They cannot be solved but only managed as effectively and thoughtfully as possible. This requires, at least by our lights, concerted efforts to be clear about the methods, vocabularies, and constructs we use when we engage in our research efforts. Some of this clarity comes in the process of actually doing the studies and interpreting the results. Some begins beforehand. Still other types of clarity arise in a dialectical process of letting our last study speak to the next one we conceptualize. All of this is to say that despite the trouble we have seen and have been unable to avoid, we have still learned many powerful lessons along the way. As we alluded at the outset, the trouble courts us as a potential blessing in disguise. It opens up unusual opportunities for us to learn, not altogether unlike a child coming to understand fire for the first time by playing with a lit candle.

NOTES

1. If Rothstein (2004) and Wineburg (2004) are correct about the nature of such school history assessments, students consistently and only superficially reproduce extant historical knowledge and without much deep, long-lasting understanding. Ironically, this appears to be part of the intentional design.
2. For more on theorizing about these touchstones, see the recent edited volume by Seixas (2004).
3. We would argue that this distinction has also been made in a related way by Lee and Shemilt (2003). Their description of it is characterized by what they call the difference between "progress" in history and "progression" in historical thinking, where the latter references investigations of the past.
4. It is possible that if students had opportunities to read multiple histories of the same events, the differences in the stories would prompt them to pursue the kinds of investigative practices at the center of studying the past.

ACKNOWLEDGMENT

Portions of this work were supported by a Teaching American History grant project funded by the U.S. Department of Education (Grant No. S215X010242). The ideas offered do not necessarily represent the endorsement or position of the funding agent.

REFERENCES

Ball, D., & Cohen, D. (1999). Developing practice, developing practitioners: Toward a practice-based theory of professional education. In L. Darling-Hammond & G. Sykes (Eds.), *Teaching as the learning profession: Handbook of policy and practice* (pp. 3–32). San Francisco: Jossey-Bass.

Barton, K. C. (2001). "You'd be wanting to know about the past": Social contexts of children's historical understanding in Northern Ireland and the United States. *Comparative Education, 37,* 89–106.

Barton, K. C., & Levstik, L. S. (2004). *Teaching history for the common good.* Mahwah, NJ: Lawrence Erlbaum Associates.

Bodnar, J. (1992). *Remaking America: Public memory, commemoration, and patriotism in the twentieth century.* Princeton, NJ: Princeton University Press.

Cohen, D. K. (1990). A revolution in one classroom: The case of Mrs. Oublier. *Educational Evaluation and Policy Analysis, 12,* 311–329.

Cuban, L. (1991). History of teaching in social studies. In J. Shaver (Ed.), *Handbook of research on social studies teaching and learning* (pp. 197–209). New York: Macmillan.

Davis, N. Z. (1988). On the lame. *American Historical Review, 93,* 572–603.

Epstein, T. (1998). Deconstructing differences in African American and European American adolescents' perspectives on United States history. *Curriculum Inquiry, 28,* 397–423.

Ericsson, K. A., & Simon, H. A. (1993). *Protocol analysis: Verbal reports as data.* Cambridge, MA: MIT Press.

Finlay, R. (1988). The refashioning of Martin Guerre. *American Historical Review, 93,* 553–571.

Grant, S. G. (2003). *History lessons: Teaching, learning, and testing in U.S. high school history classrooms.* Mahwah, NJ: Lawrence Erlbaum Associates.

Hartzler-Miller, C. (2001). Making sense of "best practice" in teaching history. *Theory and Research in Social Education, 29,* 672–695.

Hicks, D., Doolittle, P., & Lee, J. (2004). Social studies teachers' use of classroom-based and web-based historical primary sources. *Theory and Research in Social Education, 32,* 213–247.

King, P., & Kitchener, K. (1994). *Developing reflective judgment: Understanding and promoting intellectual growth and critical thinking in adolescents and adults.* San Francisco: Jossey-Bass.

Kuhn, D., & Weinstock, M. (2002). What is epistemological thinking? In B. Hofer & P. Pintrich (Eds.), *Personal epistemology: The psychology of beliefs about knowledge and knowing* (pp. 121–144). Mahwah, NJ: Lawrence Erlbaum Associates.

Lee, P. J. (2004). Understanding history. In P. Seixas (Ed.), *Theorizing historical consciousness* (pp. 129–164). Toronto: University of Toronto Press.

Lee, P. J., & Shemilt, D. (2003). A scaffold not a cage: Progression and progression models in history. *Teaching History, 113,* 13–24.

McDiarmid, G. W. (1990). Challenging prospective teachers' beliefs during the early field experience: A quixotic undertaking? *Journal of Teacher Education, 41*(3), 12–20.

McDiarmid, G. W. (1994). Understanding history for teaching: A study of historical understanding of prospective teachers. In M. Carretero & J. Voss (Eds.), *Cognitive and instructional processes in history and social sciences* (pp. 159–185). Hillsdale, NJ: Lawrence Erlbaum Associates.

Phillips, R. (2002). Historical significance—the forgotten "key concept." *Teaching History, 106,* 14–19.

Rothstein, R. (2004). We are not ready to assess history performance. *Journal of American History, 90,* 1381–1391.

Seixas, P. (1994). Students' understanding of historical significance. *Theory and Research in Social Education, 22,* 281–304.

Seixas, P. (1996). Conceptualizing the growth of historical understanding. In D. Olson & N. Torrance (Eds.), *The handbook of psychology in education* (pp. 765–783). Oxford, UK: Blackwell.

Seixas, P. (1997). Mapping the terrain of historical significance. *Social Education, 61,* 28–31.

Seixas, P. (2000). Schweigen! die kinder! or, does postmodern history have a place in the schools? In P. Stearns, P. Seixas, & S. Wineburg, (Eds.), *Knowing, teaching, and learning history* (pp. 15–37). New York: New York University Press.

Seixas, P. (Ed.) (2004). *Theorizing historical consciousness.* Toronto: University of Toronto Press.

Slekar, T. (1998). Epistemological entanglements: Preservice elementary teachers' "apprenticeship of observation" and the teaching of history. *Theory and Research in Social Education, 26*, 485–507.

Stahl, S., Hynd, C ., Britton, B., McNish, M., & Bosquet, D. (1996). What happens when students read multiple source documents in history? *Reading Research Quarterly, 31*, 430–456.

Tyack, D., & Tobin, W. (1994). The "grammar" of schooling: Why has it been so hard to change? *American Educational Research Journal, 31*, 453–479.

Thornton, S. J. (2005). *Teaching social studies that matters: Curriculum for active learning.* New York: Teachers College Press.

van Hover, S., & Yeager, E. (2003). "'Making' students better people?": A case study of a beginning history teacher. *International Social Studies Forum, 3*, 219–232.

VanSledright, B. A. (1996). Closing the gap between disciplinary and school history? Historian as high school history teacher. In J. Brophy (Ed.), *Advances in research on teaching. Vol. 6: Teaching and learning history* (pp. 257–289).Greenwich, CT: JAI Press.

VanSledright, B. (2002a). Confronting history's interpretive paradox while teaching fifth graders to investigate the past. *American Educational Research Journal, 39*, 1089–1115.

VanSledright, B. (2002b). *In search of America's past: Learning to read history in elementary school.* New York: Teachers College Press.

VanSledright, B., Alexander, P., Maggioni, L., Kelly, T., & Meuwissen, K. (2004, April). *Examining shifts in teachers' epistemologies in the domain of history.* Paper presented at the annual meeting of the American Educational Research Association, San Diego, CA.

Wertsch, J. (2000). Is it possible to teach beliefs, as well as knowledge about history? In P. Stearns, P. Seixas, & S. Wineburg (Eds). *Knowing, teaching and learning history* (pp. 38–50). New York: New York University Press.

Wilson, S., & Wineburg, S. (1993). Wrinkles in time and place: Using performance assessments to understand the knowledge of history teachers. *American Educational Research Journal, 30*. 729–769.

Wineburg, S. (1991). On the reading of historical texts: Notes on the breach between school and academy. *American Educational Research Journal, 28*, 495–519.

Wineburg, S. (2004). Crazy for history. *Journal of American History, 90*, 1401–1414.

Yeager, E., & Davis, O. L. (1996). Classroom teachers thinking about historical texts. *Theory and Research in Social Education, 24*, 146–166.

INDEX

A

Accountability measures/restrictions of, 78

Action research, 58–59, 78–79, 79n
creating change, 60–61
questioning assumptions about, 60
and critical social lens, 65–66
cyclical nature of, 59–60, 59f
and empowerment, 69
review of, 76–77
and teacher practice improvement, 57
See also Commonalities/action research and self-study; Uses/action research and self-study

Addams, Jane, 26

African American leaders in social studies, 25

Ahistoricism, rejection of, 11, 21

Ahmad, Iftikhar, 30

American Educational Research Association (AERA), 139

American Political Science Association (APSA), and social studies history, 30

Aries, social history of family life, 87

ATLAS data analysis/interpretation tool, case example, 198–202

B

Barnes, Mary Sheldon, 27

Beard, Mary Ritter, 26

The Belmont Report, ethics guide for human research, 40

Bernard-Powers, Jane, 27

Biographical investigation (interpretive framework), 14, 24–25
benefits of approach, 28
criticisms of, 27
institutional biographies, 26–27
"Old Masters" approach, 25
range in investigating broader contexts, 27
and representation from marginalized groups, 28

Blount, Jackie, 31

Bobbitt, Franklin, 17

C

Callahan, Raymond, 21

Change (research-initiated), and assumptions about, 60

Charters, W. W., 17

Child-centered progressivism, 16, 18

Childhood
concepts of, 85, 106n
child as object, 86
child as participant/researcher, 86
child as social actor, 86

Research Methods in Social Studies Education, pages 235–242
Copyright © 2006 by Information Age Publishing
235

CL

300.
71
RES

5000650118

Printed in the United Kingdom
by Lightning Source UK Ltd.
110129UKS00001B/12